MENNONITE GIRL

Mary Ediger

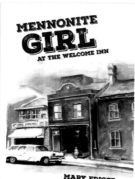

Mennonite Girl
at the Welcome Inn
by Mary Ediger

Welcome to the Welcome Inn and welcome to the life of Mary Ediger. A work of creative non-fiction, Mennonite Girl follows Mary from her life as a young girl in a quiet rural parsonage to an inner city community center in Hamilton, Ontario. The daughter of a Mennonite preacher, Mary struggles with the trials of growing up Mennonite in a non-Mennonite community, while her parents continue to follow God's call. Young and old, religious and non-religious readers alike will find themselves drawn into Mary's tale, laughing all the while as she deals with everything life throws at her.

With interminable wit and an everlasting sense of humour, this story is a coming of age story for the child in all of us.

available in print and eBook at
www.friesenpress.com

Edited by Stephanie Ediger and Cynthia McMurray
Cover Design by Mikaela Ediger © 2011

Printed and bound in Canada at Friesens

Library and Archives Canada Cataloguing in Publication

Ediger, Mary, 1959-
  Mennonite girl/Mary Ediger.

ISBN 978-1-927003-00-8

  1. Ediger, Mary, 1959-. 2. Welcome Inn Community Centre (Hamilton, Ont.).
3. Mennonites--Canada--Biography. 4. Hamilton (Ont.)--Biography. I. Title.

BX8143.E35A3 2011   289.7092   C2011-900782-7

First printing 2011

10 9 8 7 6 5 4 3 2 1

Published in 2011 by Bryler Publications Inc.
Suite 1035,
Chester, NS
B0J 1J0

Visit our website at www.brylerpublications.com

ACKNOWLEDGEMENTS

I would like to offer thanks to the following for their encouragement and support:

First, and foremost, to my immediate family. Thank you, thank you, thank you!!

To Dorothy Willms, my Mennonite friend from age 6, and the Willms family, the girls, including Cathy, (and Reg K.), on the picket lines at Durieu Elementary School during the B.C. teachers strike of 2005, Colleen Friesen, my travel writer friend and fellow Mennonite, my B.C. biking group who tolerate my stories year after year, my Liverpool, N.S. book club friends (Marcia!), The Writers Federation of Nova Scotia, and the judges of the 33rd Atlantic Writing Competition, especially Susan Kerslake.

To my sister, Stephanie Ediger, for her assistance with editing, to my wonderfully talented niece, Mikaela Ediger who designed the cover illustration and to Cynthia McMurray at Bryler Publications, for her editing, support and patience with putting this book together.

And to my dear husband, Robert Ross, who smiled through the numerous hours of writing and revisions.

ABOUT THE AUTHOR

Mary Ediger grew up in a mobile Mennonite family. She holds a teaching degree from Simon Fraser University and spent many years teaching at the elementary level in Burnaby, then Mission, B.C. She currently lives with her husband in Port Mouton, Nova Scotia.

FOREWORD

What follows is a combination of vignettes, stories and memoir. It is also a combination of fiction and nonfiction.

Many of the events did happen. I am telling these 'stories' from my perspective at the time, which was a very young girl. I cannot claim to remember conversations and the sequence of events in the order they occurred. But this was my impression.

Most of the characters are composites to protect privacy; almost all the character names have been changed. Some of the events have been intentionally altered for the same reason. The views expressed in this book are my own. Other people, including my family, may have experienced the same events in a totally different way.

I have written this because I love story telling. As well, it is in memory of my parents, who are both deceased. Though I did not always agree with their opinions and ideas, I greatly admired their faith, and their unwavering willingness to try to do God's work.

OKLAHOMA

Do you remember your first day of school? I do because I was euphoric, vibrating with giddy anticipation that day. I felt capable of levitating off my seat on the school bus and floating above the heads of the other students, like the bald man who 'loved to laugh' in Mary Poppins. It was because I had waited for so long. I wanted to go to school from the moment I understood there was such a place.

At the time, Ruth was leaving the house each morning wearing dresses tied at the back with a bow and plastic barrettes shaped like kittens in her hair. On special days, she wore a crinoline underneath, to make her dress flare out from the waist. She would return with a big smile on her face, bubbling over to tell about story time and eating frosted cupcakes on her classmate's birthdays. Then, it was the twins, Sarah and Trudy, in their matching outfits, telling about playground swings, Halloween cupcakes and singing, *'She'll be Coming Round the Mountain'* pumping their arms in unison while 'toot, tootin' and pulling back the imaginary reins for 'whoa back' while drivin' six white horses. By the time Mark joined them, talking about hot dog days, and being chosen to be the 'Cheese' when his class was playing *The Farmer in the Dell* in the gymnasium, I was bordering on obsessive.

"You aren't old enough yet," Mom said to my constant inquiries. "Your turn will come."

Upon the daily return of my siblings from this heavenly cupcake palace I imagined, I pestered them for information on anything and everything they cared to tell. They showed me pages with numbers and artwork done with paint. They read me stories they wrote. They told me about films with people and animals from faraway places and showed me boxes they decorated with red and pink hearts to collect valentines. At supper, they talked about the Empire State Building, and Paul Bunyan, the giant lumberjack who ate a wagonload of pancakes for breakfast and dug the Grand Canyon by dragging his axe. And about his blue ox, Babe.

I stayed home watching Mom do her chores and staring out the window, waiting for Tina to wake up from her nap. Once in a while I got a *muffin* for morning snack but there was never any frosting on it. All I had for art supplies was a margarine tub of broken crayons and a colouring book. I had *never* seen a film. Nor did we have a television. The only time I wore a dress was to church on Sundays and it was always a hand-me-down. And we didn't have any books with an ox that was blue.

Finally, the summer came when it would be my turn to start school. My body pulsed with expectation as I dreamed of the prospect of finally joining my siblings, wearing school clothes, sitting at my own desk and eating cupcakes.

But that same summer our family moved, and the new place, in the southeast corner of Oklahoma, had no kindergarten. I didn't learn about that right away. Mom and Dad held back on making that little tidbit known to me, perhaps wanting me to acclimatize to our new home before my year was completely ruined.

The house we moved into, on the far outskirts of Merton, Oklahoma, was the parsonage next to the Mennonite church where Dad took over as minister. From the boundaries of the church yard, all I could see in any direction were miles of crop fields, lines of fencing, and two roads that crossed and disappeared into the opposite horizons. And one faded farmyard house and barn in the distance, belonging to an old couple with an old horse, too feeble to ride.

There was little movement in the landscape but for birds floating in the immense sky and the gentle swaying of vegetation. When the wind blew, tumbleweeds rolled like giant dust balls across the wide open spaces, gathering in angled heaps against fences and walls. The church stood bold against the landscape, its tall but plain steeple pointing to heaven, its whiteness intensified by the brilliant blue of the sky, making it look huge, pure and holy.

If I could have looked at the churchyard from heaven (which I thought about during bedtime prayers, especially when we got to, *'If I die before I wake, I pray the Lord my soul to take'*) I would have seen a neatly-drawn square. Two of the sides were arrow-straight country roads joined at one corner by a stop sign. The other two sides were marked by equally straight barbed-wire fences. This big square was divided into four relatively equal smaller squares. In one square was the church building, ringed with sidewalks and dwarf shrubbery. In the second square, was the parking lot, a big flat gravel-covered nothing space, completely empty except on Sundays. In the third square, was our house and grassy yard, a vegetable garden and big oak tree. The fourth square was the best, containing another grassy area with trees and three outbuildings: a squat log house (probably the original homestead), a shed that at one time must have been a stable, and an outhouse with two seats.

Once or twice a day, a car or tractor appeared as a spot on the horizon, shimmering and trailing dust like a slow-motion comet, causing us to stop what we were doing and watch its advance, raising our hands to wave. From far off, some vehicles looked to be driverless, but as they drew close we could see the top of a head, hovering just above the steering wheel.

"Farm kids," Mom liked to say. "It's a wonder their feet can reach the pedals."

Saturday morning was devoted to chores. My sisters and I worked inside. There wasn't much cleaning or dusting to do, since we didn't have much in the way of knickknacks, or what Mom referred to as clutter. Our only living room décor was an oil painting of a mountain forest scene hanging above the couch. Another painting, which hung over the kitchen table, showed Jesus' face in muted browns and yellows gazing upward with kind, troubled eyes.

Our only clutter was a flower-rimmed plate Mom saved from her childhood in Brazil, and three porcelain Monks; two slim ones with corks in their heads to hold oil and vinegar and a short chubby one who split at the waist to hold sugar. Our most precious possession, one we rarely touched and dusted ever so carefully, was Mom's

Hummel statue: a Swiss boy wearing green shorts with suspenders, brown lace-up shoes, and a cap with a tiny feather. After tidying our rooms and stripping the bed sheets, we buffed the waxed floors with wool socked feet. If Mom got out the nutcracker, we helped pick the nuts from shells using toothpicks for her afternoon baking.

Mark and Dad did outside chores and fixed the car. Car maintenance/repair sessions always started with Dad pulling the car into the church parking lot, maybe so oil wouldn't spill on the driveway or to prevent severe damage to the house if the car blew up. Raised on a farm, Dad was a home-schooled mechanic, claiming he could make minor repairs, (those not requiring a hoist) and maintain any vehicle as long as it was manufactured in North America. Though this notion was challenged on more than one family vacation while we sat on the roadside with the hood up, Dad must have felt compelled to pass on the tradition of self-taught car repair to his only son. They leaned over the motor, Mark handing tools to Dad, who poked and fiddled, sometimes grunting. They crawled under the car to lie with their feet sticking out, Dad's scuffed toes pointing outward. The high point for Mark was turning the ignition on cue or sitting on Dad's lap to steer. They'd take the car for a few runs around the parking lot, spraying gravel and raising dust clouds, skidding to test the brakes.

When the work was done we played outside. I yearned to play inside the old log house but because it was locked on our arrival, Dad said, "No one goes inside." Mom said the shed was an ideal play spot after Dad cleared out the junk because the light came in above the half wall that was built to allow the animals to stick their heads outside. I felt comfort in the shed, imagining baby Jesus in his manger on the dirt floor, Mary and Joseph proud and intent, angels hovering in the rafters. There was plenty of room to play Orphanage, with a pile of lumber serving as a long, multi-level table. Mark wouldn't play, nor would Ruth unless she got to be the doctor, examining the babies with the plastic stethoscope from her medical case, a birthday gift I still coveted, especially the pink thermometer and two bottles of candy pills she prescribed mostly to herself.

The problem with Orphanage was that we didn't have enough dolls.

"You can't take all those outside," Mom said the first time we tried exiting through the kitchen with our assortment of dolls. "Just take the old ones out."

"But then we won't have enough for an orphanage," said Trudy.

"Surely you have lots of old dolls. You each get one every Christmas," Mom was standing at the flour-covered counter, her hands buried in a big sticky ball of dough.

"Yah, but we had to give most of them away before we moved here, remember?" Sarah said carefully.

"Oh…that's right…Well, you'll just have to pretend you have more. Put the new ones back. They need to stay clean for taking to bed at night," she said, resuming her kneading.

"Could we get Barbie Dolls this Christmas?" Trudy asked, rather boldly. "Sarah and I want one. We could trade the clothes."

"Those plastic creatures are not dolls," snapped Mom. "They look nothing like babies." She shook her head, driving her knuckles deep into the dough then yanking it back toward her, muttering while we headed back to the bedrooms, "Imagine, making dolls with mature figures... and with all that hair…"

So we did pretend, improvising with vegetables from the garden, sneaking scraps of fabric from Mom's sewing basket to drape around the babies for clothing and comfort. My favourite babies were corn cobs, already wrapped tightly in green blankets that when peeled back, revealed golden faces, like I imagined some of the 'children of the world' in the song, *Jesus Loves the Little Children*. Sweet potatoes had ideal size and shape, but they dirtied our hands when we dug them up and then the scraps of material that served as blankets. So did turnips. Cucumbers were abundant, so we used them for triplets, but they were prickly and not very cuddly. Cabbage and lettuce heads worked well as chubby, healthy babies, but were a challenge to dress up properly. Carrots were the forlorn, starving babies with long hair that flooffed outward, rescued from Biafra, a name pronounced whenever one of us tried to leave food on our plates.

We laid the vegetables along the boards, placing them apart like cribs in a nursery, twins and triplets snuggled together, naming and feeding them imaginary baby food that came in jars. Since Mom always hollered at us from the porch for meals, she wasn't aware of our extensive orphanage.

"Are we stealing?" I asked one day as we snuck along the fence with a cabbage in each hand.

"We're only borrowing," Trudy said. "We'll put them back."

"Won't they spoil?"

"Naw," she said. "The pioneers kept potatoes and cabbage in their root cellars. They'll be okay."

"I wish I could be in school to learn about pioneers," I said.

"You get to go in another year."

"So we're not stealing?"

"We're practicing," she said, "for when I get my own orphanage."

The area between the outhouse and the shed was another place to play. The house, the log house, the church and areas outside the big fence were off-limits for games, so our options were limited, as were our choices of games. Due to our heritage of pacifism, certain games were forbidden: "Soldiers" involved war, "Cowboys" required shooting, "Indians" fought with bows and arrows, and games with superheroes like Batman or The Green Hornet, since that required bad guys and villains. We were not allowed to use sticks or stones as stand-in weapons, and we were *never* to point fingers as pretend guns, or use slingshots, even though Mark pointed out that Goliath was defeated with one. That left various forms of tag, hide and seek, and non-violent pretend games in which we posed as doctors, teachers or missionaries. We were allowed to climb trees until Ruth fell and sprained her ankle.

Based on this criterion, the most adventurous game in our repertoire was daring each other to stay inside the outhouse, an activity I did everything in my power, to avoid. The length of time varied from counts of 50 to 100. It was dark inside but for the splinters of light filtering through gaps in the weathered boards and the crescent-moon hole. When my turn came, I'd stand inside with my eyes squeezed tight, hugging my chest, trying not to think of the multitude of insects that might bite me or crawl on my legs. I would will my mind not to think about rattlesnakes, since Dad told us to watch out for them, especially in dark, cool places, like right where I was standing.

Once, when I cried out that they were counting too slowly, I heard them laughing, and then Mark said, "Oops, we lost count. Now we'll have to start over." Seething with fright and rage, I fantasized retaliation, but I could never outsmart them.

I knew I had to be careful about angry thoughts since God and Jesus were always watching... and listening. They told us in Sunday school that God and Jesus know everything. Even what we are thinking. And that my sins were recorded in heaven, that one day they would stand in judgment—of me.

"How much sin are we allowed," I asked one day while wrapping a carrot, "before we won't be allowed into Heaven?"

"Just ask for forgiveness if you sin," Sarah said. "Then it's okay."

"But will it still be written down?" I asked. "Do they write it down, and then erase it?"

"Probably," said Trudy.

"But you can't do the same sin over and over and expect God to forgive you every time," said Sarah. "That's cheating. He'll catch on."

"So how many times can you do the same sin?"

"Probably lots," said Trudy.

"No, you can't," said Sarah. "If you keep doing wrong, you'll be punished."

"How do you think we'll be punished?" I asked.

"Just be good," said Sarah. "That's all."

"How good do I have to be?" I asked.

"You'll know," said Ruth. "Your conscience will tell you."

"How does the conscience tell you?" I asked.

"It's like a voice inside your head," Ruth added, "telling you you're doing wrong. And if your stomach feels a bit sick when you do something, it's probably bad. So use good judgment."

Thinking about good *or* bad judgment made my stomach feel bad. Sometimes I imagined my day of judgment. I pictured a filmy ghost-like man with silver hair, summoning me with a spindly finger, directing me to wait while he floated to a cloudy pulpit in front of heaven's towering wall. Behind him, a crowd would appear through the mist, facing me like a choir, whispering, my family and relatives among them. The man would command silence, then open a book so thick you could barely see his face. The Book of Sin. Then he would read…

"On October 5, 1964, you took the white corrective typewriter fluid from your father's study and painted your fingernails… acts of both of stealing and vanity"

"On November 3, 1964, you ate a Halloween candy from your younger sister's sack… another act of stealing…and gluttony…"

And on and on, amidst an occasional gasp from one of my aunts.

Upon completion, he'd peer at me, perhaps giving time to reflect or apologize, but I'd be struck dumb. The silence would be broken suddenly by the sound of a trumpet and a band of joyful angels lifting me like I was a feather toward the open gates to heaven's streets of gold…or the strike of lightening and my body suddenly plummeting as though falling off a cliff, my hair flying backward, tears streaming from my eyes, screams frozen in my throat, twisting and spiralling downward through a dark shaft into the fiery, black depths to suffer for eternity.

Mom said that God's House, or the church, was the central part of life. She loved to quote parts of Psalm 100 with exuberance, especially 'Make a joyful noise unto the Lord,' and 'Enter His gates with Thanksgiving,' smiling radiantly on Sunday mornings, greeting congregational members at the entrance, handing out bulletins, which she pronounced as 'bulletings', while Dad sat in a pew near the front, preparing for the service 'in quiet meditation'.

And truly, the church did draw a crowd, transforming our world every Sunday, when mud covered pickups and four-door sedans advanced along the country roads in lines like trains converging at Grand Central Station, then breaking apart and filling the church parking lot. Under Ruth's supervision, my siblings and I, at the designated time, walked from the parsonage to the church, stepping gently to stop the dust that billowed with every step from sullying our best Sunday clothes, the girls clutching plastic purses that held a coin for the collection plate, Kleenex and a comb.

The church basement smelled of mildew, sometimes making my eyes water. My Sunday school class of little kids sat on a wooden bench and listened to Mrs. Goertz read stories from the Illustrated Children's Bible propped on her tightly clasped knees.

"How could a snake tell Eve to eat an apple?" I asked one Sunday as I accepted my colouring sheet.

"God made the world and He can work miracles," she answered, putting a tub of crayons on the table.

"But wouldn't Eve be afraid of the snake if it could talk?" I asked to her receding back.

"How could Noah get all the animals to walk together into the ark like that? Wouldn't he be scared of the lions?" I asked on another Sunday, pointing at the open page.

"God is all-powerful and He can work miracles," Mrs. Goertz said curtly.

"Wouldn't it be hard to see inside the whale's belly?" I asked during the story of Jonah. Mrs. Goertz looked flustered and continued reading. She began to ignore my hand.

I cannot say whether it was truly curiosity that caused my inquisitiveness or a tad of belligerence stemming from the fact that I was still not in real school. And Sunday school was no consolation since they didn't serve cupcakes or let us play circle games.

I learned that my long anticipated dream of going to school would be postponed mid-way through the first summer after we moved to Oklahoma. One fateful evening when talk began of school starting, with my excitement growing, my questions incessant, the bomb fell. Without even the aid of a lollipop to cushion the blow, like after vaccinations, I was told—I WOULD NOT BE GOING TO SCHOOL IN FALL. THERE WAS NO KINDERGARTEN AT THE ONLY SCHOOL WITHIN FIFTY MILES. IT WAS FOR GRADES ONE THROUGH TWELVE. Once again, I wasn't old enough to go to school. I cried myself to sleep that night, the next night, and many subsequent nights, shocked and horrified at the prospect of facing another year of waiting.

The church service followed Sunday school at eleven. Our family sat in the second pew with Dad next to the aisle. Over time, Ruth, then Sarah and Trudy, then Mark, cashed in on their 'older sibling' status and were allowed to sit further back. Tina and I were told to stay put. The front pew remained empty, so I had an unobstructed view of Dad in his paisley tie, elevated in the pulpit, adjusting his black-rimmed glasses. The congregation sat solemn and still, the men wearing dark suits with white shirts and narrow unpatterned ties, the women in calf length, long sleeved dresses, simple and plain; the married ones with net-like head coverings. Mom didn't cover her head, claiming that bowing one's head during prayer was sufficient in God's eyes. She looked "sharp", Dad said, in her tailored suit, white blouse and special cameo broach.

When it was time to sing, a quiet roll like thunder echoed through the sanctuary as the congregation stood. Then came the thumping of hymnals opening and the rattling of pages turning as the pianist began to play. The sermon followed, always starting the same way, with Dad clearing his throat, then gazing for a moment at the congregation, his face fixed with an expression of either placid beguilement or silent turmoil. He'd begin slowly, pausing in and after each sentence, like he was letting the words absorb the silence, his eyes on the congregation, sometimes glancing at his notes. He'd gradually increase the pace of his words, speaking with passion, at times sternly; then he'd move to a gentler tone, gripping the sides of the pulpit or resting his elbows and pressing his palms together.

I found it hard to sit still in the heat of an Oklahoma summer when sweat pooled under my legs and flies buzzed around, landing on the same spot, again and again and again and again. I struggled to keep my neck from twisting when my head felt sore and flat from leaning against the back of the pew. I tried not to squirm when I heard the noises from the old people sitting behind us; loud nasal breathing, like horses, croaky singing and sloppy, chewing sounds like they were sitting back there eating taffy. Dad loomed close in the pulpit and I felt his eyes on me if I fidgeted or covered my ears. "It is our job," he reminded us at Sunday lunch, "to set an example". At the end of the service we bowed our heads in prayer for so long my neck felt stiff, like it was made of wood.

After church we sat down to our pot-roasted Sunday lunch dressed in our church clothes, since Mom said it showed due respect to the Lord. Sunday lunch conversations started with Dad asking questions about what we learned in Sunday school or from his sermon. Thankfully, Dad's questions were usually directed to the privileged ones who sat with their friends in the pews further back. During tense moments when responses were slow in coming, I posed questions to the table, like whether the others abandoned the lady when she was turned into a pillar of salt, and what would happen to her in the rain.

Dad said most of those stories didn't happen exactly like in the pictures.

"Then why do they put those pictures in?" I asked.

"To give us an idea of how it went."

"Why don't they put the real stories and pictures in then?"

"The Old Testament was written by prophets. Only God knows the Truth. And they didn't have the tools to make proper photographs. That's why God sent Jesus to Earth. To teach us through example."

"I thought Jesus was sent so we should not perish but have everlasting life," I said.

"Yes," he said. "And He came to teach us."

"What did Jesus say about those stories?"

"Jesus spoke in parables," he said. "It is a bit complicated. We must trust God's wisdom. And follow the teachings in the Gospels."

At bed time, I asked Ruth what parables and Gospels were. She said they were the lessons and stories about Jesus. More questions didn't clarify anything and I found her answers complicated and frustrating since each answer required another question.

After the Sunday meal, we changed into regular clothes and went back to the church to gather bulletins and wadded up tissues, and place the hymnals upright into the slots on the pews. We knew to honour the Sabbath as a day of rest but Mom said "a little picking up won't hurt."

Suppertime on Sundays meant "Faspa", either at our house or at the home of another church family. Faspa was a small, easy meal that did not take great efforts to prepare, since toiling on Sunday was breaking the Fourth Commandment. Faspa was zwieback and other baking done on Saturday, served with sliced cheese, assorted jams, pickles and preserves, and bologna or leftover ham. Mom said slicing food was not considered toil. Zwieback, she told us, means "two buns". She taught us how to make it by taking a handful of dough and squeezing a round glob between your thumb and forefinger. Then another smaller round glob is squeezed out, stacked on top of the other in the style of a snowman, and poked lightly with a finger from the top down to stick the two globs together. Other typical Faspa items were puffed wheat squares, or the ever popular 'platz'; a cake made in cookie sheets, covered with apples, peaches or plums, and topped with sugar coating and baked to a golden brown. My least favourite Faspa dish was plumi moos, a thick stewy soup made with plums, apricots, raisins and other fruit, eaten hot or cold. Fortunately, it was rarely served at our Faspa, since washing bowls and spoons required extra work.

After Faspa, the adults sat in the living room, visiting and drinking coffee. Children were politely acknowledged, then shooed away to occupy themselves with quiet activities like Jacks, Pick up Stix, or dolls. We could play Old Maid or Crazy Eights unless we were visiting those members of the church who thought playing with cards was "worldly" and might lead to gambling, which was very sinful.

Absolutely the *worst* day of my entire life in Oklahoma was the day my older siblings started school. The big yellow bus pulled into the parking lot and I cried when it drove away. Mom held my hand on the way back to the house, then let me stand on a chair to wash the breakfast dishes.

It took a long time before I realized that being miserable about not being in school wasn't doing me any good. I know I must have driven Mom crazy, following her around, probably talking way too much. She offered small tasks; drying breakfast dishes, folding wash cloths or matching socks. In the afternoons it became routine to go into the sewing room while Dad was in the study and Tina napped.

"What are you sewing?" I asked the first time.

"Baby blankets to wrap around Christmas bundles. The ladies in the Bible Study group are sewing them," she said.

"What goes inside the bundles?"

"Things for the mother."

"What things?"

"Oh, a towel, a toothbrush, a few bars of soap, a washcloth... things like that. I need to make some diapers, too. Then we'll send them overseas."

"Where's overseas?" I asked.

"These will go to Africa, where people don't have the luxuries we have here."

I'd heard a little about luxuries. Chocolate was a luxury. And banana splits.

"Are soap and toothpaste luxuries?" I asked.

"To many people in the world they are," she said. "But most people in North America don't know that."

I sat very still on the bed, not sure what to make of that. She looked at me and smiled. "You can help me wrap the bundles once we've assembled everything we need. We'll secure each bundle with a diaper pin. That way each mother has one."

Sometimes, when Mom was making clothes for us, I helped with pinning pattern pieces on fabric, but usually I sat on the single bed while she worked. I knew it was best to wait for Mom to get organized with a project and allow her a few quiet moments. Then I began to pester.

"Can you tell the story about the prince who got dropped off his royal pillow by the servant and became crippled," I pleaded.

"You've heard that one so many times," she said.

"How about Hans Brinker who kept his finger in the dike all night to save the village from perishing in a flood?"

Mom told me about Rapunzle, Hansel and Gretel, and the goose that laid golden eggs, stories with kings and queens and magic. She told them over and over.

"Tell me about when you were a little girl in Brazil," I'd ask when I wanted a real story.

'I've told you all of those stories, many times," she'd reply.

"Tell me again," I'd beg, never tiring of hearing about the jungles, with trees of the darkest green and leaves big enough to hide behind, spiralling vines and multi-coloured parrots, and snakes, longer than she was tall and as big around as I was. She told about the Corcovado, a huge statue of Jesus perched high on a hill looking down at Sugar Loaf Mountain and the mosaic beaches. I thought, except for the snakes, Brazil sounded perfect.

Mom grew up in Brazil, but she was born in Russia. That's probably why she pronounced certain words funny, like 'veelbarrow', and 'vatermelon'. She told things about Russia that I didn't like, about Mennonites being persecuted, explaining what that meant. They got persecuted for speaking German and going to church. She said her father was persecuted because he had a big farm and was rich. He was taken in the middle of the night by some Bolsheviks and sent to a work camp. That's why the rest of her family had fled, she said. And she never saw her father again.

"Was it fun on the ship?" I asked once.

"Mostly, we stayed below," she said. "It was dreadful for most of the trip."

She talked of being sick from the rolling and pitching of the boat, the crowded bunk space below deck where they had to sleep, and awful smells. She said many people were coughing and by the time they reached Brazil, she had bald patches on her head where her hair had fallen out.

When the weather was fine, Mom took Tina and me outside where we tagged along behind her, sometimes holding out clothespins or watching her weed or pick vegetables in the garden. Sometimes she let us pull carrots or pick beans. I often stared into the distance, hoping to see a mini twister or a jackrabbit, but mostly wishing for the return of the school bus.

At supper time, vibrating with equal parts of longing and resentment, I listened to my older siblings talk about pilgrims and astronauts and animals that only came out at night. Their stories about pirates and treasures and Presidents and First Ladies got me begging them for more. News of pep rallies and cheerleaders and a haunted house at Halloween had me on the edge of my chair, clenching my jaw. Accounts of assemblies with a Santa and elves and the rhythm band made me want to stomp my feet or kick something because I wasn't there to see or hear them myself. But I didn't kick or stomp, because that was not allowed.

There was a cat, Mustard, and a dog, Ginger, left behind by the previous minister's family. Ginger was a short haired, mixed breed with a bulldog face. He mostly drooled and scratched himself. I wasn't fond of dogs because of Morgan, the German Shepherd who lived next door to us in our previous neighbourhood. He ran at us, lunging and jerking from the end of his chain, barking and gnashing his teeth. Mustard was shy and hid most of the time. Mustard and Ginger stayed outside since Mom wasn't about to clean up fleas or animal hair.

Our other pets were three female rabbits; Isabelle, Molly and Daisy. Their cage was in the corner of the yard, built off the ground, the base about level with my chest, in the shade of the oak tree. Feeding them was the highlight of my mornings. Mom said it was an important job, showing me how to open and close the cage door and divide the garden scraps among them. I loved watching their crunchy little nibbles and lopsided chewing. When they finished eating, I could pet them, but I wasn't to take them out of the cage; Mom said they might leap off and would be too fast and squirmy to catch on the run.

My love of feeding the rabbits came to an end the evening that Dad came home carrying a large box.

"Come look," he'd said, placing the box on the floor as we gathered around.

Inside was a very large, fat rabbit with red-rimmed eyes, sloppy jowls and yellowing fur. I felt revulsion as Mark pronounced, "We'll call him Jack."

From then on, each time I opened the cage door, Jack leapt forward, making me drop food and pull my hand away. No matter how well I tried to divide the food, Jack always got in the way, hogging the best pieces, pushing the females away, squashing the remaining bits, making them filthy. He'd chase one of the females around, cornering her, then climb on her back with his ears plastered back, pushing at her, making the hay fall through the meshing onto the ground. If I watched too long, he'd stop moving and stare back at me, completely still except for his twitching nose. I stopped petting the girls, fearing Jack would come at me. I knew the Bible said it was wrong to hate, and that thinking bad thoughts was as bad as doing them. I began to throw the scraps into the cage, trying my best to scatter them fairly, then shut the door and leave.

One winter morning Tina was in bed with a cold and Dad was in his study.

"We should check on the rabbits," Mom said. "Isabelle is due any time and it is bitterly co-oh-oh-ld out there."

I watched my breath coming out in white puffs, aware that Jack was clomping around as we stepped carefully through the snow. When we reached the cage, Mom's grip on my hand tightened and for a moment everything was completely still. I looked into the cage, confused by some blue and pink things, like sausages, scattered in the hay.

"Oh, dear Lord," Mom whispered.

Suddenly, Jack leapt toward Isabelle, starting a rapid chase, stomping all over the little things with his big clumpy feet.

"We'll need something to put them in," Mom's voice was shaky. "I have to hurry." She turned and tried to run toward the house without slipping. I turned to follow.

As I rounded the corner, Mom was coming out the door, a tea towel and a cake pan tucked under her arm, putting on her 'church and going visiting' gloves. She hurried past me.

When I returned to the cage, I suddenly understood. Mom was placing newborn rabbits onto the towel lined cake pan.

"Are they dead?" I asked.

"Some of them might be," she said.

Jack was braced in the far corner, squishing Isabelle so her fur was bulging out, square-like, through the meshing. His forefeet swivelled side to side, his ears flattened back. Molly and Daisy cowered opposite. Mom didn't look at Jack.

"Why did Jack do that?" I asked.

"I don't understand it myself," Mom said and her tone silenced me.

My eyes darted back and forth, willing Jack to stay put, and counting the babies as Mom gathered them. There were eight. After gently rummaging through the hay for any she might have missed, Mom banged the cage door like she was mad at all of them and hurried back to the house. I followed, trying to keep up.

When I reached the kitchen, Mom was standing by the oven.

"What are you going to bake?" I asked from the doorway.

"Close the door. These bunnies are cold. We'll warm them in the oven," she said. "We need some washcloths from the hall closet. Get all of them."

My feet slipped easily out of my boots and I ran to the bathroom.

I returned a minute later, the underside of my socks damp from stepping in the tracks from Mom's wet boots. I placed the washcloths on the counter then dragged a chair to the counter and climbed up. The five bodies in the pan looked nothing like bunnies I'd ever seen. With no fur, they looked cold and ugly, the skin pink with blue spidery lines, their closed eyes bulgy like miniature marbles, the ears squashed. The only cute parts were their almost invisible whiskers. I wanted to ask where she put the others, but I stayed quiet.

With gloved hands, Mom spread a washcloth and placed a bunny onto the middle. She lifted the lower corner, then folded the side flaps as though putting on a giant diaper. She rolled the top corner down like a jelly roll leaving the tiny faced exposed.

"This will help warm the head," she said. She replaced the bundle and began to wrap another.

"How come they have no hair?" I asked.

"They're too young," said Mom "but it will grow fast once it gets started."

"When will that be?"

"In a few days," Mom replied with a sigh.

"Can I help?"

"I don't think it's a good idea to touch them," Mom said. "The mother might reject them if she doesn't recognize the smell. That's why I'm wearing gloves."

"What does reject mean?" I asked.

"That means she will turn away from them. She will ignore them and not let them suckle," Mom said.

The pan looked like an orphanage nursery. Mom opened the oven door and stuck her hand inside.

"Should we tell Dad?" I asked.

"I'll go talk to him," she said. "I think the temperature is okay now."

Mom took off her coat and threw it onto the kitchen table, then carefully placed the pan inside the oven, leaving the door ajar.

"You can watch them. But you must keep the oven door open. Else they might get too warm," she said, and left the room.

I positioned the chair so I could see inside. Soon the study door opened and Mom and Dad came into the kitchen. Dad was wearing his overcoat and holding his galoshes.

He smiled at me. "You're getting them all warmed up, are you?"

I nodded.

"I'll be back soon," he said going out the door.

From my spot on the chair, I heard Mom going into the bathroom and turning on the tap, and Dad getting into the car and turning the ignition. The car sat idling in the driveway, longer than usual. Minutes passed before I heard the slam of the door and the car driving away.

"Let's go do some sewing," Mom said, suddenly behind me. "The rabbits will be okay for awhile. Later we'll try to feed them."

"How will we feed them?" I asked.

"I need to do some thinking on that," she said. "Sewing will help me think."

Around lunch time, Dad brought home a box, lined it with hay and put it in the hallway outside his study. We put the wash cloth wrapped babies inside, under a bigger towel, "to keep out the draft". Mom let me tuck the towel under the corners.

At supper, Mom told the others about rescuing the rabbits.

"I got to feed warm milk to them with an eye dropper," I blurted out, interrupting her. "Lot's of the milk just dribbled down their faces. They didn't really know what to do," I said, now the rabbit-care expert. I relished their looks of envy. Mom hadn't let them touch the rabbits.

"We'll bring in Isabelle after supper. See if she will accept them," said Mom. "Hopefully, she'll be full of milk and want to feed them."

"Where is Jack?" asked Mark.

"I took him away," said Dad.

"Where did you take him?" Ruth asked.

Dad raised his knife and dipped it in the peanut butter jar. He made some careful swirls onto a soda cracker and placed it into his bowl of vanilla ice cream. Then he picked up his spoon and scooped the cracker and some ice cream into his mouth.

We got another scary pet the following spring. We were starting a game of hide and seek inside the shed and poised to flee as soon as the countdown began.

Mark saw it first.

"Holy cow," he said.

I flinched. We weren't supposed to say 'holy cow', so I cringed when he said it again, louder. When I turned to look where he was staring, I was so stunned I couldn't move. A tarantula was crawling along the top of the lumber pile, moving as though through water, smooth and graceful, one leg at a time. The others turned and ran, yelling, toward the house, leaving me frozen in shock for a few seconds. Then I tore out after them.

There was a near collision at the corner of the house with Mom who was charging in our direction, stern faced, wringing floured covered hands on her apron. She didn't speak but we all heard, "What is all this noise about when you know Dad is in his study preparing his sermon?"

"There's a... tarantula...in the woodshed," Mark managed between gasps.

Mom continued wringing while her expression changed to, "There had better be one if I come all the way out there to see it."

"Show me," she said and marched around us toward the shed. We followed, like geese in her wake. Fortunately, it was still there, hovering at the end of a board, two of its dark, hairy legs raised and feeling around like a tiny maestro leading a symphony.

"You can go get Dad," Mom said, looking pale. "I need to get back to the zwieback."

We ran in a pack, gathering outside the study door. We all looked at Ruth to do the knocking. Several seconds passed before we heard the slow scraping of the chair along the floor, and another pause before footsteps. Dad opened the door looking straight ahead, his lips pursing as his gaze moved slowly downward.

"There's a tarantula in the shed, Dad," Ruth blurted.

"A tarantula," Dad repeated.

"Yah, a tarantula. It's huge," said Mark. "Mom saw it. She said we could get you."

The tarantula was nowhere in sight when we got back to the shed. I tensed, thinking, 'Oh boy', but Dad started prodding and rattling, bending around to look between the boards. My sisters and I stood outside looking over the half wall, my heart pounding.

Suddenly, Dad let out a whistle.

"He is a big one!" he said. "We'll need a jar."

Mark turned and ran, accustomed to Dad beckoning.

"Dad, he might jump on you," Ruth said. "He could be poison."

"I don't believe tarantulas are adept at jumping," he said tersely.

When Mark returned with a mayonnaise jar, things got even scarier. All of our coaching and comments only seemed to delay the capture of the creature. Dad appeared to be toying with the spider, drawing the jar close then pulling it slowly away. Any movement of the tarantula toward Dad made us gasp. My breath was getting tight watching Dad's shenanigans, a word Mom used for unnecessary silliness.

Finally, the tarantula stopped moving. Dad positioned the jar while we all held our breath. Then, using the lid like a baseball bat, he flicked the spider into the jar. It landed on its back and for a moment, flung its legs wildly around in the air. Then, righting itself, it bucked up, flailing its legs against the sides of the glass, bouncing back and forth in panic. Dad held the jar up, letting the sunlight shine through to examine it more closely.

"Yes indeed, he is a big one," he said, presenting it in our direction like a prized fish while we drew backward. After letting us gaze for a moment (me in wild-eyed terror), he tucked the jar against his chest and strode toward the house. We ran along after him. I wanted to see where he was taking it. After placing the jar onto a shelf at his eye level on the outside porch, and studying it for a moment, he went inside, letting the door slam behind him.

At first Dad seemed to find it funny, smiling when we complained about the captive spider on the porch. I certainly didn't like it there. But it was one of my sisters —I won't say which one, it wasn't me — that suffered the most from having that tarantula around. For two nights, she barely slept, in constant fear that it would escape and come crawling inside the house to poison one or all of us. It got so bad her eyes were bagged and puffy. The third day, her eyes were wet when we sat down for breakfast.

"I'll take it outside," Dad announced during dinner on the third night. "I'll step on it."

"No, Dad, no," she cried. "It could bite through your shoe."

Dad had to drive it away in the car.

The spider was gone and we got back to normal, except it put a damper on our wanting to play in the woodshed.

Maybe to brighten us after the turmoil, Mom and Dad surprised us the following Saturday when a farm tractor pulled into the church parking lot, hauling a round drinking trough, bigger around than the width of the wagon. We all ran outside to watch.

"What's that for?" Mark asked. "Are we getting some cows?"

"No, it's for you," Dad smiled, as we stood mouths gaping.

"It's for swimming in!" Mom exclaimed, continuing with emphasis on each word, "Your very own swimming pool!"

"Our very own swimming pool," we chorused.

We were standing in the back yard wearing swimsuits before the farmer and Dad were able to roll it into place. Dad turned on the hose and we jumped in, stomping and splashing around in the water that barely covered the bottom. As the water gradually rose, we spent the afternoon talking about how lucky we were, having our own pool, like rich people.

At dinner, Mom and Dad went over the pool rules.

"Never swim alone."

"Ruth is in charge when you're out there."

"And don't turn into prunes."

Having a pool made that one great summer. What made it even better was that one afternoon in July, Dad brought home another surprise; a television. It wasn't new, but it didn't matter. We only got one station clearly, but that didn't matter either. Now being outside was fantastic because when it was too hot to run, we could jump into the swimming pool. And in the evening, if Mom said it was okay, we might be able to watch a television program.

Besides all that, the summer was great because I knew that when it was over, I would finally go to school. I'd been learning to read over the summer, taking advantage of enforced time "in our rooms", punishments for various things like listening in on the party phone line, or "making spotte", mocking or making fun of people or things that deserved more respect. Once, for pulling down a curtain rod. Another time, for getting caught playing tag in the church sanctuary. My older sisters were just bored enough during these times to give in to my incessant pleas to be taught to read. By the time school started, I was reading the simple sentences they printed out, which relieved some of my anxiety over not being smart enough for school.

My birthday that August was the best birthday ever. First thing that morning I was given something I had prayed for—my own Bible. A white leather Bible, with a blue satin ribbon page keeper, colour pictures, and the words of Jesus printed in red. Even better, after I read some words from my new Bible, Mom and Dad said I had another present coming and it was too big to fit inside the house. I was baffled, wondering what it could be, and how in the world did I deserve all this. After lunch, we left in the car to see the present. I could barely contain myself, nattering the whole car ride, asking question after question, receiving only smiles and smirks. It turned out we were going to the movie theatre to watch *Mary Poppins*. It was the most amazing thing I had ever seen; the scenes and characters larger than life, playing in colour, filling up the entire front wall of the theatre.

Shortly after my birthday, the whole family made a special trip into town to buy school supplies. I strutted behind, all puffed up with pride as Mom crossed things off my list, adding to the metal basket, six special thick red pencils, four erasers, round tip scissors, a double row box of crayons and a yellow cigar box to put everything in. Mom said she'd print my name on my school supplies with a Magic Marker once we got home. When I thought we were finished shopping, she took my hand and led us down an aisle of kitchen stuff. We stopped beside a pile of kitchen mats.

"It says here, first graders need to have a mat for nap time in the afternoon. You need to choose one of these," she said pointing toward the stack.

That was a not-so-good surprise. No one ever said anything about nap time at school. No thanks, I thought but I said, "I don't need to take naps".

"This supply list says you need to have one," she said.

It must have been the crayons, or Mary Poppins, that gave me courage to continue. "I don't take naps anymore," I said quietly.

"I guess first grade babies need naps," said Mark.

"That's enough," Mom snapped. "Everyone in your class will have one," she continued, sternly. "You don't want to nap on the classroom floor. Now, choose one."

FINALLY!!!

Finally, finally, finally, finally the day came.

I wore a new dress and new sneakers to breakfast and it wasn't Sunday. I rode on the school bus with the driver Sarah called a Dreamboat. I stood in my first school line up by the primary playground. I sat in my own desk with my own brand-new cigar box with school supplies, all with my name on them, watching Mrs. Shepherd.

She stood before us in her cat eye glasses that looped behind her neck on a chain, calling out names. Wearing a turquoise suit, with a white blouse done up to the neck, Mrs. Shepherd announced the school rules into the air above our heads, as though expecting them to envelope us like invisible snow. Her hairstyle was a dark mass of curls that surrounded her head like a bowl, and stayed precisely intact as she walked across the classroom, stopping in front of each row, as though checking to see if our heads lined up. Only my eyes moved, scanning my new classroom. On Mrs. Shepherd's desktop was a clear vase holding plastic daffodils, a pencil can decorated in macaroni and three pieces of chalk. Everything in the classroom was in straight lines, including the rows of readers, stacks of scribblers, the pictures on the walls and the chalk on her desk.

Some of the kids looked scared. I was no stranger to rules, and felt right at home. I thought it was the way things were supposed to be, being good in the eyes of Jesus and God applied at school, too. And I knew some of my classmates from church. At recess, I played on a swing on the mini playground for grade ones and twos. I ate a plate of beans and wieners and drank my own carton of milk in the cafeteria, at a long, white table with a bench attached.

At nap time, we rolled our mats out on the floor. I didn't want to but everyone lay right down without a fuss. I fell asleep in the middle of the story, but Mrs. Shepherd didn't get angry. On the bus home, I felt a bit dopey and disoriented, but elated. I was riding the bus from school. I would step off to greet Mom and Tina, and Dad, if he wasn't in his study. I would get to tell things at supper. And soon, I would bring home a book.

The first thing Mrs. Shepherd taught us was how to draw a circle. Then she taught us to do sticks. Circles and sticks. More circles and sticks. She said no one could print properly if they didn't know how to draw circles and sticks. We learned how important that was because if our circles weren't round and our sticks weren't straight, she threw it in the trash can. I tried my best to print carefully but she never commented, "Oh, what wonderful printing," like she did to Terry Anne Mason. Nor did she tear the page out of my book, like she did to Mark Adams. But she smiled when she read the sentence under the picture I drew. It said, 'I can jump.'

At the end of two weeks, Mrs. Shepherd began her daily inspection ritual. After we stood for the Pledge of Allegiance, we sat down, placed our hands on the top of our desks, fingers splayed, while she walked up and down the aisles, looking at our hands. As she passed our desk, we were to turn our hands over slowly. She held a ruler behind her back as she walked up and down each row. One morning we learned the reason for the ruler. Alan Smith was the first to get his hand smacked. It happened so fast I didn't really see it. But then, he let out a yowl and Mrs. Shepherd grabbed his hand and smacked him again for that. Every morning after that day we sat completely still, shoulders braced, the tension in the room relaxing only when Mrs. Shepherd opened her desk drawer to put the ruler away.

Kenny Thomas was the second person to get smacked by the ruler, but not for having dirty hands. He sucked his thumb, pretty much all the time. This irritated Mrs. Shepherd, judging by the way her voice strained whenever she reminded Kenny to take it out. Kenny would remove it and shortly after, stick the other thumb in. Since verbal reminders weren't solving the problem, Mrs. Shepherd sent him to stand in the corner. But then he would stand in the corner sucking his thumb, which distracted some of the boys, who would sneak peeks at Kenny, then snicker. Mrs. Shepherd tried telling Kenny to sit on his hands at his desk. But it never failed that one of those thumbs would end up in his mouth, as though there were an invisible string pulling it there. To make matters worse, boys and girls began to watch Kenny, waiting for the moment when a thumb would be drawn into his mouth, like they might watch a bobber, waiting for a fish to bite.

Mrs. Shepherd's next tactic was to smack Kenny's hands with her ruler. But hustling around to Kenny's desk every time he stuck a thumb in his mouth disrupted Mrs. Shepherd's flow of instruction, since she first had to get the ruler from her drawer. By the time she got there, he'd be sitting on both hands, arms cemented to his sides, head tucked down. So getting access to a thumb wasn't exactly easy, even though he was pretty small. One morning after a smacking, Kenny's thumb began to bleed, requiring a Band-Aid, causing tears from Terry Anne and excess tension in the room. Mrs. Shepherd looked the other way as Kenny placed the bandaged thumb into his mouth, but her voice grew increasingly pinched as the day progressed.

The next morning, Kenny was called forward. Mrs. Shepherd picked up a small brown bottle with a brush attached to the lid, like a jar of rubber cement glue. When she took off the lid, there was an echo of small gasps as a strong odour wafted around the room. We all watched in stunned fascination as Mrs. Shepherd took each of Kenny's thumbs and brushed them with the foul liquid. The painting of Kenny's thumbs became another morning and after-lunch ritual, giving the classroom a strange medicinal smell.

The thumb sucking stopped for several days. Every time Kenny raised a thumb toward his mouth, his face took on a sour look. He sat with his arms crossed, hands tucked under his armpits. Gradually though, a thumb could approach his mouth and stay closer to his face for longer periods, sometimes resting against the side of his cheek.

In less than three weeks Kenny had a thumb in his mouth again, at first for brief moments, then for increasing intervals, his face showing a mix of contentment and mild disgust. Mrs. Shepherd watched in disbelief as the thumb sucking resumed.

Some of the boys tried to include Kenny in games, but he wasn't eager, nor was he much good at ball games with his good hand always otherwise engaged. During recess, he sat on a swing, thumb in mouth, rocking back and forth with his feet on the ground. Many boys teased Kenny, calling him a baby and telling him to go home and change his diaper. The other kid they teased was Charlene. She was in second grade and was poor, so they said, and you couldn't help but notice her hair and clothes needed washing.

Some boys whispered about her having lice, which Mark told me were bugs that live in your hair, like fleas on animals. Charlene never said anything about lice, but she said to a group of us she once got ringworm from her cat.

The next time Mustard rubbed up against my leg, I asked Mom to check me for ringworm.

"How do you know about ringworm?" Mom asked.

"Charlene told me."

"Who's Charlene?"

"She's in second grade," I said. "She's poor."

"How do you know she's poor?" Mom's eyebrows were squinting.

"You can tell by her clothes. She wears the same dress all the time," I said. "If she was in our class she'd have her knuckles smacked at inspection time."

"Get her knuckles smacked?" Mom asked. "By whom, Mrs. Shepherd?"

"Yep. We all do if our hands and fingernails are dirty. Kenny gets his knuckles smacked for sucking his thumb."

"Have you?" she asked. "Had your knuckles smacked?"

I waited a moment before answering, "Once." It was true, I'd had my knuckles smacked, but it was for drawing sticks on a paper and counting them during addition, then hiding it inside my desk. I hadn't known Mrs. Shepherd was behind me. She had grabbed me so fast I didn't have time to be scared. It was humiliating to be caught cheating. I had trouble getting to sleep for a few nights, worrying that this lapse had been noticed and recorded in heaven.

Despite the ruler smack, I loved school. I loved the cafeteria with my own tray of food. I loved marching in the gym and playing triangle in the rhythm band. I loved my clean bread bag for carrying home my reader, and I loved reading to Tina on the couch. It thrilled me to bring home pictures I made with scissors and tissue paper, and paint. I loved telling about singing 'Oh Come all Ye Faithful' with the grade two class and Mary and Joseph in their bathrobes walking alongside a donkey made with two boys, carrying a swaddling-wrapped doll.

"Did it hurt?" Mom asked.

I nodded, afraid to look up. "I guess I'll have to check your hands before you get on the bus," she said. "Ruth, you can remind me?"

"Sure," said Ruth in a flat tone. She was setting the table. "Charlene's brother's in my grade. He's in trouble a lot."

"What kind of trouble?" Mom asked, using her 'very concerned' tone.

"He's failed some grades and he gets into fights," said Ruth. "He's supposed to be in grade eight. The boys call him a hillbilly."

"What's a hillbilly?" I asked, but Mom gave me a sharp look.

"What's their last name?" she asked Ruth.

"Myers," she answered.

At bedtime, after we said our prayers, I asked Mom if she would check my leg for ringworm.

"Don't be silly," she said.

Mom took me into Merton the next Saturday morning with a plate of raisin cookies, 'for the Myers'. I didn't really want to go along, but Mom said she needed me as a form of introduction. I'd had to ask Ruth what that meant.

"You have to go along so Mrs. Myers will talk to Mom. Mom can say you and Charlene are friends," Ruth said.

"But I hardly know her at all."

Mom's face had a frozen smile as we got out of the car. I was shocked by the poor state of the house and cluttered yard, sure Mom would say something about it being shabby, but she didn't speak as we walked past a rusty bicycle and up the beaten stairs onto the porch.

Mrs. Myers opened the door after what seemed like a long time. She stood in the doorway, not inviting us in. I could see dirty floor tiles and a toddler in a soiled diaper, his arms wrapped around Mrs. Myers' legs. After a while, Charlene squeezed out from behind her mother and we sat down on the bottom step of the porch. I tried to listen to what Mom and Mrs. Myers were saying while Charlene and I talked. Mom was talking about church and ladies Bible study group while Mrs. Myers held the screen door against her chest, her free hand keeping the cookie plate level.

"Wanna see my cat?" Charlene asked after a moment of silence.

"Sure," I said.

I followed her to the underside of the porch where a cage was sitting in the dirt. As we ducked under to approach, the cat hissed and backed into the corner of the cage.

"Are you going to let it out?" I asked.

"Uh, uh," she said. "We doan let it out."

"Never?" I asked.

"Nah," she said. "It'd run away."

Just before Valentine's Day, a new girl joined our classroom. Joanne Miller was an 'only child' with long red hair, done up daily with head bands, ribbons or barrettes that matched her many colourful outfits. Her cardigans had pictures knitted in, the buttons decorated with ducks and kittens. She wore skirts that flared and lace socks. I imagined she would get the most valentines.

"Can I try long hair again?" I asked soon after Joanne's arrival.

"It'll hang in your eyes," Mom said. "Then no one will be able to see your big brown eyes."

"But can I have it long at the back?" I asked. "For a ponytail?"

"Maybe next year," she said.

"Ruth and the twins have long hair," I said.

"When you can comb through the tangles yourself, you can have longer hair."

"I don't like to comb the tangles," I said.

"I know," she said. "That's why we're cutting it. I'll give you a nice Pixie cut."

"What's a Pixie cut?" I asked.

"You'll see when we're done," she said.

When she was done it looked exactly like it always did. In spite of my short hair, Joanne Miller and I became friends. Perhaps she sensed my deep admiration, or maybe it was the common bond of having moved from somewhere else. Mom wasn't impressed when I described Joanne's fancy clothes, but she did agree to let her mother drive me to their house on several occasions.

Almost everything in Joanne's room was pink or white and she had the most elaborate assortment of stuffed animals and dolls I'd ever seen, fanned across her lacy pillows and filling several shelves. The Millers had a colour TV and let us watch Batman. They served pretzels and orange pop on television trays in the living room. I didn't speak about any of this at home, answering vaguely when asked about these visits, especially since some of the dolls we played with were Barbies.

That spring, Mrs. Shepherd announced that our class, along with Mrs. Baker's second grade class, was going to the zoo. Everyone was eager to choose a partner for the bus ride. Joanne nodded when I turned to look at her.

The night before the field trip, Mom helped me pack a sandwich and a doughnut from Saturday's baking. Then she placed a dime and a nickel into my hand. I could hardly get to sleep thinking about spending that money. In the morning, she took me to the sewing room and showed me a change purse with a snap closure and a picture of a howling coyote, some of the stitching loose. She opened it to show me two nickels and five pennies, then she put it into an envelope and sealed it.

"Give this to Mrs. Shepherd as soon as you get to school," Mom said.

"Is this a present for Mrs. Shepherd?" I asked.

"No, but she's expecting it. She's going to give it to Mrs. Baker. I spoke to her on the phone," she said.

"It's for Mrs. Baker?" I asked.

"It's for Charlene," she said. "But it must be a secret. Can you keep a secret?"

I nodded.

"If you tell anyone, the children might tease her," said Mom.

I had never seen Charlene so excited and talkative as she was on the bus to the zoo. She was up on her knees, wearing that old dress and sneakers with no laces, playing with the change purse so everyone could see. Mrs. Baker reminded her three times to sit down. So she sat with knees in the aisle, opening and closing the snap.

After our zoo tour, we gathered outside the refreshment and gift shop where the teachers organized us into a line. Next to the shop was a partially-recessed pen containing two elephants lumbering about. Between the shop and the elephant pen was a musical cart with a man selling peanuts. A monkey in a tiny red jacket sat on the man's shoulder, attached by a long, thin leash at the neck, holding a cup. I wanted to get a closer look at the monkey but I didn't want to waste my money on peanuts.

"I'm goan' to get some peanuts. Then I'm goan' ta feed the elephants," Charlene said as though reading my mind and began moving toward the peanut cart.

"Wanna go see the monkey?" I said eagerly to Joanne. She nodded.

We approached as the monkey scrambled down the man's arm, hopped onto the ground and held the cup toward Charlene. The man scooped peanuts and handed the bag to Charlene as the monkey jumped around jingling the coin, then scampered back up to the man's shoulder. Charlene walked away and the peanut man smiled at me as if to say, 'you want some, too?' I shook my head and we turned back to the line-up. Seeing that we'd lost our place in line, Joanne gestured toward Charlene, who was moving to the far side of the elephant pen.

"Let's watch," she said.

Charlene pressed her body against the vertical bars, a peanut on her extended palm, reaching in the direction of the biggest elephant. She was patient, her arm steady. It took a moment, but the elephant, seeming to pick up the scent, began inching closer, raising its trunk toward the peanut. Very slowly, with finger-like movements of its trunk, the elephant snatched the peanut, raising it into the air and tossing it into its open mouth.

Looking pleased, Charlene extended her palm offering another peanut. Again the elephant lifted its trunk, collecting the peanut and swinging it into its mouth. Students at the back of the line moved closer to watch, and murmurs of approval echoed around the pen. By the fourth offering, Charlene was beaming. In her excitement, she put both hands through the bars of the cage to dig into the bag for the next peanut. That was a mistake.

The elephant's trunk shot up like the snap of a whip, poking and prodding aggressively at the bag. Suddenly, the peanut bag was on the ground inside the pen. The elephant was backing away, waving something in its elevated trunk. We silently watched the elephant put Charlene's change purse into its mouth and chew while coins dropped around its feet. We stared as the elephant spat the purse onto the ground and trampled it and the coins into the dirt. Charlene looked from her empty hands to the disappearing change purse.

"He took my purse," she yelled suddenly, as though expecting someone to stop the elephant. "He got my money. The elephant took my money."

Two boys started laughing but Mrs. Baker was promptly behind them, pulling them back, whispering harshly. She returned to console Charlene, looking at us as if to say, 'Please help'.

Charlene cried when she learned that neither the money nor the change purse could be retrieved. Joanne and I waited while Mrs. Baker convinced Charlene to come into the shop with us. When we left, Charlene walked out stonily, her face streaked with tears, glaring at the elephant pen while her snow cone drained of colour.

On the bus home Joanne and I talked about how we hoped our desks would be close together in second grade. She told me her mother was going to make her next birthday cake with dimes and nickels baked right in. I would be invited to the party and we would play pin the tail on the donkey and break a piñata full of candy.

But I would not be at that birthday party. Less than two years after our arrival in Oklahoma, Dad made an announcement. It was at supper, during my final week of grade one.

"I have received a calling," he said, just after we'd said grace. "A calling," he said with quiet emphasis, "comes from God." I stared at the steam rising from the casserole, wondering what God's voice sounded like.

He continued, as though addressing his congregation, using pauses, "We are going…to open an outreach centre in Hamilton, a city in Canada. The inner city. Where people are poor and underprivileged." He unfolded his hands and splayed them gently on his dinner utensils.

"I have been concerned for some time…that the Mennonite philosophy of separating ourselves from the world by living in insulated communities,…is not following the example of Jesus Christ".

He pursed his lips, shifting the napkin. "Mom and I are no longer comfortable with that kind of Christian living".

He said some more about the disciples 'laying down their tools to follow Jesus', about 'reaching out to lepers and sinners and little children', and how it was time to 'serve God by serving others'.

Finally, he said, "Let's eat."

At bedtime, at the bathroom sink, I asked what Dad was talking about.

"He means Christians aren't supposed to live together with only other Christians," Ruth said.

"Dad says Jesus hung around with lepers and tax collectors,' said Trudy. "So we're supposed to do that, too."

"That's not what he meant," Sarah retorted. "He meant Jesus wants us to help others. Just because Mennonites go to church a lot and don't dance doesn't make them good Christians. That's why we have to go live with poor people."

"What will we do there?" I asked.

"We'll go to school. You'll go into grade two, just like here," said Ruth.

"Yah, grade two with poor people," said Trudy, grinning.

"Is it far away?" I asked.

"Really far," said Ruth, "We have to cross the border."

"What's the border?" I asked, feeling a lump in my throat.

"It's like an invisible line between two countries," said Ruth.

"But there's fences and gates with guards," Sarah added.

"I heard they have guns at the border," said Trudy.

"That is foolish talk," Mom was standing in the doorway. And more quietly she added, "We do not talk of guns in this house."

I wiped hard at my eyes with my washcloth, pushing against the tears.

It might have been a joyous occasion, getting a cupcake, topped with frosting and candy sprinkles. Mrs. Shepherd gave us each one on the last day of school and wished us a happy summer. I kept my head down, licking at the frosting, trying not to cry. Before I stepped onto the bus for the last time, Mrs. Shepherd gave me a hug and handed me a package. I waited until I was home to open it. Inside was a manicure kit in a red leather case with a zipper. My sisters all looked envious, so I thought I should be happy but I wasn't. In bed that night, I cried. I didn't want to move, crossing a border with men and guns. And I couldn't imagine living with poor people... like Charlene.

STEEL CITY

On the sixth of June, 1966, our family crossed the U.S. border to settle in Hamilton, Ontario, steel producing capital of Canada. Later, Dad remarked on all those sixes. I added that at the time, I was six years old and that was really a lot of 6's. He chuckled over that.

Moving into the industrial smoke of Hamilton was a change from the clean skies of rural Oklahoma. Soon after our arrival, we drove along Burlington Street on the way to view our new home in the part of the city known as the North End. Mom told us it wasn't ready to move into yet. We'd be staying in the basement of someone from the Hamilton Mennonite Church for a few weeks, but we should go have a look just the same.

Dad wanted us to see the steel plants in the industrial area, despite Mom's referring to them as 'conglomerates', in the same tone she might use to say 'maggots' or 'filth'. I didn't know what conglomerates were; from what I gathered, *steel* was good, essential for building bridges and skyscrapers, so I wasn't clear what to think. Whatever images I'd pictured when Mom and Dad mentioned the prominent steel factories in Hamilton, nothing prepared me for the view as we drove past the two industrial giants, Stelco and Dofasco.

Dad slowed the car to a crawl, craning his neck to look, completely ignoring traffic. A tailgater honked loud and long, then swerved around us. Not a whiff of breeze came through the open windows and my legs were stuck to the vinyl seat. I was breathing hot rubber, burning oil and something that smelled like rotten eggs.

Mom was right about calling the steel mills "giants". Chain link fence rose up from the sidewalk enclosing block after block of monstrous buildings, all sprouting pipes and stacks of various sizes like weird appendages; metal walkways and stairways attached to the walls of buildings and catwalks connecting roofs. Darkened windows covered in crisscross bars stared out from upper walls like eyes of gigantic houseflies, flattened into squares. Hazard signs strung along the fence warned of unknown dangers and smokestacks high as mountains spewed and belched streams of grey and black into a hazy veil of sky. Tubes large enough to walk in turned and twisted, interconnecting and branching out in every direction. Trains of rail cars moved along tracks that lined the pavement, passing a group of oddly shaped tanks sitting high on metal poles. The scene brought to my mind a terrible story that Mom told us about camps where people were put to death in World War II.

We kept driving, passing rows of cars and trucks sitting in dusty parking lots the size of football fields. Sounds blasting intermittently from buildings and yards; big bangs of metal clanging, rat-a-tat-tatting, thumping, and steam screeching like the release valve on a pressure cooker, competed with the closer noise of busses stopping and starting in city traffic. The whole scene looked like a mad scientist had collected and connected a frenzy of metal scraps, rusty cans, tin boxes, pipes, and parts of ancient machinery, placed his creation in a cage, filled all available floor space with Hot Wheel cars and trucks, added smoke and steam to billow out every which way, then waved a magic wand to make the whole thing large enough to fill up twenty city blocks.

"The smelters are inside those buildings," Dad said pointing to several large buildings. "They keep the men working shifts all night and day."

I'd never heard of a smelter. I pulled myself forward, feeling the sweaty moisture absorb into the seat of my shorts. I wanted to get a look out the front window and better hear what Dad was saying.

"What's all the smoke from?" Mark asked from the front seat where he often sat; a privilege since he was the only boy.

"They keep the fires going twenty-four hours a day," Dad said. "Too costly to keep shutting down and starting up."

That brought to my mind another terrible place; the deep dark death place of eternal suffering.

"It must be hot inside," said Mark.

"Yah, I imagine it's hot," said Dad.

"What are the fires for?" I asked, feeling anxious.

"To melt the iron and the other metals. The temperature has to be pretty high to melt them down. I imagine they have huge vats or ovens in there to hold the molten steel."

"What's molten?" I asked.

"It means melted," said Ruth in her superior intellect tone.

"Once the girders and beams are shaped," Dad continued, "they need to be cooled so they can harden. I believe that steam," he said, pointing now toward a row of shorter chimneys, "is from the cooling process." I followed his gaze. The whitish steam billowed more forcefully than the taller chimneys, whose black smoke floated gently upward.

"One of these days I want to go have a look inside," Dad said. "We should all go," he continued in a louder voice for the benefit of the back seats. "I think they might offer tours."

I tried to imagine the interior of the buildings, envisioning a dark-clothed devil stirring a boiling vat of liquid steel, flames sputtering. I looked sideways at my sisters wondering what they were thinking. Ruth looked worried. The twins looked blankly out the window. Tina looked confused.

I turned to have one last look before the car turned into a residential area where there was less traffic. We drove quietly for several blocks, passing houses built so closely together, someone standing between the houses could reach out and touch both. The few front yards were concrete or scraggy grass with a wilted tree here and there, some with porches or 'stoops', as Mom called them. Houses were brick, most stained in soot, the wooden parts tired looking, porches and railings in states of deterioration and as Mom put it, 'in need of a good coat of paint'. A fat woman in a long skirt sat on a stoop, elbows on widely spread knees, fanning her face with a newspaper.

"How come there's so many houses but hardly any people? Tina asked.

"Probably trying to stay out of the heat," said Mom. "Or maybe they aren't out of bed yet."

The car slowed as it approached a busy intersection. "This is James Street," said Dad.

"The poorest section of the city," Mom added. "Where we are going to live."

Dad turned and pulled up behind a bus as it wafted exhaust. James Street was lined on both sides with parked cars, telephone poles, and sooty brick buildings built right up against the sidewalk, with signs everywhere; on stores, on posts, on awnings and in window displays. People moved slowly along the street, going in and out of stores. After a few blocks, Dad stopped the car.

"Here we are. Home. About a mile straight ahead is the downtown," he pointed ahead, then continued, nodding in Mom's direction. "Watch the traffic before you open the doors."

We piled out, one after the other, sisters in identical homemade outfits, assembling on the sidewalk like the Von Trapp family dressed in curtains. I pulled the shorts from the back of my legs, looking into an empty lot, large enough for two or three houses. The dry ground was hardened to a shine, bare but for garbage scattered among the weeds and against the adjacent buildings. Looking one way along the sidewalk and then the other, I could see more telephone poles, wires, bricks, pavement and moving traffic. I planted my hands on my hips and glared at Mom and Dad, wanting to shout, "*Where* is it? *Where* is home?", but they were conversing in German, which meant, "Do not disturb."

I kicked at a wad of chewing gum on the cracked sidewalk, fixing my gaze on a house next to the vacant lot. A boy sat on the single concrete step beside the small dirt patch that was the front yard, staring at us standing awkwardly on the sidewalk in our matching clothes, his mouth open like a fish. He was completely still, one hand holding a stick he'd been using to draw in the dirt. His hair was wet and combed, but his face and stomach were dirty, as were his knees, bare feet and yellow shorts. I cringed and thought about Mrs. Shepherd and her ruler. Our eyes met and his challenged mine. I lifted my chin and turned away to look across the street.

"Is that it?" I blurted, interrupting the German.

The five-story brick structure I pointed to was like a ghost-town version of the mills we had just driven past, without all the attachments or cars or smoke. As though one of the industrial giants had picked up one of its used-up buildings and plunked it down in a patch of weeds. The few windows that weren't boarded up were broken, the lower level window boards spray-painted with words and sloppy designs.

Dad turned to look. "No. That's an old sugar factory." He laughed. "Apparently, it's been closed down for a few years." He pointed to the building beside the house where the boy was still staring. "That's it, there," he said. "Let's go have a look."

"Remember," Mom said, "The place needs cleaning up.

I kept my chin down as we passed the boy's house. Thinking about the acres of field and yard we used to run around in, I looked at our new home, a three-story brick building that butted right up against the sidewalk. Hanging across the width of the storefront was an awning with *Dorothy's Dry Goods* printed in yellow italics. A mosaic-tiled entrance sloped toward the glass 'king-sized' door, between two walk-in display windows, their planked floors littered with yellowed paper and dust balls. Dad unlocked the door, flicked a light switch, and from way up high, a fluorescent light flickered twice, then lit up an enormous room.

"Wow, it's huge!" said Mark.

"Well it used to be a store," said Mom.

"Dorothy's Dry Good's," said Ruth.

The room was long and narrow with a 'church high' ceiling, its dingy beige walls scarred and nicked. The floor was a sea of garbage, much of it paper, loosely balled and thrown about. Throughout the mess were boxes, some stacked, some open, some dumped over, their contents spilling out. A calendar with curled edges hung crookedly on one wall, and opposite, a framed picture of Queen Elizabeth II hung way up high. I recognized her from some money Dad had shown us. She looked lonely, her small crowned head surrounded merely by stains and a hairline crack forking past her to the floor. Dad moved through the stuff, kicking his way along. I thought of Moses parting the Red Sea.

"This will be the main room in our community centre," said Dad. "The bedrooms are all on the second and third floors. The kitchen is back there," he said pointing to a wooden door with a large opaque window at the far end of the room. To the left, was a partially enclosed L-shaped staircase that led upstairs.

"Where does that door go?" asked Mark, pointing to another door, seemingly under the staircase.

"That goes to the basement," Dad said.

"What are dry goods?" I asked.

"All kinds of things but not food. I think they sold fabric and sewing notions. Clothing, some undergarments," said Mom.

"Is that what's in these boxes?" Sarah asked.

"I don't think so. What we have here is invoices, ledgers, store receipts…book keeping stuff," Dad said. I kicked at the newspapers and debris because Dad was doing it, but not as hard as I wanted to.

He smiled, "Yah, this place is a mess. We'll get it cleaned up before we move in."

"Look," Trudy whispered, nudging me. She was squatted over a box, with her hands inside, holding a white brassiere, putting her fist inside one cup so I could see. "D-cup," she whispered. I looked up to see where Mom and Dad were. Dad was moving slowly around the room with his ear against the wall, tapping with his knuckles, listening for something. Mom was leading Tina through the garbage toward the kitchen. Trudy elbowed me again. This time, she held a corset, rubbery and thick, with even bigger cups.

"Watermelons," she whispered.

I snickered. Trudy closed the box and followed Mom into the kitchen. Mom turned on the tap to let the water run, pointing out the double sink, the counter that ran the length of the room and the cupboards reaching to the high ceiling.

"Lots of counter space and storage room in here," she said brightly, hoisting Tina up to drink from her cupped hand. She chatted on about 'the possibilities', a fresh coat of paint, bright yellow curtains she'd sew for the two enormous windows. I stood by the side window looking into the fenced yard that belonged to the boy in yellow shorts. One tall tree provided shade to the far corner where a derelict car with flat tires sat in a mess of weeds. Scattered along the craggy ground, lay dog poop in piles and coils, a deflated beach ball, and a broken hula hoop. A bulldog was asleep on a pink bathroom mat by the back step, its legs stretched straight like a side of beef.

"Dad's going to build a bench in that corner and along the wall," Mom said, gesturing with her chin. We'll get a nice big table to eat at. Let's go see the upstairs"

We followed Mom, the wooden boards creaking as we snaked single file up the staircase. We stopped at the first doorway along the long curving hallway. The thick wooden door had a clear glass doorknob, round, but cut like a diamond with a million little edges. I held the doorknob, feeling the smooth, yet complicated surface, feeling for a moment like I was connected to something.

"This is our room," Mom said. "Out this window..." we gathered in our parent's bedroom, "it's almost like a patio. That..." she said, pointing to the "patio" floor, "is the kitchen roof."

"Can we go out there?" asked Mark.

"After," Mom replied. She used that answer a lot with us. She never elaborated on after what. But "after" was always final. We followed her along the hallway.

"This is the bathroom," she said as we stopped at the next doorway. We all crowded in.

"Look at the tub," she beamed. "It's cast iron. And look at the feet. They call this a claw foot tub. And that is a pedestal sink," she said excitedly.

"Nice floor," I said, looking at well-worn black and white mosaic linoleum. "It looks like a carpet."

"What's this room for?" Ruth asked, pointing to a door across the hall.

"That will be Mark's room," Mom answered.

We followed Mom down the hallway toward the front of the building and into the living room while Mark did an inspection of his new room.

"Look at these floors! Solid hardwood. They'll be beautiful when we get finished with them," Mom continued in the excited tour guide voice, putting emphasis on certain words, like beeeee-uuuuu-teeee-ful! She continued on about the enormous windows, the elaborate wood trimming and the circular designs moulded into the ceilings.

"What are we going to do to the floors?" Ruth asked. I looked down at the dirty, scratched and scuffed hardwood flooring.

"We need to scrape off all the old wax. Never mind that now. Let's go see the upstairs," she said.

"That's where our rooms are?" Sarah asked.

"Yes, you girls will share the two bedrooms upstairs. On the third floor," Mom said, smiling. "Wait till you see!"

We followed Mom up another enclosed staircase, each step making a different creaking sound. On the landing at the top of the staircase was a small door, like I pictured in the house of the seven dwarfs.

"What's in there?" I asked.

"A closet," Mom said.

"Why is the door so small?"

"Because the roof slopes down, see?" she opened the door and pointed inside to the sloping rafters. "The good thing is there is a light in here," she said and pulled a short string that lit up a single light bulb. "We can use it to store our out-of-season clothes." It was dusty inside, but I liked the idea of going in there. It looked like a great place to hide in a game of hide and seek. Or just a great place to hide.

The main part of the third floor was separated into two bedrooms by a dividing wall that almost reached the peak of the ceiling; Ruth and the twins had the front side, with two windows, facing James Street. Tina and I were in the smaller room facing the backyard. For once I felt privileged to be getting what I believed was a better deal. In our room, the roof slanted down toward the back so our two windows were low in the wall. They opened sideways and we could easily step through onto another flat rooftop area, which was Mom and Dad's bedroom roof.

From our outside patio rooftop we could see the garage, a portion of our dinky yard, the yard belonging to the boy in the yellow shorts, the yard of the grocery store beside us, the vacant lot and many rooftops.

"Wow, this is just like Mary Poppins!" I said.

"Oh yah, I can just see Bert and the chimneysweeps dancing all over the place," Sarah said with a smile.

"Great place to suntan," was Trudy's only comment.

"Hey, there's Dad," Mark said, walking toward the edge and pointing to the yard."

"That's far enough," said Mom, sounding harsh. "I don't want you going any closer to the edge than Mark is right now. Is that clear?"

We nodded.

"Good," she said firmly, then changed her tone back to the one of the excited tour guide and continued. "Now, as a special celebration, we are all going out to Smitty's Pancake House for lunch."

"Are we all having pancakes?" I asked.

"You can have pancakes if you want," she said, "but they have all kinds of other things on the menu."

"What's the celebration?" asked Mark.

"Our new home," Mom said. "And our new adventure!"

We followed Mom eagerly down the stairs. Lunch at a restaurant was always a special occasion.

THE CLEANUP

We hadn't yet moved in but Mom said there wasn't any point in us hanging around in our temporary basement lodgings all day, so we spent our days at Dorothy's Dry Goods, recently renamed, the "Welcome Inn". That was Dad's idea, so at the bottom of the sign, it would say, 'Well ...Come In'!

Mom said the sooner we got the place cleaned up, the sooner we could move in.

"We can't have people looking in at this mess," she said. She was referring to the state of the storefront.

In order to haul away the junk we needed a trailer, and since there was no place to put the trailer except in the garage behind the back yard, the garage had to be cleaned out. Dad had tried parking the trailer on James Street, but was told to move it by some "stuffed shirts", I'd heard him say to Mom. I asked Mom what their shirts were stuffed with, and she said some conversations were private. Maybe Dad didn't know how to say "stuffed shirts" in German. Dad tried to park the trailer in the alley that ran behind our back yard, but encountered a truck driver delivering beer to the corner tavern. The truck driver laid his hand on the horn and yelled some really nasty words. He could have just said move it like the stuffed shirts. Dad moved it anyway, looking like he wanted to yell some mean words, too.

"We need to clear out the garage so I can park the trailer inside," Dad announced at lunch. "All able bodies follow me."

"Well," Mom said. "This place has been a mess for quite some time. I guess another day won't hurt. But I need help washing all those jars on the porch. Sarah and Tina, you two can help me inside."

The rest of us followed Dad into the alley where the trailer was parked.

We stood looking into the garage. We hadn't been allowed in there because it was so cluttered with boxes and loose debris, bits of furniture and bagged rubbish, that there wasn't room to walk around. We knew from peering through the dusty window that the garage was home to two naked mannequins. One was propped on a wire stand with her arms bent like she was going for a stroll, smiling from a smudged face. The other lay stiff on a bed of garbage, her neck twisted unnaturally to one side.

"I need to get the trailer in here before supper," Dad said. "So let's clear a space big enough to hold it. Right here, next to the door."

"Are we going to throw all this stuff away?" asked Ruth. "What if some of it's still good?"

"Most of it's old paperwork," said Dad. "If you find any blank stuff that could be useful, take it into the yard."

"Can we keep the mannequins?" Trudy asked.

"What for?" Dad asked.

"We could dress them up," answered Trudy.

"I thought you had dolls for that."

"But these are better," she said. "Cause they're like real people. We could put real clothes on them."

"I think they'll be more trouble than they're worth." Ending the discussion, Dad grabbed the prone mannequin by her ankle and dragged her toward the door, her head cutting a path through the rubble.

"Yah, don't you have dolls to dress up?" Mark mimicked at the sound of the mannequin being tossed into the trailer.

"Just so we don't bump into each other," Dad said from the doorway, "You all bring the stuff over here. I'll load the trailer. Just don't try to lift anything that's too heavy."

"Mary, you can pick up the loose paper and put it in here," he said, handing me a small cardboard box. "Bring it to me before it gets too full."

I began filling my box, pleased to be given a special job, even if it was picking up garbage. I liked the cool dampness inside the garage, the dirt floor and small window, picturing Daniel Boone coming inside with a musket and a dead fox slung over his shoulder.

After I'd delivered my third boxful to the door, Trudy took hold of my arm, pulling me toward a stack of boxes in one corner. "This is for the good stuff," she whispered, rummaging through the top box to show me the contents; some panties and bras, a few nylons and a corset. "If you find something good, sneak it over here, or tell me. I'll come and get it."

"Here's one," Mark whispered and threw something that hit me in the leg. Trudy scooped a very 'big-cupped' bra into the box, closing it as

Dad came back inside. Ruth shot us a, 'Better watch out' look. As soon as Dad walked outside, she said, "I hope there aren't any rats in here."

"Do you think there's some in here?" I asked, feeling my legs growing weak.

"Rats live in the city, in alleyways...where there's garbage," Ruth said using her eyes to indicate our present surroundings.

"Would they bite?" Mark asked.

"Probably if you disturb their nests," said Trudy.

I stopped moving. "Where do you think the nests are?" I asked.

"Whose nests?" Dad was coming back in.

"The rats' nests," Mark said.

"What rats?" he asked.

"Ruth says maybe there's rats in here," said Mark.

"Don't be worrying about rats," Dad said. "There's no food in here, so I don't imagine we'll see any rats. Any rats around here will be in the alley...by the garbage next door."

"So there's no rats in here," I said, begging affirmation.

"There might be a mouse or two. Don't worry about rats," Dad said picking up another box.

I continued with the project with much less enthusiasm, worried each piece of garbage I picked up might cause a scurry of claws. I wasn't comforted by the idea of the rats being 'just' outside, imagining them sleeping inside our garage during the day, waking up at night to forage through the garbage next door.

At bathroom break, Trudy and I ran to the station wagon to change from our flip flops into running shoes. Not that either of us could outrun a rat. But I sure didn't want one running over my toes.

Unlike our previous neighbourhood, this one was full of kids, many of whom hung around, the younger ones blatantly, the older ones nonchalantly trying to see what we were doing inside Dorothy's Dry Goods. Each day, a growing crowd of young spectators gathered, pressing their hands and faces against the glass. There were tall skinny kids and shorter, stout ones, kids with blond hair and wide faces, and some with large brown eyes and curly dark hair and tanned skin. Mom called those kids, 'Eyetallian'. Many of them wore the same clothes day after day and we began to recognize some of them by their outfits.

"Why are they looking at us?" I asked.

"They're just curious," Mom replied.

"Will they go away soon?"

"I don't imagine," Mom said. "It won't be long before we'll be able to invite them in. That's what we're here for. They're not doing any harm."

When we grew tired of hauling boxes or being watched, Mom offered us scrapers, spacing us along the baseboards in the long second floor hallway.

"Just scrape the loose stuff," she said. "It's not necessary to scrape all the paint."

"Won't ridges show?" asked Sarah.

"This hallway is long and way too dim for anyone to notice a few ridges," Mom said. "When the job's finished, we'll get a frosty jug of root beer."

Working upstairs offered relief from being stared at like a zoo animal. At first, it was unsettling, kids staring in every time I looked at the front door. But after a few days, their presence became familiar. And the way they pressed themselves against the glass in the front door, it seemed they were wishing they could be inside, hauling boxes and picking up garbage.

During the first weeks of cleanup we spent the majority of our free time outside, but it wasn't at street level. The backyard wasn't much bigger than our shed was in Oklahoma, about six giant steps wide, about the same in length, so we couldn't run enough to play tag or even have a decent game of 'Mother May I". And there was no privacy since most afternoons a teenage couple sat, kissing (the twins called it necking) on the hood of the car in the yard next door, so it felt as though we were intruding.

We'd tried out Mom and Dad's patio, but preferred our third floor patio escape. It really was a great place to suntan, if we first lay down a blanket since the black surface got hot enough to burn the soles of our feet.

Mom became annoyed several times that week.

"It's quite a hike to get up to the living room and holler up those stairs every time I need one of you," she said.

"Why not holler up from the back yard," suggested Ruth.

"Oh," said Mom. "I never thought of that."

ROLLER SKATING

One afternoon soon after we moved in, Dad and Mark arrived home with a box that Dad plunked inside the door.

"Where've you been?' asked Ruth.

"We've been scouting," Mark said, looking smug.

"What do you mean by scouting?" Sarah asked.

"Well, it means looking for something," Dad said.

"What were you looking for?" I asked.

"Go have a look," he said.

The box contained a mishmash of rusty things; tools, pipes, nails, and two pairs of roller skates.

"Is this what you were looking for?" I asked.

"It's what we found," said Dad.

"Who are the skates for?" Ruth asked.

"All of you," he said.

"But how will they fit us all?" she asked.

"They're adjustable," Dad said. "First you adjust the length. Then you tighten up here, so it grips the sides of your shoes." He pointed to a small hole on the side of the rusted metal. "You use a key. It's here somewhere," he said fishing around inside the box. Then he held up the skates by the leather straps like skinned geese. "Who wants to try them out?"

A chorus of me's rang out from everyone but Ruth, who looked at the skates with trepidation, as though a list of potential injuries were passing in front of her eyes.

"How about the twins try them out," said Dad. "But let's wait till after supper. I need to oil the wheels."

A small crowd formed a line along the sidewalk, standing as though they were watching a royal procession, as Trudy and Sarah, half hanging on and half dragging each other, stomped and rolled along the sidewalk, bracing over cracks, screeching the whole way. Several kids broke ranks and ran behind, shouting encouragement and caution. The twins made it past two telephone poles before they skated into the side of a building, laughing. On their return, they each accepted a ride; each of them pulled by two kids running, so their only effort was to stay upright.

I chose the ride method to make my skating debut, requesting that I be pulled in the direction of the tavern on the corner, a much shorter distance. Adjusted to the smallest and narrowest position, the skates just managed to hold my shoes.

"Not too fast," I pleaded as I rolled along with sweaty palms, my arms and legs braced, teeth clenched, bum sticking out for balance. Thankfully, they slowed at the corner so I wouldn't be flung over the curb, and they held onto me while I did a clompy nine-point turn.

"Bend your knees a bit," suggested one of the pullers.

I bent them so my bum was close to my feet, and that got them laughing pretty hard but they hauled me back without scrapes or bruises.

"Should we let them try?" Trudy asked the third day, nodding in the direction of the door, where the after-supper roller skating fans were gathered.

"I imagine it should be okay, as long as you are out there, too. To keep your eyes on them," Mom said. She sent Mark upstairs for the first aid kit. "Just in case," she added.

One of the enthusiasts was Danny, a boy who lived in the next block. With his short, strong body, Danny proved to be one of the best pullers.

"Why don't you get your running shoes on and try them out?" "I asked one day.

"I just have flip flops, he said.

For a moment, I considered the idea of lending him my shoes, then looked at his filthy feet.

"That's okay," said Danny. "I like to pull."

"Wanna go to Hammy's?" Danny asked one afternoon as I exited the storefront. We'd just been dismissed from scraping old wax off floors. I looked into the storefront briefly for someone to ask permission but everyone older seemed occupied. Hammy's was just at the corner.

"I guess I can," I said. "But I don't have any money."

"That's okay. I have some," he said displaying two nickels on his grubby palm.

"Where did you get it?" I asked.

"My mom gives me money if I stay outside. She says she wants me out of her hair," he said like it was a privilege. We walked along the street.

"Do you know what this place is?' he asked, gesturing toward the sign with swirled letters that said Majeska House."

"Is it a hotel?" I asked.

"It's a bar," said Danny. He looked at me. "Do you know what a bar is?"

"No," I'd heard the older three whispering in their room some nights ago about the Majeska House, but they wouldn't tell me when I asked. "What is it?" I asked carefully.

"It's a place where you drink beer," he said. "Do you know what beer is?"

"No," I said feeling ashamed.

"It makes you drunk," said Danny. "Does your dad drink beer?"

"No," I said, not knowing what beer or drunk was. "Does your dad?"

"I don't have a dad," he said. "But my mom does." He looked at me, "How come you all wear the same clothes?"

"Mom makes our clothes," I said.

"How does she do that?"

"She uses a sewing machine," I answered, finally feeling like I could contribute.

"I've never seen one of those," he said, as we entered Hammy's Store.

"Hello Danny. What'll you have today?" A kind looking bearded fellow, like a disciple in modern clothes, sat on a stool beside his cane, leaning against the cigarette shelves. He picked up a tiny paper bag and small metal scoop. I gazed at the rows of candy inside the glass case, amazed that a boy with no shirt or shoes had money to spend, while he ordered, 'two green leaves, two licorice babies, two Mo Jo's, two double bubble'.

"How much is that?" Danny asked.

"Five cents. How much you spending today?" Hammy asked.

Danny held up the nickels.

"Keep going," said Hammy.

"Can I get a popsicle?" he asked.

"Yep, then you're through. You know where they are," Hammy said.

"Will you break it in two?" asked Danny. Hammy nodded.

"Now, which one are you?" he looked at me.

"I'm Mary," I said.

"How's the place coming along?" he asked.

"Pretty good," I said. "We got most of the garbage to the dump."

"Good for you," he chuckled.

That night, after lights out, I tiptoed to the other room.

"What's wrong, Mary?" whispered Sarah.

"What's beer?' I asked.

It was quiet for a minute. "Why do you want to know?" asked Ruth.

"Danny says they drink beer at the Majeska House," I said.

"Yah," said Ruth.

"But I don't know what it is. And he said it makes you drunk. What's drunk?" I asked.

Trudy laughed. "Sh," said Sarah.

"Beer is alcohol. And alcohol is bad, because it makes you drunk. Drunk means you can't talk right. And you stumble around when you walk. Or you fall down. And sometimes you go unconscious," said Sarah.

"And you can get addicted to it," said Ruth.

"What's addicted?' I asked.

"It means you keep doing it every day. And then you spend all your money on beer," said Ruth.

"Is it a sin to drink beer then?" I asked.

"Yes," said Sarah.

"Danny's mom drinks beer," I said. "So she's a sinner."

"Yah, and a whole bunch of other people around here," said Trudy. "That's why we came here, remember?"

"Are we supposed to pray for them?" I asked.

"You can if you want," said Sarah, "But you need to go to bed."

"You can pray for them tomorrow," said Ruth.

FASHION SHOW

One Sunday afternoon that summer, Mom and Dad went scouting, leaving the storefront closed and Ruth in charge.

We turned on the television in the upstairs living room, but the combination of bright light and poor reception made the experience more frustrating than enjoyable. Ruth went upstairs to read. The rest of us went down to the kitchen and closed the door, out of fishbowl staring range. We sat quietly for a few moments before Trudy suddenly stood up.

"I know what we can do. I'll be right back," she said, leaving through the back porch. She returned a minute later with the box of "good stuff" from the garage, placed it on the table and sat down. None of us moved. Then Sarah stood up, and in the style of a magician pulling a rabbit out of a hat, reached in and pulled out a very large, full length girdle, holding it high and letting it dangle by the crotch.

"Who wants to try this on?" she offered in a circus master voice.

She waved it toward Mark.

"I'm not putting that on," he said, lifting his hands in the air like he was being held up at gunpoint.

"Oh come on," said Sarah. "It's just for fun."

"No way," he said. "I am not putting any of that on. Even for fun."

"I dare you to put something on and walk around the kitchen," said Trudy standing up.

"No," said Mark, raising his voice, pointing at her, "I dare you to put it on and walk around the ping pong table."

"Mary, you do it," said Trudy so suddenly in my direction that I jumped.

"Why do I have to?" I asked.

"Okay, I'll go. But then you have to do another dare," said Trudy, all bossy-like. "Tina you can do it with me." She dug into the box and pulled out a bra. "Put this on. I'll wear the girdle."

The bra hung on Tina's shoulder like a beauty queen sash with two big lumps. Trudy stepped into girdle, squashing the cups down flat so it looked like an oversized bathing suit. She pushed Tina toward the door, then opened it slowly, to count the number of faces pressed against the glass. Five kids were milling in the entrance, not actually looking in.

"Let's go!" cried Trudy, grabbing Tina by the hand. In a mad dash, Trudy dragged Tina around the ping pong table, slipping at the corners, laughing while they burst into the kitchen and collapsed onto the bench.

When they composed themselves, Trudy looked at me. Still panting, she sing-songed, "Now it's your turn."

"Okay, but Sarah has to come with me," I said.

"I didn't say I'd do it," said Sarah.

"Then you have to do something by yourself, after Mary does hers," said Trudy.

"Okay, we'll go next," said Sarah. "Mary, you wear the girdle. I'll wear the bra."

As soon as we were dressed, Trudy crossed her arms and said in a menacing tone, "You two have to do something different."

"What do we have to do?" I asked.

Trudy looked at Mark, but he remained quiet. She pursed her lips and smiled.

"You two have to go into one of the display windows." She let that sink in. Sarah was about to open her mouth and Trudy added in a lighter tone, "Just walk around once and come out," she said. "But you have to touch the glass on the front window."

Mark nodded. "Yah."

Tina nodded. "Yah."

Sarah looked at me.

"I don't want to," I said.

"Come on," said Sarah. "Let's get it over with."

"Wait till it's your turn," Sarah said to Mark.

"No way. I'm not putting that stuff on."

"We'll see," Sarah said. "Come on, Mary." She took my hand and led me to the kitchen door. The kids outside must have heard the commotion because they were at the front door, pressing their faces against the glass.

"Come on," Sarah urged, "Before more of them come."

"Wait," Trudy was approaching with two dishcloths. "You're not ready yet, Mary." She wadded the cloths and stuffed them into the cups.

"There," she said. "Now you have bosoms." I didn't want bosoms but I knew if I objected, she'd make my bum bigger, too.

We tiptoed through the storefront to stand at the entrance door to the south-side window, out of sight for the kids still watching through the front door.

"Wait till we get outside," said Trudy, marching past us. "We have to watch to make sure you touch the front window." She unlocked the front door, and she and Mark and Tina joined the kids outside.

"Ready?" Sarah asked. I nodded, thinking I was absolutely *not* ready as she opened the window display door. She stepped onto the platform, scrunching to make herself small, hauling me up behind her, leaving the door open. As soon as I was inside, Sarah let go of me and leapt forward, covering the five or six steps forward to touch the front window before I could think to follow. As she turned back, I jumped up, following her path and touched the front glass. When I turned around, I saw the door closing. Sarah was gone.

I ran to the door and stood for a second in complete shock, then began banging and pushing, searching for a non-existent knob. When I stopped pounding for a brief moment, I heard laughter outside, growing louder.

I kept banging on the door, almost in tears, calling for Sarah to let me out. Wild eyed and panicky, I watched Sarah, minus the bra, join the group outside the window as they started to clap and chant, "Ma-ry, Ma-ry, Ma-ry."

I crouched against the locked door, hiding my face for several seconds. I felt like crying but I knew that was the worst thing I could do. I got up and began to walk slowly, keeping my eyes averted, swaying my hips like I'd seen in movies, turning at the front. The clapping got louder as I swaggered back. I stopped then, and bowed. They continued clapping, while I stood waiting for someone to let me out. That didn't appear to be happening, so I placed my hands on my hips, put my chin up, and made another circuit with exaggerated hip movements, taking an extra turn near the front. I paused, keeping my eyes elevated so I didn't have to see their faces, praying someone would have mercy and open the door. I wanted to plead and yell but my throat was choking with tears. I later wondered why it didn't occur to me to just take the girdle off, since I was fully dressed underneath. It must have been stage fright.

I did two more walks with decreasing fanfare, hoping they would get bored with my show and let me out. Still, they clapped, so I began to pour it on, stomping my feet and wiggling my hips. I was beginning an arm-extended, slow-motion twirl when I saw the blue station wagon.

My movements stopped as the car doors opened. The audience carried on, perhaps thinking my pose was part of the act, then started booing. The clapping slowed. They followed my gaze, heads turning until they saw Mom standing on the sidewalk, staring in disbelief. It grew very quiet as Dad walked up beside her, his eyes blazing.

I could see Dad's lips moving slowly. His face was still and stern. I tried to cover myself with arms and elbows while Trudy, Sarah, Mark and Tina walked inside with bowed heads, and the neighbourhood kids fled.

"What could you possibly have been thinking?" were Mom's first words behind the kitchen door. "Where is Ruth?"

Dad was shaking his head slowly back and forth, looking at the box of undergarments on the table. Nobody spoke.

"Mary, what were you doing in there?" he finally said in his 'very disturbed' tone.

"I didn't want to," was all I could mutter.

"Then why were you in there?"

"The door got closed," I said.

"Who shut it?" Dad asked, slowly.

I looked down. "Who put her up to this?' he asked, scanning each of our faces.

Nobody spoke.

"Shame on all of you," he spat. "You will go to your rooms until supper...and think about what kind of message we are trying to share with this community. Tell Ruth to come down here."

Dinner was tense.

We got the big lecture at bedtime. The overall theme was 'setting an example'. It could have been stated as simply as that, but it took almost an hour. Words like irresponsible, shameful, disrespect, disappoint, disgrace and such were thrown in. We were blamed equally; me of course, for my performance, the others for clapping and locking me in, and Ruth for neglecting her responsibility.

Mom and Dad were really angry, but partly I think because they really couldn't think of a suitable punishment for us. It was abundantly clear that this type of charade would never, I repeat never, happen again. The best they could come up with was we weren't allowed to watch television for a week.

THE VS'ERS

After we had been in Hamilton a couple of months, Voluntary Service workers started to arrive to help set up and run programs. These 'VS'ers' were young men and women, most of them Mennonite, usually in their late teens and twenties, who signed up for a term of service with projects sponsored by the Mennonite Church. The Welcome Inn was one of a long list of projects run by the General Conference of Mennonites to support and aid groups and individuals affected by poverty, conflict, oppression or natural disaster in North America and many countries throughout the world. Terms of service ranged from a few months to two years.

There were usually around six or seven VS'ers at the Welcome Inn at any given time. They arrived from all parts of North America when positions were posted. The first came in August of '66. Two houses were rented to house them, separated by gender and distance in accordance with unspoken rules of piety and propriety. Many churches encouraged young adults to go into voluntary service before settling into a career or marriage. It was a good way to see another part of the world and serve God at the same time. Several young American men were "conscientious objectors". Mom explained that they could do voluntary service instead of being drafted and going to war in Vietnam.

Some volunteers did service work full time at the Welcome Inn, while others held down regular paying jobs and donated their paycheques to the programs, assisting with Welcome Inn activities in the evenings and on weekends. All Voluntary Service workers received free room and board and a small allowance (about $30 a month) for personal expenses.

At mealtime, the VS'ers ate with our family in the Welcome Inn kitchen for reasons of efficiency and to avoid potential issues around cooking, grocery shopping and clean up in three kitchens. The Welcome Inn's kitchen could seat a small crowd with two tables pushed together against an L shaped bench built along the walls. The larger table comfortably sat eight or squeezed 10, and the smaller table could accommodate six. Sharing meals allowed for efficient communication within the community centre since each meal provided an opportunity for a meeting. My siblings and I sat at the smaller, shorter table and were encouraged to listen or talk quietly amongst ourselves.

Schedules were arranged so Mom wasn't strapped with the brunt of the meal preparation and clean up, though she was the main kitchen manager. Some of the volunteers helped with cooking and cleanup. My siblings and I helped out with less taxing kitchen duties; setting the table, peeling potatoes, cutting fruit and vegetables and doing dishes.

Mom faced some hurdles when working with young adults in "her" kitchen, especially when it came to practices that challenged her thrifty mindset, like using excessive amounts of cheese or mayonnaise, or wasting good food by not scraping pots and bowls properly before washing them. I wonder if Mom struggled with finding the right tone so that she could give advice without sounding shrewish. At times, rather than voice her frustrations or happily demonstrate the merits of a spatula, Mom used the "heavy sigh, excessive banging of pots or loud closing of cupboard doors" approach to express her angst, which left some VS'ers raising eyebrows and treading softly in the kitchen.

It wasn't long before Mom and Dad appointed themselves chief food shoppers. This decision was made after several grocery shopping trips by well-meaning VS'ers resulted in what Mom deemed frivolous spending; purchases included unnecessary items like exotic fruit, expensive brands, or small, therefore "more expensive in the long run", jars and canned goods. Once the food shopping issue was resolved, Mom enjoyed the fellowship in the kitchen. It was a good time to talk with volunteers in a casual and relaxed way while kneading zwieback dough, rolling out pie crust, or mixing meatloaf.

Louella was among the first volunteers to join the Welcome Inn staff. Mom told us that Louella would be staying with us for one year, and would be doing an internship at the Hamilton Psychiatric Hospital during her stay. She'd work at the hospital during the day and help at the Welcome Inn in the evenings and on weekends.

"What's a Psychiatric hospital?" I asked that night after lights out.

"It's where crazy people go," said Trudy.

"No, not crazy. Mom said unstable," Ruth corrected her.

"What's unstable?" I asked.

"It means they don't think right. They do strange things," she said.

"What kind of strange things?"

"Like talk to themselves and get scared about everything. Some of them pull their hair out."

"How come they have to go to a hospital?"

"They're kind of sick in their heads," Ruth said. "So it's not like a regular hospital, cause they don't do operations and stuff. They just talk to the people," replied Ruth.

"Or they put them in a straight-jacket," said Trudy.

"What's that?" I asked.

There was silence.

"Why do you tell her stuff like that?" I heard Ruth whispering.

"What is it?" I asked.

"Oh it's just a jacket with really long sleeves," Sarah said after a moment. "They make the person cross their arms and tie the sleeves together behind their backs so they can't move their arms."

"Why do they do that?" I asked, trying to picture it.

"So they don't hurt themselves, or anybody else," Ruth said. "Now go to sleep."

"How do they hurt themselves?" I asked more quietly.

"Go to sleep," said Ruth, sounding just like Mom.

I had trouble going to sleep after that conversation, and wondered what this Louella would be doing at the hospital. I wondered whether she'd have to tie people's arms behind their backs. I pictured her as short and hefty with a mean face. I was completely surprised when Louella walked into the Welcome Inn storefront with a three-piece set of matched luggage, looking like she'd just stepped out of a fashion magazine, tall and slim in a peach jumpsuit that zipped up the front.

She had a deep golden tan and long blond hair that reached the middle of her back in a vee, and flowed with her confident, graceful movements. The first VS'ers, two boys from Kansas who were just settling in, jumped forward, practically pushing each other aside to help carry her bags. My sisters and I, awestruck, sat on Louella's bed and watched her unpack. We had never seen anyone so glamorous, not in person. She showed us the contents of her satin-lined accessories suitcase, neatly organized in three layers that popped into tiers when opened. Inside were lipsticks, mascara, eye shadows and pencils, moisturizing cream, eye cream, hand cream, and assorted nail polishes and perfume. She talked to us about her home in Pittsburgh and how she was interrupting her third year of college to see if she was making the right career choice, while she placed these items into one of three wicker baskets on the doily-topped dresser. She told us she would be staying for one year and shadowing at the hospital, helping where she could. She said that she hoped that working in the hospital would help her decide if she really wanted to go into counselling.

"Are you afraid?" I asked shyly.

"Afraid of what?" she looked at me, tilting her head.

"Of… work…working at the hospital," I stammered.

"Oh no, there's nothing to be afraid of," she said, looking at me quizzically, then smiled and got back to unpacking. Ruth pushed an elbow into my ribs and I lowered my chin. Louella placed items from the lowest layer of the case into the other two baskets; hair bands, coloured bobby pins, silky scarves and a silver charm bracelet, which she held up, stretching it out for us to see. The numerous charms bobbed and shimmered, among the most prominent a heart, with the tip and tail of an arrow protruding at an angle, a tiny gem sparkling from its center.

Initially, Louella's pattern of showing up late for breakfast and eating just a single slice of unbuttered brown toast annoyed Mom. "If she wasn't so busy putting on make-up she could be on time," Mom said one morning. "I don't know why she needs to look so fancy around here. I hope she isn't filling your heads with silly ideas. There are more important things to do around here than standing in front of a mirror."

I USED TO BE EXCITED ABOUT SCHOOL

That summer, I wasn't sure whether to be excited about starting school or scared. I would be going to a new school, newly built because a fire destroyed the previous one. The old building was still standing, the whole thing so charred you could smell it from the sidewalk. It was boarded up with plywood fencing sprayed all over with graffiti, and not much of the roof remained. One night, I dreamed I was inside a burning school, but it looked just like the sugar factory and I couldn't find my way out. I saw stairs through the smoke but my feet wouldn't move and I yelled but no sound came out. I told my dream at breakfast when Mom asked her usual question about how we all slept. Dad said, "Oh, they have alarm bells at school and there's plenty of time to get out." Mom said that everyone has those kinds of dreams, so I should just try not to worry. But I did worry and I wasn't sure if it was school I was worried about. I loved school in grade one.

I knew I'd have to walk by the Majeska House on the way to school. Mom said, "Don't worry, it's closed in the morning, and you can walk by with Mark after lunch." Worse than the Majeska House, though, was the old lady around the corner whose house we had to pass to get to school. Some of the kids said she was a witch. I didn't know if that was true but she certainly looked like one, with her long, dark dresses that cinched at the waist with a belt and her long scraggly, grey hair. And, there was the black cat that did figure-eights around and through her legs while she swept her vine-covered veranda with a corn broom. Some kids threw stones at her house and ran off, drawing her outside to wave a bony fist and yell in a raspy voice. I'd seen this happen. I hadn't thrown any stones, nor would I ever; she was clearly not someone to mess with, even though nobody seemed to understand her hoarse shouting. Maybe it wasn't English.

When I mentioned her to Mom, she said, "Don't talk like a fish," which was her way of saying, "Don't bother me with nonsense." I always walked on the opposite side of the street after Danny said she put curses on kids, and decided, just to be on the safe side, never to even look at her house again.

School and fires and the witch and straitjackets and the sugar factory, weren't the only things keeping me awake at night. I was having trouble getting to sleep after our visit to Niagara Falls. I'd been excited on the way after hearing Dad call "the Falls" one of the seven wonders of the world. The first thing we saw after parking the car was the rusty remains of a boat stuck on some rocks at the crest of the falls. Dad said it was a blessing the boat got hung up like that and no lives were lost, but one of the passengers' hair turned from brown to white in the time it took for rescue to arrive.

We ate baloney sandvitches, (that's what Mom called them) in a heavy mist, listening to the thunder of the water falling. Dad told us about a stunt man going over the falls in a barrel.

"But wouldn't he fall out of the barrel?" I asked.

"They'd nail the lid on for that stunt," he said.

"But how would he breathe?"

"Oh, I imagine they drilled a hole or two."

"Then wouldn't the water get in?"

"Oh, maybe a bit. He'd be getting fished out at the bottom before much water got inside."

I couldn't stop thinking about being scrunched inside a sealed up barrel with only tiny air-holes, being churned and slammed around inside while tumbling over the falls, maybe to crash on rocks below. What if he threw up? And I couldn't fathom how a man's hair had suddenly turned white. Like the lady turned to a pillar of salt.

After the picnic and a walk along the main street we visited Madame Tussauds Wax Museum. Mom and Dad weren't too keen on paying the entrance fee but we were all gathered by the front entrance, staring longingly at the display figures. I think Mom felt we deserved a treat for the hard work scraping floors and hauling out garbage, so she nuzzled Dad's ear till he got out his wallet.

The first exhibit inside was The Beatles. Mom wasn't pleased, most likely since the entry fee was pretty 'steep', that's Dad's word for expensive, and the first thing we saw were beatniks, a potentially damaging influence. But next to them were JFK and Jackie, who were dear to Mom, then the Royal Family, so she softened some. We moved along to a pioneer exhibit, some astronauts and knights in armour before finally Mom said we could wander freely. Fortunately, Mom took charge of Tina who needed to use the bathroom, because one of us, not me, discovered the Chamber of Horrors. And if Tina had gone down there, Mom would have had a cow. Tina hadn't yet started kindergarten.

Mark whispered to me while I was studying the cave people, entranced by their monkey-like faces and hairy backs. I tore myself away and followed him down the stone staircase to the dungeon, then stared between the bars at a scene so gory and I couldn't tear my eyes away. Inside the massive jail cell were wax men, all filthy and gaunt with wild, tangled hair. Two were chained by their wrists and ankles to the walls, their skin sucked tight over their rib cages like plastic wrap, wearing filthy ragged jailbird pants so loose they seemed likely to slide off, while furry wax rats with bloody snouts gnawed their toes. Another man sat with hands chained, so his arms extended above his head in a 'v', his head hanging so far forward, it looked like his neck might break.

On the other side of the jail cell, a man was stretched on a rack, his neck twisted, his face contorted, his arms and legs extended so forcefully it seemed he might, at any minute, be ripped apart. Two bodies hung on meat hooks from the ceiling, blood trailing around their mouths and various wounds and pooling beneath them in waxy red puddles on the floor. I stared for quite a while before I heard Dad, who'd stopped on the stairs in mid descent, his face taking on a look of surprise and shock—either from us being there, or the exhibit itself, or both, while Mom muttered angrily behind him, using phrases like "horrid nonsense" and "ruining the effect of God's most magnificent natural wonders" and "utter foolishness".

The ride home was sombre at first. It wasn't exactly that we'd done wrong to go down into the dungeon. I guess we should have known better, used better judgment, but I imagine Dad was anticipating the argument that we really couldn't have known not to go if we didn't go down and to see first. So, after about thirty minutes of induced quiet self-reflection, Dad began spouting off facts about how much water fell over the falls on a daily basis and how that generated all kinds of hydro electric power going all over the place.

During Dad's conversational lectures, I generally went into daydream mode: during the rest of the ride home I fantasized about being a pretty circus trainer in a tasselled mini dress, directing a band of chimpanzees dressed in overalls or frilly dresses, doing tricks to loud applause.

TAVERNS AND ROOFTOPS

The Majeska House Tavern was on the corner of our block, five doors away from the Welcome Inn. Mom and Dad generally ignored the fact that it existed, always glossing over or discouraging talk of any matters related to it. My siblings and I walked past it several times a day because that was the direction we walked to go almost everywhere, including school.

The outside walls of this "seedy bar", as Ruth referred to it, were stucco, dirtied in various hues of browns and yellows on the lower section with chipped and stained, faded mint-green concrete bricks above. The surface of the stucco was marred by bug landings, scuff marks and mud puddle splashing from city busses, but when sunlight struck it the right way, random sparkles gleamed through the stains and splotches. This made me think about the glittering buildings I imagined lining the golden streets of heaven. I had a habit of running my fingers along the rough exterior as I passed until Mark told me he thought the yellow stains were from pee.

A neon sign in red italics reading *Gentlemen* hung above the main entrance, which faced the corner of the block at a 45-degree angle. A sign on a smaller door around the corner read *Gentlemen and Escorts*. Sometimes, when we passed the main door would swing open and men would stumble out, wafting aromas of nicotine and beer, at times, almost colliding with us. I'd try to look past them into the bar, but if I was obvious, laughter or snide commentary followed like, "Go home, little girl. You're mommy's waiting", or "Ladies entrance is over there," jabbing toward the other door.

It was easier to look in as men were entering, but that offered only a brief and partial view, since the inner door immediately swung back like a saloon door. Sometimes I caught the odd glimpse spotlighted beneath the light fixtures; figures huddled around partially filled beer glasses in a cigarette haze, and red terry cloth tabletops. Mostly, I saw the backs of men.

The Genesee House was the other tavern in our neighbourhood, two blocks north on James Street. It had a larger blinking neon sign, perhaps indicating a step up in class and standards. It appeared to attract a larger clientele, judging by the rowdy activity at the entrance door in the late hours of the night. This, we would witness from our bedroom windows in later years, after we moved into the townhouse development that replaced the torn-down sugar factory on the other side of James Street. We walked past the Genesee House to get to Hamilton's "bay", a famously polluted body of water at the narrow western end of Lake Ontario, where we went on summer evenings to play on the swings or catch tadpoles and salamanders if we could find any alive in that toxic, swampy environment.

Walking past the Genesee House bothered me, but not because of the men who hung around there. It was the women. They paced outside the bar or stood leaning against the hydro pole in tight fitting pants and high spiked shoes, glaring if I glanced in their direction. Some of them slouched against the walls, barely able to stay upright. The younger ones wore pirate-like eyeliner with blue shadow and clenched-teeth expressions that seemed to be asking for a fight. Many had blond hair, but it was not the kind of blond hair you'd see streaming in the wind in a field of buttercups on TV. These women had straw-like hair, so brittle and dry that I worried whenever I saw them strike a match to light up a cigarette. The older, puffy-eyed women had paunchy stomachs and smudged red lipstick and were more likely to ignore us or be unaware of us as we hurried past. They all smoked, needing some form of activity while they leaned and slouched, waiting for cabs or their mates to come out from the bar. Whenever a man entered the picture, one of three things was bound to occur; foul language, kissing and groping, or a nasty argument.

Summer nights were hot and humid, so we slept with windows open. From our bedrooms we heard things happening on James Street, late at night, especially around closing time. Sometimes the sisters and I stuck our heads out the windows to try to catch conversations, but if it sounded really interesting, we set out on a little trek.

By going through the back bedroom window, we could access the front balcony by going over the roof from the back fire escape. Mom had shown us how to do this, though she would have had a fit if she knew we were going over in the dark, in our pyjamas. There was a short brick embankment on the south end of the roof that we could hold onto, so it wasn't actually dangerous. The trickiest part was right at the start; pushing ourselves onto the upper roof, which was hard for Tina and me, and treading softly on Mom and Dad's bedroom roof so as not to alert them of our escapades. The first treks were thrilling for me: I felt like I was in the story of *Peter Pan*.

From the front balcony, we had a perfect view of the street below. We could see the sidewalk in front of the grocery store in one direction, and because the house on the other side was set back from the sidewalk, we would see a ways up James Street toward the downtown. We couldn't see directly outside the bar because of the angle, but we could hear all kinds of laughter and talking, much of it slurred and foul. Sometimes, bar patrons stumbled into our viewing area, walking by or waiting for cabs heading uptown. Once we saw a man pee against a telephone pole right below us.

Mom and Dad didn't know about this. Their bedroom at the back of house was shielded from much of the late night racket. Being privy to these "drunken shenanigans", a term I had once heard from Mom, was fun at first, because it was a bonding thing with my sisters. We were drawn to watch, maybe because we knew that if Mom and Dad had known about it, it would have been forbidden, shut down the way the TV was turned off whenever the shooting started, even if it was Bonanza and we were in the middle of an episode.

One night, late in summer, I was awakened by Ruth and the twins sneaking through my bedroom. I sat up.

"There's something going on outside," Ruth whispered.

"Should I come?" I asked.

"Hurry up," said Trudy.

"Should Tina come?" Sarah said.

"Let her sleep," said Ruth.

On the sidewalk below were two men, spotlighted under the streetlight. They were facing each other, shifting their weight from foot to foot, moving in a slow circle like animals I'd seen facing off on *Wild*

Kingdom. One man was short and stocky with a plaid shirt partly unbuttoned and hanging out of his pants on one side. The other was tall and slender and wore a baseball cap. The short man's thick legs were bent and his arms outstretched like he was ready to give a hug. He took a shaky lunge at the tall man, and then another.

We watched in silence.

The short man's speech was slurred and angry. I tensed each time he swore, as though he were speaking to us. The tall man leaned backward with each advance, raising his arms protectively in front of his face. Suddenly, the short man sprang forward, grabbing hold of the tall man's forearm, tugging and twisting, nearly pulling them both down. The tall man managed to break free while the short man spun back to face him. I wished the tall man would take the opportunity to run, but the short man charged again, this time landing a punch. I heard it thud. The tall man hunched over, turning away, and the short man wheeled around, panting like a dog, his mouth open and sloppy, waiting to face him again.

Then I heard voices, approaching quickly. I wanted to leave, but not alone, so I stayed, praying the fight wasn't going to get bigger. Just as the short man was winding up to throw another punch, two men ran into view. One of them shoved the tall man aside while the other grabbed the short man from behind, pulling him away. The two men took hold of his arms, one on each side. They ushered the short man along the sidewalk, saying things like 'wasting your time', 'not worth it', 'let's get outta here', while he struggled to pull away from their grip, swearing over his shoulder. The three disappeared from sight, their voices trailing, leaving the tall man swaying under the streetlight, one arm clutching his shoulder. He stayed like that for a minute, then pivoted clumsily and staggered out of sight in the opposite direction.

"Do you think he'll be alright?" I whispered.

"He's not going to die or anything," said Trudy.

"Yeah, he'll just have a bruise," Sarah said.

Just the same, it made me feel sick inside. And before each late night excursion after that, I asked Ruth if she thought there was going to be a fight. If she thought there was, I stayed inside.

GRADE TWO

In mid-August, Mom took Mark and Tina and me to register at our new school, which was still under construction. The principal, Mr. Becker, got up from his desk and gave us a full tour of the building, leading us around ladders and over cords. He and Mom chatted like old friends.

"We have a very large and diverse student population," he said. "It sounds like you've already met some of the children from the James Street area. The children from the south and east side neighbourhoods tend to come from more stable homes. Many of their fathers work at one of the steel factories."

The new smell of the fresh cement and the cleanly painted walls was a nice change from all of the other buildings in the North End. None of the teachers were there yet. Mr. Becker said there was still too much dust and construction equipment to move in, but he assured us everything would be ready on time. He asked questions about the Welcome Inn and Mom managed to answer them while bragging about how smart we all were.

A few days before school started I asked Mom what I should wear the first day.

"Something clean and respectable," she said. "How about the blue shorts set?"

"Will the twins be wearing theirs?" I asked.

"You can ask them, but it wouldn't matter," she said. "They're not going to the same school."

"I wish I could go to their school," I said.

"Now, why would you want to go to their school?" she asked. "There'd be no one your age."

"They always learn the good stuff first," I said all whiny. "I never get to tell something good at supper."

"You can tell, too," she said.

"Yah, but it's not good stuff, like they tell."

"You can still tell."

"Yah, and they laugh and say, 'We already learned that ages ago," I grumbled.

Mom looked tired of this conversation and said, "No they don't". And I thought, "Yes they do", but knew saying it wasn't going to help.

On the first day of school, I was surprised to see so many of my new classmates dressed in regular, store-bought clothes. I was expecting most of the kids to be poor but not even half of the kids looked ragged. The shabbiest was a boy, with stinky socks, thick scabs on his neck, and snot crusted under his nose. When Miss Jones told us to take off our shoes and gather on the rug, nobody would sit next to him. Anyone he sat beside inched away and made Miss Jones grimace.

We stood up each morning to sing *God Save the Queen*, but Miss Jones didn't check fingernails or ask if anyone had brushed their teeth and not once did she pick up a ruler, except to draw a line on the chalkboard. She wore peasant blouses, long gauzy skirts and sandals. Each day after recess, we chose a book from the shelf to take to our desks or the rug to read with quiet lips, while Miss Jones picked one student to read to her at her desk while she made notes. I grew less nervous waiting for my turn. I'd parked myself close to the front, listening to each classmate read. There was a lot of hesitating, stuttering and making things up. I could tell. Miss Jones smiled and thanked each student after their turn. It was Friday before she called on me. Having chosen the same book all week, I read confidently.

"Wonderful job, Mary," Miss Jones whispered and gave my arm a gentle squeeze. Some students sitting close by saw this. One of them was Lily Chan. She looked me in the eye and gave the smallest of grins when her name was called next to read. She sat down beside Miss Jones.

"I've noticed you've chosen a chapter book, Lily," said Miss Jones. "Did you bring it from home?"

Lily nodded.

"Would you like to choose a book from the shelf?"

Lily shook her head and began to read. I was stunned. Miss Jones sat with her mouth open. When Lily was on her second page, Miss

Jones interrupted, asking if she would skip ahead to another page. Without looking up, Lily turned to a page near the end of the book, and continued on like she was Ruth's age.

The following Monday, Miss Jones put us into reading groups. Lily and I and two boys were put in a group called the Rabbits. Our name cards had green stickers. After the first week, Miss Jones spent most of her time with the other four reading groups, primarily the Raccoons and Hamsters, one of whom was my neighbour, Danny, whose name cards had red and yellow stickers. It was natural that Lily and I should bond, especially since the other two Rabbits wanted nothing to do with us.

By the end of September, Lily and I were together all the time, sitting at the classroom carpet, lining up one behind the other and walking to and from school. We spent recesses leaning against the wall by the kindergarten window. A white line divided the playground; boys played on the far side away from the windows, girls nearest the school, while the supervising teachers patrolled with whistles.

Lily noticed other divisions on the playground and pointed them out to me; the poor kids played on the monkey bars or by the walls. The girls with better clothes played in the middle of our side, the older well-dressed girls closer to the dividing line. I found that mildly interesting but it was a girl named Liz Harrison that drew my attention. Liz was in grade three. She had curly blond ringlets that hung past her shoulders and wore the best clothes I had ever seen. Better even than Joanne Miller's because they were hip, like the clothes girls wore on television commercials. Maybe, it was the way she wore them. She looked perfect as she walked by with three friends who jostled to position themselves closest to her.

One day, while watching Liz's group pass by, I realized *Lily and I* were being stared at. Three girls were standing by the center line of the playground and looking at us. Not in a friendly way. Suddenly nervous, I stared back, the sense of threat growing. I nudged Lily, then looked at my feet.

"The one with the pony tail is Darlene. The tall one is Erica. The red head is Tammy," Lily said, her lips barely moving. "They're in grade three."

"Who are they?" I asked, trying to keep my lips tight while the staring girls leaned together, talking and looking at us.

"They're mean. Especially Erica," said Lily.

"What do they do that's mean?" I asked.

Lily didn't answer my question, "Let's go," she said, pushing herself away from the wall. As we walked away a chill ran through my body, even though it was hot.

On Monday when I called on Lily for school, I suggested we play hopscotch at recess.

"Maybe they don't like us watching everything," I said. "Nobody uses the hopscotch courts."

"Maybe," Lily said. "So you know how to play hopscotch?"

"Yah," I said. "We used to play in the parking lot in Oklahoma. We made the court lines in the church parking lot with a stick. My mom showed us how."

At recess, I kept my attention on hopscotch and tried not to think about those girls. We had fun and played again the next day. By the next day, Wednesday, some girls from our class were watching, and started playing next to us. Thursday, more girls were watching and on Friday, all three courts were occupied. The following Monday, there were line-ups at all three courts. Before long, there was a recess frenzy of grade two and three girls running to the courts as soon as their feet hit the playground, lining up with rocks. It got so busy girls began standing in line with partners to play two against two.

Lily and I became a team. We returned to the playground after school, and practiced with pieces of roofing shingle, which landed flat. This gave us an advantage over those who threw stones into the squares because stones could roll when they landed and if the piece you throw rolls out of the square, you lose your turn.

Mom knew what I was up to. I had brought Lily home to introduce her, and Mom liked Lily right away. I stood by while they carried on a conversation about the wonderful public library up the street. After that, Mom told me I could play with Lily after school for an hour or so but not to neglect to play with the children at the Welcome Inn.

One good thing about hopscotch was it kept my mind off of Darlene, Tammy and Erica most of the time. The bad thing was I missed watching Liz. Now and then, I'd glance up to scan the playground, looking for her shiny curls, but sometimes I saw the mean girls staring in my direction.

They made their first approach in the last week of September. Lily was poised to shoot when the atmosphere at the hopscotch court became suddenly charged, as though a thunderstorm were brewing. I looked up, startled to see them standing at the head of our court, Erica's shoe well over the line. Seeing them up close, my body went rigid.

All movement stopped. Lily, her face tight, tossed her shingle just inside number eight. She steadied herself before hopping, turning carefully to avoid kicking Erica, her eyes never lifting. The spectators watched as though Lily were hopping on glass. She missed her next shot. On purpose, it seemed.

I stepped up to the start line, eyes fixed on the shingle inside square seven. I needed to hop the court and pick it up on the way back. I felt heavy, like I was back in my burning school dream. I wasn't sure if I could move. As I willed my foot to lift, I heard swishing and looked up to see Miss Everett, approaching purposefully, a whistle bouncing on her ample bosom. She stopped just behind Erica.

"Enjoying the game?" she asked cheerfully to no one in particular.

Erica moved her foot, watching me with her eyes narrowed, like a hungry wolf.

There was a lot of talk about prayer in our house, and praying was done routinely and often. I was starting to have some struggles around the idea of prayer. I believed it was right to pray for people and for answers and for things I wanted or needed. In Oklahoma, I prayed for a horse. I prayed for a bicycle. I prayed for a monkey and a surprise birthday party with a live clown performance. When my prayers didn't get answered the way I wanted, there was an explanation that made reference to the difference between 'wants' and 'needs'. I didn't need a horse or a bicycle, and should NOT be praying for fancy birthday parties when so many people were going hungry. Sometimes, I felt guilty when I prayed since I couldn't stop thinking about stuff I wanted.

After we moved to Hamilton, my prayers started to change. I began praying that I wouldn't have nightmares about the taverns, or the sugar factory or the witch, or getting trapped in the basement. I prayed the drunks would be quiet and go home. I prayed for the mean girls to leave Lily and me alone.

But I was troubled by the idea that so many people in this neighbourhood were 'in need' and seemingly weren't getting their prayers answered. When I asked Dad about it, he said we need to trust God's wisdom and sometimes these lessons were difficult to understand, but we must have faith in the outcome. Those answers didn't really help. I waited for time alone with Mom when her mind wasn't occupied.

"Why don't these people pray for the things they need?" I asked one day while I helped her peel potatoes.

"Many of these people don't know how to pray," she said. "They don't even know about prayer. That's why we're here. To show them. But it takes time."

"How long does it take?" I asked.

"It depends," she said.

"What does it depend on?"

"On so many things," she said slowly and then smiled at me. But she looked tired. "People need to understand first. And then they need to have faith."

"What do they need to understand?" I asked, wondering if I understood.

"That God will take care of them."

"How will people understand that if they don't go to church?"

"We need to show them," she said. "Telling people doesn't always work."

"Danny doesn't have any sheets on his bed," I said. "He doesn't even have a bed. Just a dirty mattress. And his clothes are all on the floor."

"When were you over there?" She looked alarmed. "I'm lucky to get three minutes of talk out his mother on the doorstep."

"Yesterday, after school. Mrs. Grabinski wasn't home," I said.

"Where was she?" Mom looked me in the eye.

"She was at the doctor's," I said. "That's what Danny said."

"She left him alone?" she asked, like it was my fault. "How old is he?"

"He's in my class," I said. "But he said she told him to come here if he had a problem."

"Oh," she stuck out her lip. "How'd she get to the doctor's?"

"Taxi," I said.

"What did you do over there?" Normally Mom wasn't so curious about my activities.

"He showed me some of his toys." Really he had, though that lasted about 10 seconds.

"How long were you there?"

Longer than I wanted to be, but I said, "Not very long."

As soon as I had stepped inside Danny's house the day before, I was sorry I had agreed to come. It was dark with the curtains drawn and I squinted to take it all in, having never seen anything like it. We passed a lumpy couch, ripped and frayed as though scratched by wild animals, with a faded pillow on one end and a heaped blanket opposite. The only other furniture was two ratty kitchen chairs facing a television set on a wooden box. A full ashtray sat on the floor amongst scattered magazines near the squashed pillow end of the couch. I followed Danny into the kitchen, where dirty dishes and cups were piled by the sink and on the counters. A cereal bowl, filmy with milk and soggy fruit loops, sat on the table opposite empty milk cartons.

Danny didn't seem embarrassed, so I didn't say anything. Apprehensive, I followed him up the stairs, "That's my mom's room," he said, pointing at a closed door with a poster of a grey kitten hanging upside down, its hair sticking up, and claws embedded in a tree branch. We passed a small bathroom with a running toilet and entered a room with no door.

The only furniture was a grubby mattress on the floor. The wallpaper was faded, bubbled and peeling and a small closet had hinges but no door. A blanket and some clothes were scattered in small heaps. Danny kicked them around, bending over and picking things up with one hand and hiding them behind his back with the other while I stood mute.

He kicked away a couple of piles to clear a spot on the floor, sat cross legged, and lined up four grimy Hot Wheels and the sorriest teddy bear I'd ever seen, with matted fur and both eyes missing. I smiled, and encouraged by my feigned enthusiasm, he got up and leaned into his closet, returning with a plastic gun. Even though it was a toy, it made me more uneasy, mostly because I couldn't think of anything to say, so I asked if we could go watch television.

He shrugged. "Okay, he said. *Dark Shadows* is on."

I sat down on the couch, right away noticing animal hair stuck all over the fabric and on the wadded up blanket, wondering if there might be fleas around. Danny sat on the floor, really close to the television set. Mom would never let us sit that close to our television. She said it would damage our eyes. We watched *Dark Shadows* for a very short time before I realized the show was about vampires. I didn't want any more nightmares so I closed my eyes each time the vampire came on the screen and as soon there was a commercial, I said I had to go home.

"Do you think I should tell Danny to ask his mom to pray for some sheets?" I asked. "It really looks like he needs some."

Mom didn't answer for a moment. "Mrs. Grabinski could buy some sheets, but she chooses to spend her money on other things," she said. "Like cigarettes. I've invited her to Women's group, but she hasn't come. I think if we give her time, she will, but until then, I don't think we should bother her or Danny about sheets."

"Why would that be bothering her if we ask her to pray for some sheets?" I asked.

"Because she might think I am telling her she isn't being a good enough mother," she said. "I think it would be better if we quietly pray for Danny. We can do that together."

THE STOREFRONT

After school was a busy time in the Welcome Inn storefront. There were tables for games in the smaller of the two sections at the back by the kitchen, with chairs scattered around. Two couches, the cushions ripped and stuffing coming loose, shaped an "L" in one corner, looking shabbier as each day passed and they were picked at and occupied by more kids than they were meant to accommodate. We called this section "the games area" or "the library", depending on whether it was noisy or quiet. Stacks of puzzles and board games, many of the boxes reinforced with masking tape, filled shelves, along with books for lending or quiet reading on the off chance it was actually quiet enough to concentrate. We had many board games to choose from, but if too many came out at once, the Monopoly houses could end up in the Parcheesi box. The biggest challenge in the games area was getting a group of kids to learn the rules of the game, and play properly. A successful game was one that did not end up with kids arguing and throwing pieces around.

Books and magazines were donated to the Welcome Inn by the box and bagful from various sources. Before being added to the library, all reading material was perused for appropriateness of content. Any romance novels with covers showing large-breasted heroines or cleavage were removed. Books containing foul language or with any reference to sex, drugs or violence were ousted.

Sometimes Ruth and the twins smuggled "choice" selections to the third floor before they'd been seen by the censors. Their favourites were *Cosmopolitan* and *Vogue* magazines, but they took other ones, too. And *Harlequin Romances*. I would have joined them in this, but I was still too young to exactly understand what criteria they used to make their choices. When I asked them to explain things from the books or magazines they laughed or ignored me. I thought about threatening to tell on them, but knew that would be unwise in the long run. Fortunately for them, Mom didn't make many trips to the third floor other than to supervise our prayers and say good night, and many nights saw her yelling "goodnight" up the stairs from the living room. My sisters kept their purloined stash of racy literature well hidden, tucked under their mattresses, taking it out only when they were sure Mom was completely out of range.

In the larger storefront room, a ping pong table was set up in the middle, with chairs arranged against one wall for visiting or watching games. Sometimes, kids chased each other around the table, slapping each other with the paddles or playing tag by winging the tiny ball around to tag the next 'it', though not if Dad was in the room. He encouraged us to get the kids engaged in board games or civilized ping pong matches. It was part of our service project, he said, to engage the neighbourhood kids in worthwhile activities. If kids were too rambunctious, they were shooed outside to play in the vacant lot. Skipping ropes were on hand for outside play, though they were mostly used for inappropriate activities, like tying each other up. The other piece of outside equipment was a basketball that was often returned partially deflated.

Among the regulars in the storefront were Carol Davidson and Jeanie Tufts.

Carol was in second grade but not in my class. Jeanie was a year older. Carol had a scratchy voice, and sounded older than her years. She was the kind of girl who could stand around or sit, doing nothing, not even talking, and was always happy. She was at the Welcome Inn whenever it was open. Her dad had a disability, she said and didn't go to work. He didn't have a car and his legs tended to swell, forcing him to keep them elevated, which meant Carol was in charge of getting his smokes when her mom was at work. Sometimes Carol called on me to go with her when her dad gave her an extra nickel to buy herself some candy, which she shared with me.

Several times, I walked with Carol to her house when she needed to deliver cigarettes. Her dad was always in the same plaid armchair, smoking, his thick legs up on a hassock, a pedestal ash tray stand smouldering next to him, radio blaring. Though his fingers were yellow brown, his face was pasty white, like the underbelly of a fish, and so were the bare parts of his feet that puffed out around his tight slippers. He always greeted us jovially, asking questions about school. We had to shout our answers because of the radio. The air was a thick bluish haze and though I enjoyed visiting, I struggled with the smell and the noise level. But I felt the need to make an occasional visit, because I enjoyed the candy.

Jeanie Tufts lived around the corner, five houses from the witch. Jeanie was often around but she was the type of girl that was only happy if she was doing something. Jeanie was what Mom called a chatterbox, and was one of the first neighbourhood kids to try out the roller skates. She took to those roller skates like a gopher to burrowing and continually asked to use them. The rest of us seemingly forgot they existed, content to leave them hanging on a nail on the way down to the basement. But those skates drew Jeanie as though they were an extension of her feet…and weather permitting, she'd be rolling out the door.

Club nights started fairly early on. The club for the young girls met on Tuesday evenings. That was my group. I always seemed to be in the "young" group.

Our group of young girls, which included Tina, Carol and Jeanie, sat around the ping pong table making "young girl' crafts, like bleach jug birdfeeders and macramé bracelets. Dad made wooden frame squares with nails sticking up all around so we could weave potholders with Phentex yarn. We filled baby food jars with coloured water and plastic flowers, covered the lids with fabric, and placed them upside down for table decorations. We carved pumpkins, taking turns digging out handfuls of pulp and seeds, and decorated paper sacks for collecting Halloween candy. At Christmas, we made toilet-paper-roll candles painted green, with a yellow paper flame.

Ruth and the twins got to be in the "older" girls group, which looked and sounded way more interesting than our group. They met on Wednesday evenings. I watched enviously from the staircase or the library room while they made better crafts, but I had to be quiet or Mom would make me go up upstairs to read. They made wall hangings of macramé owls framed between tree branches with beads for eyes. They tie-dyed hankies and used them for bandanas. They made bigger-than-life orange, purple and pink flowers with wire and tissue paper and green tape stems to put in vases for their bedrooms. For Christmas, they made freestanding Christmas trees by taking old telephone books and folding the pages into points and gluing the front and back covers together.

Mom saved all the empty apple juice and extra-large soup cans and the older girls used them to make hassocks. This was accomplished by sewing together seven fabric-covered soup cans; one can was the centre and six cans surrounded it like petals. Once they were stitched together, the hassock was traced onto a large piece of fabric. This piece was cut out and sewn around the top with cotton batten padding underneath for comfort. From the top, the hassocks looked like great big flowers and made me think of the "Flower Power" slogan that was printed everywhere on walls and on T-shirts. There were all kinds of different fabric pieces available to make their hassocks colourful and groovy.

Boy's Club met on Thursdays. Sometimes I watched them, too. The Boy's Club also made better stuff than the Young Girl's Club. Such as log houses and forts with Popsicle sticks. They made pictures by burning into slabs of wood with electric wood burners—even the smell was exciting, reminiscent of campfires. And they also made wallets after Dad scouted some leather and a hole puncher, then plastic twine to weave through the holes. Dad even got his hands on a fancy rig that embossed pictures into the leather. I looked at Mark's wallet with its depiction of the head of a horse with such envy that finally, Dad punched one up for me and let me weave it together upstairs.

SHOPPING EXCURSIONS AND SEWING CLASS

A common problem among neighbourhood women was being married to husbands who drank or smoked excessively. A common complaint was the difficulty of feeding families when the money rarely lasted to the end of the month. Mom recognized the need to educate the North End women on home economics. She kept a running commentary on the spending habits of the North End women. "Most of those women have never opened a bag of oatmeal," and "They buy expensive packaged cereal, probably the sweet stuff. No wonder they run of money."

"Can you imagine buying cigarettes, instead of milk for your children? What can they be thinking?" she would say. "They're in dire need of cooking lessons. Some of them don't know a thing about making a piece of meat, never mind making it last. Imagine throwing away a chicken carcass or a ham bone!!" and "They claim they can't afford a whole chicken, so they end up buying the pieces. What kind of nonsense is that? Don't they understand that they end up paying more? Land sakes. I bet they even throw the carcass away with meat still attached to the bones."

In order to achieve her goal, Mom organised regular monthly meetings followed by shopping excursions. These were timed to coincide with paydays and days when welfare cheques were deposited. The idea was to buy the bulk of food supplies in quantities large enough to last an entire month, shopping as a group to help each other make wise choices.

Since Mom had been feeding large numbers around the Welcome Inn table, Dad was becoming an ace scout for food bargains, the best source being Hopper's Wholesale, where dry and canned foodstuffs came in extra large bags, cans and boxes, and by the case. The ladies could get better value by sharing in purchases of case-lots of things, like canned soup and toilet paper, or chipping in for a share of flour, sugar, potatoes or rice from extra large bags. It wasn't exactly open to the public, but Dad did some finagling to allow them access.

The meetings began with the group gathered at the rollaway chalkboard. With Mom as chairperson and Anita standing ready with chalk, they made lists and tallies of who would contribute toward a case of canned soup or tuna, or a share of rice or sugar. Once the shopping lists were organized, cookies or muffins and coffee were served at the kitchen table, giving the opportunity for "fellowship", (Mom's favourite word for visiting) and cooking demonstrations. This ritual before shopping was vital, according to Anita, a VS'er who had majored in Home Economics in College and who believed strongly that "one should never shop when tired or hungry", since this can lead to hasty decisions and/or binge shopping. The snacks also kept the ladies content, and thus more likely to listen to tips and recipe ideas.

With a happy crowd at the table, there were many hands for chopping, slicing, and mixing, while Anita talked of the nutritional benefits of fresh produce, or Mom gave step-by-step demonstrations on making borscht or a casserole. With caffeine levels boosted, appetites satisfied and lists ready, the group piled into the van. When they returned, the goods were divided and the women ferried home with their groceries.

Anita played a key role in forming a women's sewing class, making arrangements to have her sewing machine sent from Wisconsin by Greyhound bus. That began a quest for used sewing machines locally and through the church system in southern Ontario. Dad helped by bargaining for and collecting sewing machines, and became the chief repair person, creating a special "gulch pile" for sewing machine parts.

The women's sewing group started with six members who set up sewing machines on the ping pong table. Word spread and the group increased in size as machines were acquired and new dresses were flaunted. Card tables were added and extension cords were rigged up under and around the ping pong table, like massive sleeping spiders, to support the growing number of machines.

Dad was on call, and busy during the sewing groups. As the class size increased and sewing machines put to the test, he needed to be within earshot, and was often summoned to secure a zipper foot, apply oil, or replace fuses when the circuits blew. An ironing board, set up for the purpose of pressing seams, became a source of contention. Anita insisted on teaching this step in the sewing process. Mom wasn't picky about seams being ironed, and claimed it was the iron that caused the fuses to blow constantly. They compromised by using the iron for short periods of time, quickly unplugging it after every use.

It soon became apparent that when it came to basic knowledge about sewing, nothing could be taken for granted. As the size of the group grew, Mom and Anita were having trouble keeping up with the demand for help with both major and minor problems. We would hear about their Tuesday morning struggles when we came home from school at lunchtime and found them at the kitchen table, worn out and staring into space.

Mom told us it was taking time to reinforce the basics, like how to change a needle in the sewing machine, or how not to sew over pins, or through too many layers of fabric. Even though sewing machine needles were inexpensive, Mom couldn't help being frustrated by the number that needed replacing. She was also annoyed when anyone began "fooling around with the tension dial", which resulted in loosely stitched or bunched up seams that needed to be torn apart and re-sewn. Anita was bothered by careless use of seam rippers, which left tiny holes in the fabric, and even more bothered when people did not use them at all, instead ripping seams apart using sheer force, "compromising the integrity of the fabric". Both were frustrated with the careless laying out of pattern pieces, which led to wasting fabric.

"I was speechless when I went over to help Louise," Mom said, shaking her head one Tuesday at lunchtime. "I didn't even know what to say," she continued with her arms crossed by the soup pot while we sat waiting with empty bowls. "She sewed the top of her skirt together, so she couldn't even get it on."

Another time,

"I wish they could just learn to fold the fabric in two equal pieces, so they can lay the pattern on properly and cut all the pieces they need," Mom talking. "Trisha Wilson started cutting before she'd laid out all the pieces. And she didn't lay them out carefully, so she only had enough fabric left for one sleeve. She'll either have to use a different piece of fabric for the other sleeve, or have a sleeveless dress!"

And another,

"I could not believe it when Donna Carter showed me the pieces to her dress. The stripes went up and down in the front and sideways on the back," Mom again. "I can't believe she wouldn't have figured that out. We did talk about that last week, didn't we? Didn't we talk about that, Anita?" She sounded shrill. "We may have to stick to solid coloured fabrics."

And another,

"Donna sewed her dress together today...but she sewed the seams on the wrong side, so it looks like it's inside out.'"

One Tuesday Mom and Anita were sitting at the table bent over and shaking. They were laughing so hard, Mom had tears in her eyes.

"What's so funny?" I asked.

It took a minute for her to speak, every time she opened her mouth, Anita laughed and that got her going again.

"Gina Masters sewed her sleeve in upside down," she said.

"And... she modeled it for us... She couldn't figure out why... one arm had a bell sleeve," Anita was having trouble talking.

"Anita told her she'd sewn it in upside down. That she needed to take the sleeve out and sew it back properly," Mom was shaking.

"But she wouldn't," Anita said, practically in tears. "She said it was okay. She wore it home, she was so happy."

The best lunchtime report occurred the day the Tupper sisters joined sewing group. The two sisters were so big they arrived in separate cabs. We later guessed their combined weight to be in the 800-900 pound range. Anita was still reeling with the shock of taking their measurements. The five foot measuring tape hadn't fit around either of their waists, so she'd asked each sister to use her hands to mark the places where the tape measure didn't reach and add 60 inches. One of them was 77 inches around her mid section and the other a slightly slimmer 72".

"I'm not sure I'll be able to expand any of our patterns enough to fit them," Anita said. "I may have to order one." She shook her head sadly. "I don't think I've ever seen a pattern in a size like the one they'll need."

"I wonder if we have pieces of fabric big enough to sew them each a dress," Mom said, looking genuinely concerned. "I may have to pick up another bolt of fabric."

The Tupper sisters didn't live far away, but their idea of "walking distance" differed significantly from ours. They participated long enough to make two dresses each, simple sleeveless shifts, then they stopped coming.

Despite all the trials and tribulations around sewing class, some of the women made rapid progress, and a buddy system formed, providing additional support. Anita printed basic steps on paper and hung them on the wall, and inspired by some of Louella's outfits, the women gained confidence and skill.

The women were so excited about wearing their outfits that after they had been meeting for about a year, one woman suggested they have a fashion show. Mom's comments after the fashion show betrayed a similar level of pride;

"The ladies were beaming."

"Did you see Jeanie's new haircut? She even had it curled!"

"Did you see the way Donna walked through the storefront? I've never seen her walk with such confidence."

"The men were proud. You could see it in their eyes."

Sewing group was so popular that a Bible study group, and then a quilting group grew out of it.

SMART LADIES

Lily rarely came into the Welcome Inn. I didn't ask why, so we played at her house, always outside, even in winter. Lily spoke Chinese at home but didn't talk about her family, except her older brother, who was in high school. She had a way of clamming up when she didn't wish to comment, and she accomplished this by setting her jaw, raising her chin and averting her gaze. Then she changed the subject.

Darlene, Tammy and Erica continued to torment us at school. I was grateful they lived in a neighbourhood on the other side of the school, and had never come to the Welcome Inn, or even ventured into the neighbourhood. For some reason, Lily and I were interesting to them— maybe because our differences made us stand out— me because of my homemade clothing and Lily because she was the only Asian student at school. They seemed to relish opportunities to make sudden appearances, asking questions in loud voices and in such a way as to make themselves appear genuinely interested.

"Does your family eat everything with chopsticks?"

"Do you have to go to church every Sunday?" and

"Do you have to pray at home every day?"

"Do your parents speak English?"

"Do you have to eat rice every day?"

"Where do you buy your clothes?"

We tried ignoring them, moving away, but they'd follow us, repeating the questions, sometimes splitting up to corner us. Lily was better than me at ignoring them. She'd glare back, so I was usually the one to stammer a response.

"I heard your parents get old clothes from churches and give them away for free," Erica said on one occasion.

"Sometimes," I replied.

"Is that where you got that dress?"

Maybe because of this, Lily and I invented an activity that became our favourite pastime. We called it Smart Ladies. We acted rich. We always played at Lily's, and if we saw anyone coming, we stopped playing until we were alone again.

At the beginning, the sessions were short and repetitive.

"Oh Daphne dawwwling, you look so beautiful in that fur coat. Where did you get it?

"Oh thank you Penelope. It is divine. I got it in France."

"How much did it cost?"

"It was two million dollars"

"It looks so fabulous. I must buy one of those on my next trip to France."

"Are those alligator shoes? I simply must know where you bought those."

"I bought them last time I was in France. Aren't they just divine?"

"How much did they cost?"

"Only three million dollars."

"Do you like my necklace?" I say, gesturing toward my neck. "It has sixty diamonds."

"I will simply have to go out and buy one, too. But I will also get a matching bracelet for five million dollars."

I loved Smart Ladies so much that I began to take an interest in the habits of rich ladies on television. I begged to watch *Green Acres* to observe Lisa Douglas, and *Gilligan's Island*, to look at Mrs. Howell's suits and Ginger's gowns, since it was majority rules around choice of television show, and viewing time was limited when Mom felt like enforcing it. I asked questions during commercials.

"What do you think is the most expensive food in the world?"

"Caviar."

"No, it's lobster."

"What is caviar?"

"They're some sort of fish eggs."

"How much would they cost?"

"Caviar is not a 'they'. It's an 'it'."

"How much does 'it' cost?"

"Depends on what kind you want."

"What's the most expensive kind?"

"Maybe caviar from whales. Beluga, I think."

"How much it that?"

"Probably about two hundred dollars for a can."

"What's another kind of expensive food?"

"Lobster,"

"Where does lobster come from?'

"From the ocean."

"How much does lobster cost?"

"I don't know. More than we can afford. Mom sure would like to have a lobster some day."

"What else is expensive?"

"Champagne. But that is a drink. It's alcohol."

"Is steak expensive?"

"Yah, and so are hors d'oeuvres."

"What, are you planning on going to some fancy restaurant or something?"

"No. What about cars?"

"What kind of cars do rich people have?"

"Rolls Royce," said Mark. "What? Are you planning on being rich? How you going to do that?"

"Just wonder what her life would be like in New York," I say.

"Who?"

"Lisa Douglas."

"Well she wouldn't be driving," said Ruth, "She'd be taking a taxi. Or she'd be getting picked up in a limousine."

How she knew these things amazed me. Must've been all her library books, or the magazines she smuggled into her room.

Lily and I played Smart Ladies several times a week, always at Lily's. We stuck our noses in the air or walked with library books on our heads, jabbering in clipped voices about clothing and accessories, makeup and hairdos, naming shampoo brands we knew from television commercials. We talked of mansions and yachts with built-in swimming pools and bowling allies, all with maids, ponies and poodles. We planned parties and fancy menus. Lily told me about shrimp cocktail, T-bone steak, soufflé and Black Forest cake.

"Oh Eva, that blouse is magnificent! I must know where it came from," said Lily, looking down the nose at my imaginary fancy blouse. A perfect lead-in for me.

"Oh I'm so glad you noticed, Michelle!" I answered with as much French accent as I could muster. "I just got this. It was a gift, sent by a luxury liner from the Orient. It's made from raw silk."

Just days earlier at dinner, Mom was talking about a play she said she'd give her eye tooth, whatever that was, to see, called 'The King and I'. Her eyes longing, she talked about the music and the beautiful silk costumes. That led to a conversation about the Orient being famous for silkworms, and the process of making of silk fabrics, which were very expensive. Two male VS'ers from Kansas, started joshing each other about how one would love to see the other dressed in clothes made of worm spit.

"The silkworms are kept by the King's attendant and they only make royal silk," I told Lily smugly, swaying my hips along the cement walkway. "This blouse is a birthday gift from the King of Siam." I paused to run one hand gracefully along the inside of the sleeve. "And he sent some tea. The only kind of tea the Queen of Siam allows in the palace. Would you like some?"

"I would love some tea. But you wouldn't dream of making it yourself. Surely, you'll get one of your servants to bring us the tea," answered Lily, haughtily.

"Molly…Molly…" I called briskly to the brick wall. "Bring us some tea. And bring us some finger sandwiches made with butter. And be sure to trim the crusts. I would also like some caviar in a side dish. Use the china. But don't bring too much. We need to watch our figures."

"Oh, I do hope she remembers to bring sugar cubes and cream for our tea," said Lily. "But I must be careful not to spill on this dress. The sequins are real diamonds and it costs one million dollars to have it cleaned."

"Only one million. Goodness. I just had my mink cape done and the bill was two million dollars. Surely, you can afford the bill."

"No, no, of course I can, but I am planning to wear this dress to the President's Ball tonight and I simply cannot get it soiled."

"Why don't you just get a new dress for the evening?" I said with my nose pointed upward. "I saw a splendid red satin gown with rubies embroidered around the neck. It would go well with your new beehive hairdo. We can have Charles pick it up with the limousine."

"Well then, I will have to dash home after tea to try it on," she smiled. "I wonder what will be on the President's dinner menu this evening?"

Lily invited the Beatles to her parties, seating Ringo next to her at the table. Out of respect to my parents, who declared everything rock and roll "sickness", I did not invite them to my parties, rather, inviting Hoss and Joe Cartwright—without their guns, who rode in on horses that were led away by jockeys to eat exotic grass dishes at the stables. Julie Andrews and Dick Van Dyke were on my party list along with other Disney stars like Snow White and Bambi.

Some Saturday afternoons, when the weather was good, Lily and I walked to the public library, where we chose books by Beverly Cleary (Lily's favourite author) in duplicate, so we could read them together. We formed the exclusive membership of my very first book club, with Lily starting the discussion as soon as she finished a chapter. This was a problem for me, because she read much faster than I did. Rather than admit to my weaker reading skills, I chose to skip sections to keep up. If Lily laughed, I'd wait about four seconds and laugh even if I had no idea what was funny.

Consequently, I didn't have much to add to our literary discussions, since many times I was fuzzy on the plotline. At times, Lily asked me questions and watched me slyly while I stammered out an answer. I could tell by her face that she was on to me, but she didn't say it right out. I always planned to read the sections at home and add some intelligent piece to the conversation the following day, as though the idea just came to me, but that rarely happened due to the busy nature of the Storefront. By the time night rolled around I wasn't in the mood to read, preferring to listen to the conversations from the other room or to daydream about being Liz.

Our third Beverly Cleary selection was called *Ellen Tebbits*. I decided to try a new tactic, since Lily was aware of my cheating anyway. We sat down at a table in the library, and I asked Lily if she would read to me, saying I would follow along in my book. Lily nodded and began to read. When Ellen Tebbits snuck into the broom closet to change into her ballet outfit so the other girls wouldn't see her woollen underwear we laughed. When Ellen Tebbits emerged and started her ballet lesson, the wool panties started sliding off, and we broke into fits of laughter. We laughed so hard, our eyes were wet and Lily was having difficulty continuing. Our laughter brought the librarian to our table. She told us to behave quietly or we'd be asked to leave. We tried to laugh quietly but that didn't work. So we left.

It turned out Lily would end up reading me that whole book. She said it was way more fun laughing along with somebody else. Mom was pleased about my treks to the library with Lily and my interest in books, even though we were mostly reading about a bratty little kid and a skinny dog. So in winter, when it was too cold for walking too far, Mom had Ruth ride with us on the city bus to and from the library so we could learn to go ourselves, along with instructions to sit up front and inform the driver of our destination as we deposited our tickets.

If Lily and I were together and we weren't at school, or playing hopscotch, or reading, we were playing Smart Ladies. The game remained a secret. Mom and Dad would have been appalled had they known, since one of their favourite topics for discussion and/or lectures was "how resources weren't shared properly", and how North Americans had all the wealth and the multinational giants were taking advantage of poor countries. Even though I really didn't understand about multinational giants, I heard about them repeatedly. I understood inequity; some people had more and some people had less. Dad had it drilled into our heads: most North Americans were getting more than their fair share, causing others to suffer, so I knew I was not supposed to want. Yet, playing Smart Ladies with Lily was one of my favourite things. I was actually quite good at it. Lily said so.

THE CLOTHING PROJECT

In, and before the sixties, many Mennonites were farmers, living off the beaten track, set apart from the worldliness of modern society. Hamilton, with 'big industry' jobs, was too much in the mainstream for the life of simplicity honoured and pursued by the Mennonite culture in places like Kitchener-Waterloo and Vineland. Our Mennonite Church had a small membership. Some of the church members supported programs at the Welcome Inn by volunteering time. The churches further away helped in other ways.

One of these efforts came in the form of clothing donations. It became the job of my sisters and me to sort and organize these donations in the basement. When boxes arrived, I was excited in the same way auctions and barn sales thrilled me, for the chance of finding something new, for cheap, or free, since Mom often let us each choose an article or two for ourselves. It was kind of like a treasure hunt.

In the beginning, I sorted through boxes enthusiastically, imagining that deep within the boxes were dresses like the ones Shirley Temple wore on the Good Ship Lollipop. Instead, I found dresses that were long and plain, and looked as though they had come from the closets of someone's deceased grandmother. I dug through each new box praying that my hands might touch denim, or I might find a brightly coloured sweater or a peasant blouse. But I pulled out older women's skirts and jackets made from durable permanent-press fabrics in solid bland colours. I persevered through the years, hoping to find a pair of jeans or a tie-dyed T-shirt. But I found 'slacks' with elastic waists and blouses in ladies sizes, with no frill or lace. And they smelled of stale floral cologne or mothballs.

Most of the clothing we unpacked was for mature women. And most of it was homemade. You could tell by the lack of labels on the clothing, as well as the telltale large seams and ample hems that allow for easy alteration. We did find articles of children's clothing, but not many and not very often, perhaps because Mennonite mothers tend to mend, patch and pass clothing along from the older to the younger ones until they end up in the ragbag. I was familiar with this tradition. Many of my dresses were handed down from Ruth or one of the twins. So sorting clothing was both fun and disappointing. Fun because we could have found something hip or stylish. Disappointing because we generally didn't. For the most part, the children's clothing was similar to the stuff we already had. Plain and practical, because it was home-sewn by other Mennonite moms whose collective view was to keep wardrobes basic and unadorned, in order to discourage the sins of pride and vanity.

All but the smallest adults needed to duck for clearance as they descended into "the dungeon" where the donated clothes were sorted and stored. It always took a moment to get used to the dank smell and the dim lighting of the one exposed bulb in the room at the bottom of the stairs. This room, which we named *The Department Store*, was the main clothing and display area. Trudy said the poor lighting was good since the flaws in the clothing were less obvious.

Dad assembled shelves with concrete blocks and rough boards salvaged from the garage, which had me stacking clothes with caution after several incidents of feeling faint while Mom removed a splinter from one of my fingers. These makeshift units were the type of shelving I imagined cave-men might have built to hold their stone bowls and water vessels, as they tilted and swayed, not quite flush against the walls due to dampness and lumps in the ancient plaster. Dad's solution to the need for shelves in the middle of the room was to build a multi-layering of hanging boards attached to chains suspended from the exposed ceiling beams. The hanging shelves tended to swing when bumped, sometimes dislodging their contents, scraping skin, or causing bruises. If one got swinging and bumped into another, we could end up tidying up quite a mess.

Dad created coat and dress racks with wire and piping, fashioned like hanging parallel bars, or trapezes. These were less dangerous since they were well padded when full, except for the pipe ends which might take out an eye if we made a sudden turn. Dad strung Christmas lights from protruding nails in the beams to add extra light and festivity to the main display area, which we organized into sections; women's, men's and children's, marked with cardboard signs we made by cutting the backs off cereal boxes.

In the corner of the room, a bathroom was roughed in using vertical boards that did not quite meet the ceiling. This tiny room was the only part of the basement with an actual solid floor. Most of the basement floor surface was made up of relatively smooth sections of solid concrete, surrounded by crumbling bits. The raised bathroom floor was covered in plywood and ancient yellowed linoleum, its worn edges tapering like pie crust rolled too thin. The toilet bowl was rust coloured from the water line down, and since no amount of scrubbing could clean it, it was never clear if the toilet was flushed or not. A lone pedestal sink stood out in the corner of the small room. A constant trickle of Hamilton's iron-tinged water leaked from the worn silver faucet, leaving a permanent ring of rust around the drain. The only added room décor was a small mirror hanging crookedly above the sink and an extra large nail, banged into the wall to hold a roll of toilet paper. The bathroom door was hinged to open outward, and because of the imbalanced nature of the room, it swung open into our display areas. Thus, hooks needed to be installed on both sides to keep the door closed, both when it was and when it wasn't in use. Of course, this also made it easy for people to take advantage of the opportunity to lock the door from the outside when someone was inside. More than once I was locked inside while an older sibling went upstairs and turned off the light, leaving me in complete darkness. At least the outhouse in Oklahoma allowed some light to penetrate through the cracks...

There were two other rooms in the basement. Like the three stories above, the basement was long and narrow, one room running into the next and accessed through open doorframes with low clearance. The middle room was the largest, occupied on one side by a black metal furnace large enough to cook both Hansel and Gretel. Opposite the furnace was the laundry area containing a sink, a wringer washer and a dryer, which Dad had made level by propping the corners with blocks of wood. Occasionally, the dryer jiggled itself off one of the blocks, and vibrated precariously at an angle, making rumbling sounds like thunder. Whenever I walked through this middle room, I looked straight ahead and quickened my step, in case the dryer slipped, or the furnace suddenly blasted on, raising the hair on my neck.

The "Billiard Room" at the front of the building was the only place in the basement I liked; unfortunately, it was also the farthest to get to. It was the room the neighbourhood boys used for pool games, lit by a florescent light over the table, and scary dark when the lights went out since the two tiny windows that faced James Street from under the walk-in windows were thick with years of yellowed residue.

The pool table took up most of the room and was our clothing organization station when it wasn't in use, its large surface providing an ideal folding and sorting area. Once it was arranged into piles or put onto hangers we carried the clothing back to the display room where it was added to the shelves and racks. Since space was at a premium, a shoe department was created in a very small, very dark space behind the furnace, not my idea, and a place I did everything in my power to avoid. Nor did I ever go into the basement alone in case someone turned off the light at the top of the stairs, leaving most of the basement in complete darkness. With the rough floor, finding your way to the stairs was a potentially dangerous situation, like stumbling blindly along a bumpy, pebble strewn path in a dark, dense forest.

The clothes were for people who needed them, most of whom were "going through hard times" as Dad put it. It was mostly women who came in quietly asking for clothing, many looking worn out or jittery, often with children, rumpled and dishevelled. I had never seen many of them before, some wearing sunglasses they didn't remove.

When this happened, Mom immediately took the woman into the kitchen, shooing away anyone who was in there, summoning one or more of us, either to tend to the children, or to go downstairs with instructions; 'Get two dresses, some pants, a skirt, a few blouses and an outfit or two for the children'. She'd give the name of someone who was close in size to the woman and close the door.

Early one morning, a woman with bruises on her face and three children arrived looking completely exhausted. Mom took Mrs. Bishop into the kitchen and closed the door, leaving the kids sitting timidly on the couch. Debbie was around my age but she looked much younger. Timmy sat on her lap wearing a soiled diaper, his nose runny, his head droopy and his legs splayed like a rag doll. They were all thin and frail and looked like they hadn't washed or combed their hair in ages, especially Annabelle, who looked miniature, and would have been adorable if she were cleaned up and wearing a nice dress.

 They didn't say much or seem at all interested in our questions. Finally, Mom came out and said, "Go downstairs and find some clothing for this family", which was a relief to me. Mom told us later that Mr. Bishop spent most of the welfare money on drink. After that day, the Bishop family came around the Welcome Inn quite regularly. Many times they left with a bag of groceries. Sometimes with food right off our table if they happened to knock during mealtimes.

Not all women who asked for clothing looked miserable. Some came looking shabby but chipper; clearly not candidates for Mom's private kitchen sessions with tea. They asked to pick clothing for themselves, using the basement bathroom as a change-room. At first, Mom allowed them free reign down there.

None of us girls liked that. They inevitably left a mess, but our comments fell on deaf ears. Rather than sympathy, we'd hear words about these "poor people who have struggled, who have no this, or have no that…"

Since complaining was not effective, we tried insisting the women stay upstairs and relax, browse through the magazines, while we went downstairs… that we knew exactly what might look nice, naming a specific garment, like 'a nice beige sweater' that would 'fit just right'. Sometimes it worked, but when it didn't we were left to clean up after them.

 "You probably have a point," Mom said one day after Ruth showed her a sizable pile of clothes on the bathroom floor, right up against the toilet. "If these women really need the clothes they'll be grateful for the bag they're given."

She became even more agreeable after it was pointed out that if allowed, these women took only the best quality items. That idea really irritated Mom who had taught us to put together bags with a variety; one or two "choice" items along with some of the regular stuff, and a few worn things for house cleaning and chores, thereby keeping our stock at least a little bit classy.

Initially, Mom was easy about giving clothing to anyone who asked, handing out bags joyfully, since we "were blessed with such an abundant supply". Her attitude changed when two younger women returned three times in a short period asking for more clothes. When Mom questioned them and discovered they were throwing the clothes into the garbage rather than washing them, she was beside herself.

"Can you imagine?" she exclaimed, "Throwing away perfectly good clothes because they need to be washed! Can you believe someone would actually do that???" She repeated variations of this line for days, at meals, or muttering to herself while sweeping.

For entertainment, we tried clothes on, playing dress-up in men's suits and high heels, parading around the pool table as though we were in a Paris fashion show. Mom didn't know about this activity. She would have had a fit, especially after my performance in the storefront window. But we always posted a guard to watch the stairs and give enough warning so the ones dressed up had time to duck behind the furnace to strip off the clothes, leaving a pile to clean up later. Or they could just hide there. Mom didn't usually do a head count, and there were so many places in the house we could be at any given time. And we never did it with neighbourhood kids around, since they might blab. As for being sneaky and doing things that Mom might call sins of pride or vanity or showing off, I was growing less and less worried about these activities being recorded in heaven, mostly because I knew I wouldn't be standing alone up there, being judged. From what I was witnessing on a daily basis, I'd be in good company.

THE SUMMER OF '67

Before there was Red Green, there was Dad. Except Dad preferred nails over duct tape. If there was any way Dad could drive a nail into something, he would. Otherwise, he'd use wire to wrap and twist.

He built us a tent travel trailer, completed in time for a family vacation that summer to Expo '67 in Montreal, Quebec. It was a two-wheeled, enclosed trailer reminiscent of a spruced up, oversized, donkey cart. The wooden box of the trailer was painted stellar-jay blue, purchased from the discounted paint rack at the hardware store to loosely complement the colour of our car. The box, enclosed on all sides, served as a storage compartment for luggage and sleeping bags, accessible through a hinged tailgate at the back and secured with a padlock. The view from the top was a six-by-six-foot square platform, a perfect size to accommodate Dad laying down in either direction, the flat top designed to accommodate our canvas tent.

The tent was nailed at the four corners to the top platform, inside a 'lip' around the edges, in the style of a shallow sandbox, leaving a gap at the front entrance. Dad built the lip so we could feel secure inside the tent while we were camping. A piece of foam covered the floor of the tent, "for comfort", with a golf ball sized hole cut into the middle for the centre pole. Four shorter poles supported the corners. When we travelled, the tent lay collapsed in the shallow box, covered with a tarp.

"We won't need to pay for a campground," Dad said. "We can stop whenever we want. All we need is a level spot."

Dad gave us a demonstration of his self-designed tent trailer in the alley behind our garage where it would attract the least attention from neighbourhood kids. He chose a Sunday afternoon so there would be no chance of interfering with a truck delivering beer to the back door of the tavern.

"Suitcases, sleeping bags, cooler, go underneath here," Dad said, showing us the inner compartment. "In the morning, we throw our sleeping bags underneath, take down the poles, flatten the tent a bit and we're ready to go."

He pulled a short wooden post from the compartment and stood next to the trailer hitch. We fanned around to watch.

"With this post placed under the hitch," he said, lifting the tow bar and positioning the wooden post under it, "the top will be perfectly level." He wiggled the tow bar until it slipped into a notch to secure the 'third leg' post. "Like this."

Then he stepped onto a narrow ledge that was built across the front of the trailer, level with the bottom of the 'box' for easy access to the tent platform.

"Hand me that pole," he said, pointing to the ground. I reached down and handed up the pole. It was a little taller than me.

"Is this the only pole?" I asked.

"The others are inside the tent," he said.

Holding the centre pole, he pulled at the canvas with his free hand until he found the tent door. Using the pole to prod his way through the entrance, he crawled forward, leaving his behind and feet sticking out. We watched the tent take on the shape of his kneeling form, a jerkily moving brown mass. It reminded me of the monsters from the movie, 'The Day of the Triffids' and a shiver ran up my spine thinking about what Mom would say if she found out we'd watched it. With a series of abrupt elbow jabs, pole pokes and grunts, the silhouette transformed, lifting to form a vertical peak. The point jiggled back and forth for a few seconds before it was planted with one final grunt. I had to cover my mouth to stifle a laugh. Dad did not like us to 'spotte' as he called it when we mocked, or made fun of his handiwork.

"Hold open the flaps," his muffled voice yelled out. Mark and I stepped up to the ledge and grabbed one flap each to open the door, giving Dad light and air. Then, the corners emerged, one at a time.

"Wow," said Mark.

"Yah, wow," said Ruth, rolling her eyes. Trudy stood with one hand on her hip looking on stone faced.

"How long do you figure that took?" Dad asked, poking his head out through the door.

"Oh, I'd say less than two minutes," answered Mark.

"That's not bad," said Dad. "I'll practice a few times to get the feel for it. That way I can put it up in the dark."

"Are you going to practice now?" I asked, eager to watch the Triffid show again.

"Come inside and lay down first," he said. "I want to see how we all fit."

"So, you think it's going to be big enough?" Sarah asked.

"Two or three will sleep in the station wagon," Dad said. "We'll work out who goes where." Mark climbed in nodding approval. I followed, lying down close to the pole. Mark took the side opposite Dad who was flat on his back, his brush cut just meeting the wall of the tent, his heels flush against the opposite side.

"Pretty comfy," I said, rocking gently on the foam. Actually, it was dim and stuffy and smelled like mildew. Sunlight shone through the tiny net window, creating a yellowish brown hue. It made me think about what it might be like to sleep in a ditch. The flap opened and Ruth crawled in, followed by Tina, who sandwiched herself between Mark and me.

"Not so comfy anymore," said Ruth. Sarah's head appeared followed by Trudy's, "I volunteer to sleep in the car," she said. "That goes double for me," said Trudy.

"All right, everybody out," said Dad. "I want to take her down."

"Maybe we should show Mom," said Tina. "She'll want to see."

"I'll get her," said Sarah, removing her head. "Me, too," said Trudy.

We lay there discussing possible sleeping arrangements while we waited for Mom. A few minutes later we heard them.

"Oh, how cozy," Mom said. She stuck her head in, beaming like a mother bird returning to her nest with food.

"Want a try?" I asked, sitting up. Mom took over my position, bear-hugging Tina at the same time as I exited clumsily. I listened to Mom's exclamations about the luxurious and cheap accommodations we would have while en route to Expo, while I circled the trailer, running my hands over the rough wood.

"Why are all these nails sticking out of the side?" I asked during a lull in the interior conversation. For a moment I wondered if the horizontal row of nails was to safeguard us from climbing nocturnal rodents.

"To tie on the fishing poles," Dad called out. "And for bathing suits."

We were all excited about going to Expo. Because of what I'd heard from Mom and Dad, and commercials, I was really excited. When we first heard about Expo, Mom and Dad had talked about it as a wonderful "possibility" in the same way they had discussed a family adventure to explore South America in our station wagon, stopping to visit Mom's sisters.

Shortly after our first Christmas in Hamilton, Mom received a small inheritance. None of us put the two ideas together right away, as we discussed options for spending the money.

"How about a summer cottage?"

"I don't like the idea of going to the same place over and over," said Mom. "Where's the adventure in that?"

"And we'd have to look pretty far from here to find one we can afford," said Dad.

"A new car?" That would be Mark.

"We have a car," Dad said curtly. "I don't know how to fix those modern cars. I prefer the older models. Easy to fix as a tractor."

"How about a colour TV?" I was waiting for that one. It was one I had been thinking about.

"We need to agree on something that will make us all happy," Mom said, emphasizing every word, making it clear that a colour TV was not something she thought would fit into that category.

"How about a horse?" My suggestion, and the expression of something I prayed for often. The truth was, I really wanted a monkey. I prayed for that, too.

"A horse!" Mark burst out. "Where we gonna put a horse? There's about ten blades of grass around here. It couldn't take three steps across the back yard without bashing into a fence."

"Yah, we could tether it up in the lot," said Ruth. "It could walk around in a circle and live on weeds."

"Or garbage. Maybe it would be better to get a goat," added Sarah.

"We could take a horse for a ride on the sidewalk. Real good for the hooves," said Trudy, smiling at me. "And you could clean up the horse poop."

"That's enough," Mom snapped. "How about a piano? I've dreamed of witnessing you all playing the piano," her tone changing to her sing-song voice.

"A piano is boring," said Ruth, bringing on a tense moment of silence. I thought a piano was boring too, but knew better than to say it.

"All the great composers were masters of the piano," Dad said, leaving just enough space between each word to drive the point in. "A piano is one of God's most amazing creations."

We sat shamefaced over the boring piano comment. Tina broke the next silence, "We could go to Expo."

"That is a wonderful idea," said Mom, suddenly all smiles, then repeating, punctuating each word. "That is an absolutely wonderful idea."

We all echoed choruses of agreement.

"Maybe we can do both," said Dad, glancing sternly in Ruth's direction. "I think we might be able to manage both."

At bedtime, Ruth muttered through gritted teeth, "God did *not* invent the piano. Someone else did. Not sure who, but some human… invented the piano. Dad doesn't even *play* the piano… I *never* heard him say one word about wanting a piano."

We did in fact manage to do both. It was the Mennonite way, stretching resources, getting good value. We got an "as is", out-of-tune piano with two sunken keys. Dad began his tent trailer project and we made plans for our trip to Expo.

Getting ready for family road trips—which we embarked upon at every conceivable opportunity, since Dad loved driving, and Mom loved adventure—was done with reasonable calm.

The parents were comfortable with their self-appointed routines, Dad gathering the cooler, lantern and camping pots with grease-stained forearms and blackened fingernails from the recent car tune-up, Mom removing rust from the Coleman stove with steel wool and airing out the sleeping bags.

Menu items rarely changed on our car trips. Staples such as peanut butter, jam, mustard and a roll of bologna were packed along from home, along with any over-ripe bananas and apples from the fridge. Apples were for munching in the car, on the off chance they were fresh enough to munch. Mostly, they induced flatulence and accusatory glares, unless we suspected either parent, in which case, we quietly rolled down the windows. Since Mom was generally too busy to bake before a trip, she packed a large box of Nilla Wafers or

Ginger Snaps. These quickly became more wilted than snappy when they were placed in the cooler with the decaying fruit, taking on the smell of apples and becoming soggier as the cardboard absorbed the water pooling around the melting ice block. Sometimes, we got to eat store-bought white bread on our vacations, which I begged to eat un-toasted since burning it over a Coleman stove ruined the thrill. Mom made efforts to keep the more expensive loaves elevated in the cooler, propping them up on bananas, floating apples and the carton of milk. We kept a thermos full of Kool-Aid, splurging on an extra bag of ice cubes to keep it 'ice-cold'. A selection of small bony fish, caught en route, added to our holiday meals. We never left home without fishing poles; for the Expo trip, they were attached to the trailer with wire.

We shopped for additional food along the way. Mom and Dad liked to detour into areas where fruit was grown to scout out roads beside the large orchards of the "fat rich" fruit growers, where there might be a possibility of finding apples, cherries or peaches on the ground. We kept a stack of ice cream buckets in the car for this eventuality and margarine containers for wild blueberry or blackberry picking along the highways.

When "free" fruit was scarce, Mom and Dad tried their hands at fruit stand bargaining. Like a tag team, they approached a market or stand, scouting fruit and vegetables Mom referred to as "needing to be eaten". Once they spotted such a stash, the process would begin.

"I'll give you fifty cents for that basket of plums," one of them would offer.

While they bartered, we browsed the souvenirs or gazed longingly at displays of maple leaf-shaped fudge. More often than not, they'd return to the car with a box of assorted mildly shrunken or wrinkled fruits and vegetables, with a fruit fly or two hovering.

Perhaps to compensate for eating around bruises on our fruit, we occasionally got a round of ice cream cones or a meal at a restaurant. Mom and Dad figured, sometimes out loud, that the money they saved on grocery and produce shopping should go toward family treats. The question then became whether to stop for a daily ice cream or forego a few days in order to eat a meal at a restaurant. Mathematically, it worked out that three days of ice cream equalled one dinner at a restaurant and two ice cream days equalled a lunch. So, if we chose a restaurant meal we had to do without ice cream on some days, a practice I found painful.

We had lively discussions on the benefits of the various options and decided democratically, but with a family of eight there was always a chance of a tie vote. Somehow things worked out and 1 loved both options, except on the forfeited ice cream days. On those days, all talk in the car quieted as we drove past large cardboard cones that typically depicted the strawberry flavour, Dad keeping his eyes straight ahead, the mood in the car momentarily sombre, as though participating in a funeral procession.

But we could sometimes be placated with a basket of peaches. Everyone in the family had an obsession for sucking on peach pits. No other form of fruit experience entertained each family member quite so much as the process of removing each tiny sweet fleshy bit from each tiny crevice in a peach pit. This provided hours of car-driving enjoyment, each of us sucking, using finger nails, teeth, sometimes even small tools like safety pins or toothpicks to excavate every morsel of fruit. The concentration required for this effort was huge, and once started, was difficult to stop. I believe Mom introduced this activity as a way to keep us quiet. At varying intervals, each family member would bring out the pit for careful examination, sometimes resting them in our cheeks like squirrels to give our tongues and eyes a break. Sometimes we showed each other.

In lulls or in further attempts to quiet us down, Mom and Dad put on CBC radio. Several of us would complain how boring it was to have to listen to that.

Mom's reply was, "One day, you'll all love listening to it".

We'd all give each other the "she is so wrong" look, and I thought, "Never in a zillion years will I willingly listen to that mind-numbing chatter. Turns out, Mom was right.

We left for Montreal early one morning shortly after school closed for summer. Really early. Cranky, early. It seemed to be a policy that our family vacations had to begin in the wee hours of the morning, while it was still dark. The reason might have been to avoid a prolonged farewell by whomever we were leaving or to cover our daily driving quota and still have time to fish. In later years, however, I suspected Dad may have wanted to get us into the car in a groggy state, so that he could get some miles under his belt in relative peace and quiet. By the time the inevitable whining and squirming began, we'd be well on our way to wherever we were going.

En route we sang all the Expo songs we knew from the radio and television, Ca-na-da...one little, two little, three Canadians, we love thee, now we are twenty million...' My favourite was the Ontari-ari-ario song. The older sibs learned good songs at school and taught them to us in the car. We sang old songs we knew like Old Dan Tucker, Oh Susannah, The Titanic and both versions of This Land is Your Land. Sometimes Dad interrupted with hymns, drowning us out with volume and exuberance. While we sang we kept our 'eyes peeled' to seek license plates. Mom kept a running list and a pencil in the glove compartment so she could add to it a new state or province when one was spotted on the road. Another game we played in the car was the alphabet game. We had to start when someone said 'Go' and find the letters in order, starting with 'A' on signs that we passed on the highway. When someone claimed to be finished they'd have to report where they saw the 'J' and the 'Z' before they were given credit for winning. I never won. Not once.

We pulled into the "campground" in the early evening. Driving around Montreal had been more taxing than Dad had anticipated and we were all hungry and tired. We arrived to find our accommodation near the Expo sight was a farmer's field with about one thousand other family campers.

"Don't be too concerned with the campsite," Mom said, as the car manoeuvred over bumpy grass through the maze of vehicles and tents. "We'll only eat breakfast and sleep here. We are here to see Expo."

After all my anticipation, I might have been disappointed with Expo 67 but it was more amazing than I could have imagined. The exposition was housed on two islands, connected by bridges, with buildings and structures like none I had ever seen or conceived. Everything was new and huge and clean. The pavilions were enormous; structures of glass and chrome, a gigantic glowing sphere, an upside down pyramid, assorted triangles bunched together like mountain ranges, roofs with curves and slopes and beehives, one like gigantic wings in flight, all assembled like some futuristic city. It was a fantastical smorgasbord of shape and colour with flagpoles and structures like statues: some like rockets, others twisting and spiralling, and everywhere, benches and walkways, flowers and trees. Garbage cans and walkways were spotless. People were everywhere, on trains and in cable cars, in boats, walking along sidewalks and paths and in line-ups where pretty ladies with uniforms like airplane stewardesses smiled and pointed.

Within minutes of paying our first admission fee, we stood outside the Australia Pavilion next to a pen of live kangaroos. A mother kangaroo had twins in her pouch, their mouse-like faces peering out and their tiny paws, so cute I wanted to jump into the pen with them. Mom began gesturing that we were leaving and I pretended not to notice, moving around to the far side of the pen so she practically had to drag me away, after which we gathered for a lecture from Dad about staying together, during which Mom noticed a family, each child with the string of a green balloon attached to their wrist.

"Now that," remarked Mom, "Is a very good idea. Wait here." She bee-lined in the direction of a clown selling helium balloons, returning in less than a minute, the look on her face saying, "If he thinks I am going to pay that much for a balloon, he's got hay for brains."

Her face grew less disturbed as she studied us, her five daughters dressed in matching yellow shorts sets similar to the one she wore, Mark and Dad in short sleeve shirts made from the same fabric. We were certainly easy to spot in a crowd. Mom had a thing about sewing our outfits from the same bolt of fabric, especially in summer when we all wore elastic waisted shorts and V-neck shells. All the same, she reinforced Dad's lecture about staying together and keeping an eye on each other.

I didn't mind wearing a carbon copy of the shirt and shorts sets worn by my sisters and Mom. It was kind of cute, our family parading around like a singing group. The uniformed attendants who controlled the velvet line dividers monitoring the flow of patrons into the exhibits couldn't argue and divide up our family.

"Can't you tell we're together??" I wanted to yell at one of the line-up officials when he almost clipped the cord in front of Mom and Tina and I after the others had passed through. "Look at our clothes!"

And people did. Perhaps not with quite the looks of admiration they might have bestowed upon the Dionne quintuplets. But they did notice. It happened that the twins got separated from us later that day, and while the rest of us looked around frantically, a pot bellied tourist with a sunburned nose called over, "I think I saw two of you people over by the paddle boats."

Mom was right about not minding the campsite. That evening we were too exhausted to worry about where we were sleeping. We spent a total of six days at Expo. Our lunches were picnic style, packed at the campsite. For dinners, we splurged on chili-dogs and hamburgers. Oddly, my thoughts of food were few and far between. There was so much to see and do. Each time we saw another pavilion I had to rethink my favourite. Each time I left one I'd ask if we could come back, but there was always something new to see. I wanted to memorize it all; the talking robots, the fireworks, the movies and songs, the exotic animals, the waterskiing shows, the gondolas from Italy, the monorail that went right into the U.S. pavilion, the carved wood figures at the Czechoslovakia pavilion, the bumper cars. Even while we waited in line-ups, there were clowns and jugglers, fire eaters and magicians performing, so it seemed we didn't really wait at all.

After lunch on the second day, Mom and Dad gave us each eight dollars to spend. To say we were ecstatic is putting it mildly and we all begged to go directly to a gift shop, where I bought two post cards for Lily. In another shop I found the most beautiful monkey puppet on four strings attached to a wooden X. I stared at it and almost cried when the saleslady took it down from the display hook and told me it was seven dollars. Mom was shaking her head, telling me to think on it for a day or two, that spending so much of my money on one item might not be wise. That we had more travelling to do and I might regret having spent all the money. I did cry then, worried someone else might buy the monkey. But the lady was looking at us kindly, and whispered she had more just like it.

I wanted that monkey so bad that I didn't buy ice cream or a lucky rabbit's foot. Mom made me wait two more days, and then we went to check whether he was still there. On the fourth day, after another talk on wise spending, Mom took me to get the monkey. I'd already named him Herkimer. He had black fur, and real-looking marble eyes. The only part that looked fake was the red cloth tongue. I walked him around all day, using the strings like he was a real monkey. After that, Mom made me keep him in the car, saying that we needed to keep him from getting tangled or trampled in a crowd, but really it was because I was slowing everybody down. But I felt so happy, like I'd got an answer to my prayer for a monkey, even though it wasn't real.

After lunch one day near the end of our week, Dad and Mark left to watch some fellows building a dory boat, so Mom took the girls to look at the restaurant at the Maritime Pavilion. She was curious to see how much it cost for a bowl of lobster chowder. The restaurant was fancy with table cloths and extra glasses on the tables and when Mom looked at the menu, she laughed, but not in a funny way. Then she sighed.

"Some day," she said, in her dreamy, "possibilities" voice, "We'll all go to the Atlantic Ocean. And my dream when we get there is to eat a lobster. A whole lobster, all for myself."

Driving home after a visit to Ottawa, with curly top ice cream cones in hand, we noticed cars pulled over on the side of the road. Dad slowed. Never one to miss free roadside entertainment, and seeing a herd of deer gathered and a crowd of people taking pictures, he pulled onto the shoulder and stopped. We piled out, momentarily startling both the herd and the onlookers with our noise and matching attire.

Mom was thinking out loud about what kind of scraps we might have in the cooler to contribute to the communal feeding, and began rooting around in the back of the station wagon with her ice cream cone-free hand, inviting annoyed looks from some of the spectators. I licked my cone, moved closer to the herd, and counted seven does standing in two groups and a very large buck.

For a minute I became wistful, thinking about Bambi. About how we couldn't all sit together at the matinee since we arrived late, me sitting a row ahead of Mom and Tina, crying at the end when Bambi's mother died, feeling sad and foolish without a Kleenex, wiping snot and tears on my bare arms.

It appeared that one family was taking the lead in the feeding proceedings with the larger herd. The mother was holding a box of crackers and the father making little coos and tut tut noises, enticing a doe toward his outstretched palm. A young boy and girl stood close to him, watching with pride as the doe took the cracker.

The buck stood alone, closer to the forest. His head was high, holding a rack of antlers big enough to hang Christmas lights on. Two elderly people were trying to lure him closer with a carrot.

Groups of people stood close to their cars watching, some taking pictures, the cracker man looking wise and adventurous, whispering instructions to the kids like he was Marlon Perkins from Mutual of Omaha's Wild Kingdom, one of the few TV shows we were allowed to watch. The boy stretched his palm forward, looking scared and hopeful while the mom dug a camera out of her bag. At the same time, I heard Mom and Dad approach.

"I found some bread," Mom said, ripping a slice apart. The larger deer pack startled and resettled, focusing on the crackers. The boy beamed as a tongue lapped the cracker from his palm.

A doe began to move toward the elderly couple with the carrot while the buck watched. Dad was smiling, perhaps remembering his boyhood on a Kansas farm. He crunched his cone, ready to take the final bite, but stopped with the cone midway to his mouth.

He gazed at the buck.

"I wonder," he said quietly. The elderly couple gaped as Dad carefully approached the buck. When Dad was within arms' reach, he stopped, gently raising the cone toward the buck's mouth. The buck looked down his nose until Dad's arm steadied. Then the buck inched toward the cone, stopping when he and the cone were a lick apart.

The action from that moment was a series of photographs, each action frozen for an extended moment. Snap: the buck moving closer, nose extended to smell the offering. Snap: Dad and the buck motionless. Snap: Dad, impatient, pushing the ice cream cone into the buck's nose. Snap: the buck again motionless, as though attached to the cone by its nose. Snap: the buck rearing its head violently, Dad stepping backward. Snap: the buck holding its head up, cone pointing straight up to the sky. Snap: the buck with head dropped, cone shaken off and lying on the ground. Snap: another still of the buck not moving, aware now that the cone was no longer on his nose. The rest went a lot faster. The buck suddenly swung his head away from the road, and as though hearing a gunshot, he took off into the forest, running at a full gallop. The does turned and followed, stampeding toward the trees, as though chased by demons. The crowd stood with mouths agape. The girl standing with her palm extended started to cry. The mother wrapped her arms around her.

Dad smiled sheepishly, "I guess bucks don't like ice cream." He turned toward the car. We followed looking apologetic. The doors slammed and we drove away.

We got home after our Expo trip, and got back into our routine. All-in-all, I thought that summer was fantastic. I was excited about starting school with Lily in my new class.

Near the end of second grade Lily's parents, and then my parents, had been called to a meeting at school. Lily and I were told that we would be accelerating. Which meant that rather than going into third grade in the fall, we would be going into fourth grade. When I saw Lily after that meeting, I asked her what she thought of that.

"I think it's good," she had said.

"But those three mean girls will be in grade four," I said.

"Yeah," she said. "But you and I will be in the same class. We'll stick together."

Two weeks before school started, the phone rang. It was Lily. She told me her family was moving to New York. They would be leaving by the end of August.

LIMBO

The first day of grade four was the worst day of my life up to that point, closely tied with all the other days of that September. One of the mean girls was in my class. Darlene. I would have wished to be in the other grade four class with Liz Harrison, except the other two awful girls, Tammy and Erica, were in there, too. I cried silently in my bed every night that September. Between sobs, I prayed for someone to help me. Then I prayed for forgiveness for my sinful thoughts about those horrible girls, like wanting crows to pluck their eyes out. Then I imagined being like Liz, with green eyes and shiny blond ringlets, wearing white bell bottom hip hugger jeans.

Each morning that September, I sucked on Tums that I snuck from Mom's drawer to settle a stomach that seemed to be in constant turmoil, and not only because Darlene was in my class, but because I couldn't read the handwriting on the board. That first week I learned what it's like to be treated like I was one of the stupid kids, kept in one recess because I couldn't do the work. Finally, Miss Montgomery listened to me choke out that I was just coming out of grade two and I hadn't been taught how to hand-write. I was humiliated and angry that she didn't know, and wondered why she didn't. She apologized with a box of Kleenex and sent me outside, but I knew my eyes were red and puffy, so I waited in the washroom for the bell. But she was extra nice to me after that.

On the playground I didn't know who to play with, since my old classmates might wonder why I was in grade four. Or they might not be concerned at all because I only hung out with Lily, so who cared? The grade fours already had friends, so why should they bother? I was learning a valuable lesson: that it's better to have more than one good friend. I tried moving slowly around the playground, watching hopscotch games, trying to look like I was having a grand time when my stomach was clenched, trying to stay ahead of the three hags who sometimes followed me without saying anything, making me want to scream.

I did not believe that "sticks and stones can break my bones, but names can never hurt me." When it came to Tammy, Darlene and Erica, I might have preferred sticks and stones. More than anything, I was afraid they would make me cry. Every day, I vowed not to let them, because if I got labelled "cry-baby", it would stick. But that resolve was weakening.

One recess, near the end of September, I saw them headed in my direction, Erica in the lead, looking at me like cats prowling a lone mouse. I took a deep breath, my thoughts racing—"what will they say?", "what can I say?", "what will they ask?", "what can I do?"— feeling the world slowing, my body wanting to curl up on the pavement and go to sleep. They were almost within speaking range when an incredible thing happened. Two girls approached from the opposite direction and stood in front of me. Rita and Sophie, from my new grade four class.

"Do you want to play double-dutch?" Sophie asked, holding up a skipping rope.

I was too stunned to speak.

"Do you know how to turn the ropes?" she asked.

I nodded.

"Do you want to play?" she asked, tilting her head slightly as though looking at a simpleton.

"Yes," I said. "I do."

"Come on," she said. "You and Rita can turn. I'll jump first, because it's my skipping rope."

I followed them to a vacant spot, not bothering to look at the three girls I knew were staring after us. I was overwhelmed with the kind of joy Mom demonstrated on those Sundays when she exclaimed the psalms with such glee. I felt more elation than I'd felt at Expo or when I got Herkimer because this gift was completely unexpected and perfectly timed. One minute I was being thrown to the sharks and the next, I was skipping.

I could have wept with happiness, but knew not to do that either. Tears were tears.

I turned the ropes in rhythm with Rita, collecting my composure, watching my hands as though in deep concentration, though I'd practised skipping double-dutch with the twins in the empty lot beside the Welcome Inn. It wasn't long before I was counting by two's and chanting along. On my first turn, I skipped to a count of 48 before taking back the ropes. When the bell rang, I stood in the line up between Sophie and Rita, and said a silent thank-you to heaven for another prayer answered.

The next day at recess, like flies to sugar, other girls flocked around us. It wasn't as though skipping was new, but double-dutch was just catching on and Sophie's footwork attracted attention. She could turn in circles as she jumped, hopping on one foot, then alternating feet. Rita wasn't bad either, and other girls began asking to join us. Sophie said yes to Patricia and Beverley in order to free Rita and me up from turning so we could jump in two at a time. I was jumping, literally for joy, thinking, "Five-to-three on the playground. Five–to-one in the classroom."

Skipping became the new recess pastime. I occasionally looked to see if the hags were lurking, but they made me feel unsettled, so mostly I pretended they didn't exist. Sophie and Rita caught onto this, and when they asked if I was scared of those girls, tears welled up and they had their answer. Sophie and Rita lived three and four blocks from the Welcome Inn respectively, so they rerouted their walk home so we could walk together, splitting apart at the corner by the tavern.

Sophie was Yugoslavian. Her mother spoke almost no English but she welcomed Rita and me into her steamy kitchen, the pots on her stove rattling or sizzling, emitting fishy or sauerkraut odours. She offered us thick slices of bread slabbed with margarine and sprinkled with sugar, then conversed boisterously with Sophie in Yugoslavian, slamming cupboard doors and banging pot lids. Rita and I watched and chewed. After snacks, we sat on their brightly coloured, fancy-patterned, plastic-covered couch, talking about boys.

Rita didn't have us over, saying her mom got headaches. Sometimes, Rita and Sophie came to the Welcome Inn, where we sat on the fraying-edged couch. I never told them about the basement, knowing Sophie would want to watch the boys play pool. I didn't want them to see the clothing department, and hoped there'd be no traffic up or down while they were there.

Sophie had a crush on a boy in our class who she called a "hunk". From what I could see, he didn't feel the same way, but that didn't stop her from discussing him at length. She also talked about boys from the Junior High, telling us the names of 'hunky' boys her sister knew. I was tempted to mention these names to the twins, but imagined that would backfire—afraid they might be reminded of the incident when they talked me into writing a letter to our school bus driver in Oklahoma, telling him I thought he was handsome, even helping me with the spelling, and then convincing me to give it to him. They got all kinds of mileage out of my innocent compliance, asking me over and over if I "had gotten a letter back asking for a date? Or maybe a phone call?"

RICHARD

Coming down the stairs one morning, I sensed something was different. While the sound of snoring registered, I scanned the storefront and saw that the roll-away bed, usually stored in the closet, was set up beside the ping pong table. Its occupant was curled up facing the wall, covered by a grey wool blanket. I tiptoed toward the bed, my nostrils working like a dog's following a scent. The nicotine smell wasn't unusual; it lingered in the clothes and hair of many people who came in, but the smell of liquor in the storefront was cause for concern. I got close enough to see thin strands of grey hair plastered against a flat-backed balding scalp, spotted with freckles. Footsteps from the stairway didn't cause the man to stir and I remained still while the siblings joined me, their facial expressions curious, like Dorothy's when she first saw the Munchkins approach. The kitchen door sprang open suddenly and Mom's wildly gesturing arm summoned us.

"Who's that?" I blurted out as soon as the door was closed. Instantly, the tavern odour was replaced by the all-too-familiar smell of burned pancakes. Dad stood by the stove in a meditative stance, a spatula in his hand, staring into a smoky fry pan.

Mom sat down and started to rotate her coffee cup as though she had some heavy burden to bear while we arranged ourselves at the table. A silence followed, as was custom before we said grace. We sat and waited while Mom stared into her cup, but not for a prayer. I watched Dad's back as he flipped a pancake, using a quick jerk of the elbow and more force than necessary, causing a hiss and a billow of smoke from the sizzling grease.

Dad turned to face us, pursing his lips the way he used to do in the pulpit before sharing thought-provoking or controversial ideas with his congregation. Holding his gaze steady, he took a deep breath and spoke without expression, "I found him outside this morning. Propped up against the front door." He turned back to his fry pan. A flip. A splat. A hissss. He half-turned, leaning against the counter, and continued. "I tried knocking on the door from the inside to wake him up, but he was out cold. So I opened the door and he fell right onto my feet. Still snoring."

"Dad pulled him inside and then got me," Mom said, looking up, her brow furrowed. "We couldn't just leave him there, and he was in no condition to be outside."

"So we set up the bed and managed to drag him into it," said Dad, a hint of a smile appearing on his face. "It's a good thing he's not very heavy."

"Why didn't you call the police?" asked Mark.

"He wasn't doing any harm," said Dad. "He needs to sleep it off."

He turned abruptly, opened the oven door and reached bare-handed toward a Pyrex pie plate stacked high with pancakes. He yanked the plate out, practically throwing it on the counter. I heard the trace of a moan, which was as much admission of poor judgment as we would witness. We all waited for more information while Dad piled on the last of the pancakes. Using his shirt tail as a pot holder, Dad brought the plate to the table, plunked it down, and picked up a fork.

"Drive your trucks under," Dad's standard instruction when serving food. One at a time, we lifted our plates toward him as he called our name. Stabbing two pancakes at a time, he raised them high and let them drop; our job was to catch them with our plate before they fell into someone's juice.

I looked at the two blackened pancakes on my plate. Turning the heat up high was one of Dad's time and energy saving cooking practices. He reasoned quick on high was more efficient than slow on low. Batter oozed as I cut into a pancake. I didn't like pancakes. Not even the fluffy, golden, silver dollar pancakes at Smitty's Pancake House… never mind burned pancakes with raw centres. I concentrated on keeping my face impassive, since even non-verbal complaining summoned lectures about "hungry people in Africa" and about "our good fortune to partake of three hot meals a day", at which point the food in question was ingested into a stomach wracked with guilt.

"Would you like tomato or noodle soup for lunch?" Mom asked. No one responded, the question an obvious tactic to change the subject.

"Is he sick?" asked Tina, her mouth full.

"Is who sick?" asked Mom.

"That man out there," said Tina, pointing at the door with her fork.

"I imagine he'll be feeling bad for a while," said Mom. "But I don't think he's sick. We'll know more when he wakes up."

"What's his name?" I asked.

"Don't know," said Dad. "He wasn't awake enough to talk. Did a bit of muttering. Nothing I could make heads or tails of."

"You could check for a wallet," Mark suggested.

"We'll find out when he wakes up," said Dad in his "closing of the sermon" voice. The talk went back to the chicken noodle or tomato question, while I focused on the imminent problem of finishing my breakfast.

I balled a napkin loosely beside my plate hoping for an opportunity to dispose of a few bits. This was risky, since detection would invite not only the starving Africans lecture, but an additional speech on wastefulness and dishonesty. Mom seemed intent; her gaze so close to my plate that I mashed the burnt pancakes with my fork instead, hoping to dissolve some bits in the warm homemade syrup. Mom's cost-efficient substitute for Aunt Jemima was water and brown sugar boiled into thin syrup, a dollop of margarine melted in to make it "rich". Finally, I gathered pieces of the mush, put my fork as far into the back of my throat as I could, and swallowed.

We left for school, moving slowly past the rollaway cot to get another look. All morning I kept wondering about the sleeping drunk man and what he'd have to say to Mom and Dad. And what they'd say back. At recess I told Sophie and Rita about him.

"Those are age spots," Rita said. "My grandfather has them. He has dandruff, too."

"The guy was probably out late at the bars," said Sophie. "Maybe he didn't have enough money for a taxi."

"Probably at the Majeska House," said Rita.

"Yah, probably," I agreed.

"My dad doesn't like that place. He goes to the Genesee. When he stays out too late, my mom doesn't talk to him in the morning," said Rita. "She wants to get a new couch. She hates it when he buys drinks for his friends, spending all that money."

"Yah, my mom gets pissed at my dad, too. She yells at him the next day if he stays out drinking," said Sophie.

I couldn't contribute to the conversation, as I couldn't relate to any of it. Not to a Dad drinking in a bar or a Mom saving money for a brand new couch. Or to using words like "pissed". I tried to picture Dad in a tavern buying beers for his friends.

"What do you think your parents will say to him when he wakes up?" asked Sophie.

"I don't know," I said. I could only imagine. I wondered if they would try to pray with him or something, like the Reverends did after the alter calls at the Billy Graham crusades.

"Your parents never drink do they?" asked Rita.

"No," I said. "They never do".

At lunchtime we hurried home, anxious to hear what Mom would have to say about the drunk. Running through the storefront past the now-vacant "cot spot", our headlong burst into the kitchen was halted by a combination of Mom's wide-eyed, "that is no way to behave" look, the sight of the drunk man hunched over a bowl at the kitchen table, and the sound of a long, loud slurp. The slurp was followed by about four seconds of silence during which the man turned his head toward us, tortoise-like, while we stood frozen like a herd of stunned sheep. My attention was fixed on the prominent hump that was the man's back. I thought about a scene from "The Hunchback of Notre Dame", the one where Quasimodo gleefully tips cauldrons of boiling water from the bell tower onto his attackers below.

"This is Richard," Mom said. She released the wooden spoon she was using to stir the soup and picked up a stack of bowls from the counter. Holding them against her midriff, a word I knew from the Playtex bra commercial, she gestured toward the table.

Richard moved his head slowly in a circular motion and I made myself not look away while he tried to focus on us. His blue eyes were glazed, like they were floating in corn syrup, red around the lower rims. Thin hair ringed his bald head like Friar Tuck, and the skin below his narrow cheekbones hung loose, forming jowls around his narrow chin. His cheeks were gaunt, accentuating thick rubbery lips wet with soup, and his red nose was bulbous, spider veined, and rough, like the skin of a pickle.

He looked as though he had recently woken up and showered, as his hair was damp, combed back, and tucked around his small protruding ears. I recognized the shirt draped over his hump and hanging loosely at his sunken chest, as one that belonged to Dad. Returning his attention to the table, Richard clutched the bowl with one hand as though trying to keep it grounded while his other hand resumed guiding a shaking spoon from the bowl to his mouth.

"He's joining us for lunch," said Mom, as she spread the bowls around the table. As she rattled off our names he gave a small grunt and smiled, then lowered his eyes and got back to his noisy eating. We sat down, adjusting the bowl placements, none of us wanting to get too close. Normally, Mom served us at the stove, but we were too bewildered to follow the routine. She brought the pot over and started ladling, asking questions about what we were learning at school. Richard continued chewing with exaggerated, circular motions, like a cow grinding up grass, but sloppier. I ate my soup, trying not to stare. Without asking, Mom refilled his bowl and placed another slice of buttered bread on his napkin, like they were already old friends.

After school, I arrived home to find Richard slumped over a puzzle in the storefront. His forearms were on his thighs, his head inches from the table top, his mouth slightly open. I saw that he had connected a short row of edge pieces on the London Bridge scene he was attempting to reconstruct.

I joined Carol on the couch and picked up a book, using it the way Maxwell Smart would, to spy. Richard sat completely still, moving only his eyes, staring at one piece for a moment and then shifting to another. Then his head swayed slightly and he fixed his gaze on a piece to one side. He stared at it for a moment, as though willing it to move. I studied the thick tufts of grey hair that sprouted out from his ears. He lifted one arm above the table in slow-motion, pulling his torso up slightly, and reached forward like his arm was full of lead. The skin under his chin wobbled turkey-like while his fingers hovered unsteadily above the selected piece. His hand, landing clumsily, grasped the piece and deposited it near the centre of the table. With great effort, he moved his arm back under the table to rest on his thigh and resumed his slumped position. I decided to go see if Mom wanted help in the kitchen.

Richard, joining us for supper, was suddenly talkative. He seemed to be telling us about a war, though the details were hard to understand due to his mumbling and the fact that Mom and Dad tried repeatedly to steer the conversation in other directions. As pacifists, they didn't condone talk of war, especially at the dinner table with children present, so the conversation was difficult to follow.

After supper, my siblings and I followed Richard into the games room, shutting the door, while Mom and Dad sat around the table with the other VS'ers discussing business, as they often did after supper. These impromptu meetings allowed us to have some "free of neighbourhood kids" time in the storefront, which we enjoyed even though several were always hanging around the front door. We got used to their presence outside between "open door" times; it was kind of like having a television on in the background that we could glance at from time to time to see if there was anything good on.

Richard was cleaned up, but still smelled of nicotine and stale alcohol, so when we pulled up chairs to join him at his puzzle, I sat on the far side of the table. Richard's mumbling was quiet and garbled and didn't make much sense, but it sounded like he was talking about a time when he was in London, which was probably what had prompted him to choose this particular puzzle from the stack. Though I was not a fan of puzzling, I didn't mind gathering the edge pieces into a pile. He continued to mutter, almost under his breath, and then laughed suddenly like someone had told a joke. I pushed my few edge pieces closer to him, relieved when the kitchen door opened and the adults emerged to open the front door and let in the after-dinner stampede.

The next morning, I noticed Richard's rollaway cot, still up in the storefront, was more neatly made than any of the ones upstairs. He joined us for breakfast and then lunch and was perched at the piano when I got home from school. Not playing it, just staring at the keys. He was wearing his own clothes again, newly washed. His wardrobe included a knee length grey button-down overcoat, and it was soon apparent that Richard liked to keep this coat on regardless of the place or temperature. Seen in profile, he was the shape of a question mark, his hump at the high point, his hunched back forcing him to lean forward. With the grey overcoat, his bald head and his prominent nose, he looked like a kind, harmless vulture.

"Hi Richard," I said, as I walked past. "Can you play the piano?"

In response, he lifted his arms slowly and began to plunk out "Chopsticks", not quite in the right rhythm, but recognizable.

"Wow," I said. "That's really good! Want me to play the top part?"

He turned his head and nodded, so I pulled up a chair. Ruth had taught me chopsticks; she'd played the top part to make it jazzy. Then she taught me the top part.

"Go ahead," I said. "I'll join in."

He began to play again. I began my part but then he seemed shaken and got confused with his notes.

"Just play chopsticks," I said. "I have to play my part at the same time. It'll sound neat."

He mumbled something, then laughed.

"Go ahead," I said. "Try again, but don't stop. Just keep on playing."

We tried again three times before we got going with any finesse, after which we got a round of applause from some spectators on the couch.

Richard joined us for dinner, again talkative. It was difficult to understand him, since he muttered and exhaled noisily through his nostrils, his words thick and liquid, as though he were having trouble with his tongue. It was rarely clear who he was talking to because his back was so hunched forward, he was usually looking down and hardly ever made eye contact with anyone. Often laughter, coming out of his nose, punctuated his mumblings, like tiny bursts of smoke from a dragon, making us all laugh along even when no one knew what was funny. Sometimes he interrupted when someone else was talking, but his voice didn't have much volume, and it didn't seem to bother anyone.

After dinner, Richard excused himself and left the table with us. As usual, kids were gathered outside the storefront door, pressing their faces and hands against the glass, leaving smudges, which irritated Mom, who loved clean windows so everyone could see "God's beautiful creation" outside. At least they knew not to knock during meal hours, since that didn't sit well with Dad, who did not like being unduly disturbed. While they waited for the doors to open, they took turns pushing toward the front to get the best view.

I assumed we'd go back to the puzzle table, but Richard seemed jittery, his body and arms twitching nervously. Apparently, not in any mood for sitting, he began pacing back and forth in front of the couch, grumbling with little snorts and heavy breathing. He stopped for a moment while his eyes settled on the broom standing by the basement door. As he stared, the broom appeared to draw him nearer and picking it up by the handle, he looked it over like he was inspecting it for quality. Suddenly, he swung the brush side up, holding it up to his shoulder like a rifle. Standing as straight as he could, he turned, soldier-like, to face us, then did a ninety degree turn and marched to the far side of the ping pong table. He turned to face us again. This began a demonstration of army stances and manoeuvres with the rifle broom, while he muttered commands. I stared from the couch, thinking of Gomer Pyle marching and drilling while Sergeant Carter bellowed.

After the brief demonstration, Richard stopped, standing as tall as he could, broom resting on his shoulder and barked, "Fall in." His voice had command, but not much volume.

None of us moved.

"Fall in," he repeated and stomped one foot.

We remained still.

"On yur feet," he ordered.

Mark jumped up, then my sisters and me. Cautiously, we approached.

"Atten.......shun!" he called into the air.

Mark got into position beside Richard and the rest of us lined up. When we were standing quietly, Richard took two steps forward and did two ninety degree turns to face us, his expression serene, still holding the broom/rifle. His left arm suddenly flew up and angled into a salute.

"All shalute!" he slurred, his cheeks wobbling.

We saluted. He seemed pleased. His arm went back to his side.

"About fashe!" he snapped and swivelled on one foot to face the other direction. Then he swivelled again to face us.

"Company....about fashe!" he repeated, spittle spraying. We mimicked his turn and stood in a line-up facing the front door. Danny was there, Carol, Jeanie and Debbie Bishop, among others, all with pleading looks that said, "Can we come in and play?"

Richard marched to the front of the line.

"Forward…..marsh!" he called and proceeded forward.

Holding imaginary rifles against our shoulders, we followed as Richard chanted, "Left…left…left, right, left, (Pause) Left…..Left…" Making sharp turns at the corners, we marched around the ping pong table. We began quietly chanting along. After two circuits, Richard stepped out of line, calling, "Continue marshing!" He stood to the side, nodding approval or pointing his rifle broom if our footsteps were out of sync. When he was satisfied, he fell into step at the back of the line and picked up the pace. This created havoc, with all of us trying to stay in step and turn sharply without getting trampled by the soldier behind. It seemed our chanting grew louder and our footsteps heavier, because suddenly we heard the kitchen door open and a very loud and exaggerated clearing of the throat.

Dad stood at the door, Mom behind him, with her mouth slightly open and her neck tensed. They stood for a moment while we slowed our marching and quieted our chanting, like toys winding down.

"Richard, why don't you come and join us for another cup of coffee," Dad said tersely.

"There's still some pie left," said Mom, her cheerfulness sounding strained.

Dad gave us a "shame on you" look while Richard put down the broom and followed them into the kitchen. The door closed.

The rest of us sat down sheepishly and pretended to work on Richard's far-from-finished puzzle. About ten minutes later, the door opened and Richard emerged smacking his lips, followed by Dad. Everyone was smiling, so Richard must have gotten the happy pep talk version of the "we are pacifists and don't condone any type of military activity within these walls" speech. Either that, or he got a brief but harsh lecture, sweetened up with another piece of pie.

Richard sat down with us, looking coy, while Dad unlocked the front doors to let the kids in. "Can we do some marching?" asked Danny, as he bounded in.

Dad ignored him.

The next morning, when Mom and Dad woke up, the rollaway bed was empty, maybe because it was Sunday and they had mentioned church to Richard a few times.

Richard was back about a month later, sleeping outside the front door. And so began a pattern, repeated often, but not every month. After three stays with us, we were no longer surprised to see him on the rollaway bed some mornings. Dad tried to talk Richard into moving his sleeping quarters to the basement but Richard argued that he'd have trouble with the "shtairs", with the "drink and all that", or if he woke up suddenly in the middle of the night he'd wonder, "Where the hell am I?" I overheard that conversation, and sympathized: if I woke up in that creepy basement in the middle of the night, I would surely think I'd died in my sleep and gone to hell. So, his sleeping quarters remained beside the ping pong table.

Mom and Dad soon noticed his visits often occurred about a week after he received his monthly welfare and pension cheques. Richard generally spent a day or two with us before he disappeared, always leaving with some donated items of clothing, usually a shirt or pants and a pair of socks. Mom tried to entice Richard into trying on coats from the selection of men's wear in the basement, but Richard would not be coaxed out of his grey overcoat. Mom washed it once when she was able to get it off of him while he was out cold, but he was not pleased, and told her so.

After the first visit, Richard's military talk was done privately and in a loud whisper, directed toward one of us when Mom and Dad were elsewhere, as though telling us a secret or participating in some conspiracy or engaging in espionage. He continued his military drills with us in the vacant lot when he was having a "fag", pausing into "at ease" if anyone happened to pass that might report these covert activities to our parents.

Mom told us between Richard's visits that we needed to be mindful of his dignity... treat him with due respect since he was an adult and because of his drinking problem. For Dad, it was a fine line between allowing Richard to "maintain his dignity" while insisting he follow the Welcome Inn rules. So having Richard around, was a bit of a dilemma for Dad especially, who liked order. As long as it wasn't being imposed on *him*, by "bureaucrats". Like everyone else, Richard had to go outside to smoke, but he needed a table to roll his cigarettes. Dad wanted Richard to roll in private, but the Welcome Inn was always busy, so there was no private area other than the rooms upstairs, and they were off limits.

Dad learned to cope with Richard rolling cigarettes at the kitchen table, usually by leaving. Mom would stay to supervise, making urgent movements all around to speed up the process, though his progress didn't seem at all affected. Rolling was clearly something Richard did well, starting with the removal of the pouch of tobacco and papers from his overcoat pocket, his hands moving in a confident, professional manner while he rolled and licked. It was the only time I ever saw his hands not shaky.

We all liked to watch Richard roll cigarettes, but that only happened if we were already in the kitchen. Mom didn't take kindly to any of us being present, but didn't want to make it an issue since it might compromise his dignity. What really bothered Mom was when one of us asked a question to encourage talk about tobacco brands or rolling techniques. We enjoyed a long lecture on these matters one night. From then on, we watched him mutely, smiling encouragement and giving silent nods of approval to his tightly rolled "fags" if Mom's back was turned.

For me, Richard's fingers were hard to look at, stained a sickly brownish yellow. Mom said that was nothing compared to the horrible effects nicotine had on the throat and lungs. A series of deep scratchy coughs would shake Richard from time-to-time, turning his face red and making his eyes water. It was painful to listen to, since this was the kind of coughing that would warrant hitting or stroking his back to relieve the congestion, but in Richard's case, with the hump, it was difficult to know how one might do this. I was grateful he covered his mouth with his sleeve and his aim was always toward the floor. Mom and Dad didn't talk much about that cough. I think they were letting Richard's lungs speak for themselves, a living example of the dangers of smoking.

Mom and Dad tried talking to Richard about God and invited him to participate in Bible study group. They might as well have asked him to leap over a tall building. If Richard was present on a Saturday, he always slipped away before breakfast was served on Sunday mornings. So after a while, they stopped asking, knowing if they pushed too hard, Richard wouldn't return, and there'd be another lost soul out there.

I don't know where he went when he wasn't with us. I think I asked and Mom told me something about a rooming house. For over two years, he came and went. Around that time of the month, there was always speculation about whether he would or wouldn't arrive. During the cold months, Mom worried if he didn't. And so the last winter when three months went by without a visit from Richard, Dad made some phone calls. He reported that Richard had recently spent several days in the hospital, but had been released. When another month passed with no sign of Richard, Dad made more phone calls. He was told Richard's body had been found in an alley shortly after he was released from the hospital.

We were all saddened by this, imagining that he died alone, though the details were never shared. Richard had become part of the larger Welcome Inn family. I remember Richard for opening my eyes to things like tolerance and acceptance, how to handle a rifle, efficient cigarette rolling techniques. And how to laugh at nothing.

ICE CREAM BONANZA

Dad had a knack for finding deals. It was an opinion widely held that the best deal he ever found was the ice-cream. As it turned out for me, this deal was the best and the worst.

Dad said he was "led" to the Dairy Rich Distribution Centre. He used to preach about being "led" and "called" by God or Jesus. I had a hard time understanding this, and would ask Dad questions like, "How do you know where to go? How does God speak to you? Did God give directions? How did you get the calls? Were they at night? In private? Did you actually hear the voice of God, out loud?"

Dad said he didn't exactly *hear* the calls out loud; rather, it was a quiet message, within. I asked him, "Where within? What part?" and he said, within his heart. When I asked how he knew it was God, he said he just knew.

I wanted to hear the voice of God, too. I began to pray for a call, doing my utmost to listen. I heard all kinds of things inside my head but it didn't sound like God. It sounded like Mom. I began to wonder if God only spoke to adults, so I asked Dad more about being "led". Do you see God and follow Him? Or is it more like an angel? What did the quiet voice sound like? And could you see a path?" But Dad said that being led was like being called —you didn't actually see or hear anything. Rather, God had a way of leading you "from within".

"You have to listen," he said. I tried again and again, picturing Jesus with his hands pressed together, his long wavy hair flowing down over his shoulders, an expression of longing on his face and his kind eyes looking upward. I waited to hear him say something, but the words in my head were Bible verses or lectures about the poor or lessons from Sunday School. Nothing new.

Then, one evening it dawned on me to wonder what might happen if I did get called. What if God wanted me for a special job? What if He bid me to recite Bible verses during Show and Tell or asked me to invite everyone I met to church? I decided to stop asking for calls because I might not follow His instructions, in which case, He might get angry and inflict punishment, like He did upon Job, giving me blistering boils from head to toe for ignoring His call. The more I thought about it, the more frightened I became. So I made my prayers quick, thanking God for health and strength and daily food, asking Him to bless the sick, poor and elderly, and immediately saying "Amen".

Dad was led to the ice cream in early February. I was with him on the first part of his journey and didn't even know it. I'd come downstairs after being called "a suck" for complaining about the current choice of television show. Mom was leaning on the counter writing something, but stopped when I slumped onto the bench.

"Dad's taking a quick trip to Hopper's Wholesale to pick up some stuff," she said. "Why don't you bundle up and go along for the ride? He's warming up the car but he'll be back in to get the list." I sat up, suddenly thrilled. "I can take the list outside."

"The important thing is the soup bones. I'm showing the sewing group how to make soup tomorrow. I want to send a bone home with each of the ladies. See how many you can get." I grabbed my coat, snatched the list, and ran out of the kitchen.

Dad was jabbing at the ice-crusted windshield, white puffs spewing from the tailpipe and from his mouth. My hands vibrated in time with the idling of the car as I zipped up my coat and put on my mittens. I held the stocking hat I'd tucked under my arm high and let it unroll, watching the bright colours ripple down. Pulling the hat on my head, I grinned, coiling the tail around my neck like a cozy snake. I crossed my arms over the pompom, not minding the cold because people going by might look and think, "What a lucky girl to have a hat like that!" And, I was lucky to have it. No one I knew had a striped stocking hat that hung down below their knees.

We had shown Mom pictures of stocking hats in a magazine, hinting that she might consider them for Christmas gifts. She shook her head whenever the subject came up, saying things like, "they look silly", "like something worn by Sleepy or Dopey", and "will quickly go out of style". We tried convincing her they doubled as scarves, thus saving hours of knitting, and required fewer hooks when drying, and, due to their bulk, were less likely to be lost.

There were no such hats under the Christmas tree, but we found an incredible Boxing Day sale in the States. Mom relented when she saw our pleading eyes—or the unusual occurrence of a Canadian dollar being worth more than the American dollar or maybe, because of the hat/scarf/save-on-knitting-thing. I loved wearing my hat, especially after Ruth showed me the trick. "Watch," she'd said, just after we left the store. Drawing her arm backward, she threw the pompom like she was throwing a baseball. It shot forward then arced around while she circled her head like the pompom was a hula hoop, letting the tail circle her neck two and a half times before it lost momentum.

Dad looked at me and raised his eyebrows. "Mom said I can come along," I said. "I have the list." He gave a half smile and motioned for me to get in. "Just a minute," he said. I heard scratching sounds and watched while a jagged viewing space opened in front of me. A few minutes later Dad got in, throwing the scraper onto the back seat.

"How was school today?" he asked. It took a second before it registered that this question was for me. Most questions like this were posed at supper time and to the table at large.

"Not so good?" he asked, looking at me.

"No, it was good," I said quickly.

"How are you getting along without Lily?" he asked. I thought, "Now you ask!" It was about five months too late for that.

"Okay," I said. I could have said "For a while it was horrible actually." But I didn't, maybe because of the hat, or because I was finally getting along without Lily, but more likely because "bellyaching" (i.e. complaining) was rarely tolerated.

"What are you learning at school?"

I thought about complaining that I was sick and tired of *never* getting to learn anything interesting first, that I always heard about everything from the older siblings. I'd already learned about Marco Polo, about his travels through China and Mongolia in his quest for spices and tea and his battles and tribulations in crossing the Gobi desert. It was mostly my fault since I pestered them endlessly for information, but still it made me mad. "We're learning about Marco Polo," I said, mindful of the bellyaching prohibition.

"What do you know... about Mar-co Po-lo," he said, like he was reciting a poem. So I told him a few things about Marco and Genghis Khan. He remarked that it was an awful long way to go all the way across China for tea and spices and that he was happy with sugar and Ketchup. Then he burst into song, as he did whenever the inclination struck. *"Oh come, come, come, come...Come to the church in the wi- iiiiild wood, oh come to the church to-oo-day, ay, ay, No-o spot is so dear to my chi-yild-hood as the li-ttle brown church in the vaaale"*

I wasn't sure what train of thought led him from our conversation to this song, but I sang along on the chorus because the windows were closed and because I liked the thump, thump, thumpy marching-band rhythm of the song.

"What's on the list?" Dad asked when we got to Hopper's.

"Soup bones. Mom said to get all we can... mayonnaise, Puffed Wheat and flour. And a case of Kool-Aid," I said, holding up the surprisingly short list. Usually Mom and Dad came home from Hopper's with the station wagon full. Mom must have added Kool-Aid to make the list long enough to warrant starting up the car. Dad yanked the cart along the aisles, stopping occasionally. The cart was really a moving platform a couple of inches off the floor. I almost asked for a ride, but Dad's erratic manoeuvrings made me reconsider. I was prone to motion sickness.

Following behind, thinking about the Friendly Giant, I tilted my head way back to see the shelves lined with crate-sized boxes of paper towels, Styrofoam cups and toilet paper. The middle aisles held gallon-sized jars of pickles, mayonnaise, and condiments, fruit cocktail in pails, and extra large cans of soup. On the cement floor, were pillow sized bags of rice, cases of canned goods, and buckets of peanut butter and cooking lard. Mom loved Hopper's for the good value that she associated with purchasing in large quantities, which she could do because she had the good fortune to be "blessed with abundant storage", most of which was on the rickety back porch that she fondly referred to as "the pantry".

We were ready to check out when Dad suggested we check the price on ice cream. I practically skipped to the giant glass freezers where the five gallon pails were arranged in neat rows. This, apparently, was where Dad began to be "led". I'm not sure whether you could call it a journey, but whatever it was, it started in front of those freezers.

When Dad opened the freezer door, maybe to get a sniff since the prices were clearly visible on price cards, he happened to notice two tubs lying on the floor under the bottom shelf. Those fallen tubs, separated and excluded from the tidily stacked group, must have piqued Dad's curiosity. His inner tendency to support the underdog, the shunned, the outcast, must have compelled him to get a closer look. He leaned in, pushing a space between two containers on the lower shelf.

"There's little gashes in these two," he said. I stuck my head inside the door, curious to see the gashes. Each tub had a narrow puncture about as long as my hand with ice crystals crusted around the tears, one revealing a rich golden colour with dark spots inside. "Probably Butter Pecan or Rum and Raisin," said Dad, following my gaze. The other tub showed gloppy streaks of bright red and green in a yellowing vanilla base, clearly a Christmas Candy Cane variety that hadn't sold over the holidays. "I wonder how much they want for these," he said, sounding like he was talking to himself.

"Excuse me," he called toward the meat freezer where a white-jacketed clerk was making notes on a clipboard. "I'm wondering what kind of a discount I can get on these tubs of ice cream," his bargaining voice, chipper and hopeful. The clerk clipped his pencil to the clipboard and walked toward us, looking in the direction of Dad's pointing finger.

"I'm sorry sir," the clerk said, "Those aren't for sale. The containers are damaged."

"They don't look that damaged to me," said Dad. "What kind of discount are you willing to offer?"

"I can't sell them. They're going back to the distribution centre."

"I'll save you the trouble of sending them back. How much do you want?" Dad asked, beginning to sound impatient.

"I am sorry, sir. Damaged ice cream is returned. That is our policy."

"Then your *policy* should be changed," Dad said with an emphasis on "policy". He breathed out deeply, and with an effort to be calm asked, "Where's the distribution centre?"

"It's down on York Street," the clerk said, turning away.

"How much will they charge me there?"

The clerk turned back to face Dad. "Oh, they won't sell it to you, sir."

"What will they do with it?" It sounded like an accusation.

"It'll be thrown in the garbage," said the clerk.

"They throw away perfectly good ice cream?" Dad almost yelled.

"The damaged ice cream will be thrown away, sir," the clerk said, backing away. He turned and hurried through the swinging storeroom doors.

Dad didn't sing on the way home. He muttered about ridiculous policies, bureaucratic nonsense and sheer wastefulness. Any conversation involving the word "policy" tended to get him agitated. Other words of this nature were "capitalism", "capital punishment", "military", "regulations", and any mention or glorification of "war" in general and the "Vietnam War" in particular.

When we got to the Welcome Inn, he kept the car idling while we unloaded the stuff. Dad laid the box he was carrying on the ping pong table. "Tell Mom I have an errand to run. I'll be home in time for supper," he said. "Ask Mark to help with this box." I heard the car door slam and the car drive away.

"Where's Dad going?" Mom was standing in the kitchen door.

"He has an errand to run. He said he'd be home for supper."

"What kind of an errand does he need to run now? Did you forget the soup bones?" She looked at me puzzled.

"No we got the bones." I suspected Dad might be going to the distribution centre to tell them not to throw away ice cream, but I didn't know for sure and didn't want Mom to get agitated, too. I shrugged and carried the Kool-Aid into the kitchen. "Where is everybody?" I asked. It seemed unusually quiet with no one in the storefront.

"There weren't too many kids in so I shooed them home. The girls and Mark are upstairs. All of the VS'ers are getting ready to go to a social evening at the Jansen's. So, it's just us for supper tonight." She continued in a faraway tone, "It is quiet, isn't it? It's almost strange. I wonder where Dad went."

"Can I open this?" I asked, putting down the Kool-Aid, hoping to catch her off guard.

"Sure, go ahead, but we aren't having any with supper. That's for weekends," she said absently.

Dad arrived just as Mom's irritation was beginning to show. "Wait till you see what I have in the car," he announced. "I'm going to need helpers once I get the boxes in."

"What did you get?" Mom asked, sounding wary. The siblings were ogling the Kool-Aid packages, speculating on what flavour combinations to experiment with. I'd folded back the top to showcase the smiling frosted Kool-Aid pitcher man pursued by brightly coloured cartoon-faced fruit characters displayed behind the hundred packets, which were sectioned and tiered in flavour groups.

"You'll see," and he was out the door, leaving it wide open.

"I bet he got some ice cream," I said, and got a few eye rolls that said "enough already" and "shut up about going to Hopper's and setting up the Kool-Aid display."

Dad came back, straining under a huge box that he plunked on the floor at our feet.

"WOW!" echoed through the room. We were staring into a box filled to the brim with ice cream novelties. My mouth dropped. "There's more," Dad said and went back out the door.

We all looked back and forth from the box to Mom, wondering if it was okay to touch. She looked like she was staring at a pot of gold, and was trying to decide whether or not it was real. Nobody moved.

"Where did you get this?" she called trance-like, but Dad was gone. She stepped forward to shuffle through the top layer of assorted boxes of ice cream treats — Ice Cream Sandwiches, Popsicles, Drumsticks and Eskimo Pies, the boxes ripped at the corners or slightly squashed.

"Must be from the distribution centre," I said and got more looks.

"What distribution centre?" Mom asked, looking at me.

I didn't answer because Dad walked in with another large box and plopped it down beside the first one. The second box held five gallon tubs of ice cream, with loosely scattered Creamsicles and Fudgesicles lying on top and in the spaces between.

"Holy cow!" yelled Mark and Mom gave him a cross look. She did not approve of calling anything other than God and socks holy.

I could see Butterscotch Ripple printed on one of the rims and Strawberry on another. Dad was smiling, clearly loving this.

"Where did this come from?" Mom asked again.

"There's one more box in the car. I'll be back in a minute and tell you all about it," and he left again. He was still smiling.

"Where are we going to put all this," Mom said to no one in particular. Dad returned with a much smaller box, filled with an assortment of loose ice cream bars, Popsicles, Drumsticks and little Sundae cups. He looked at Mom. "I think we can put all the food we have in the chest freezer. We can put this ice cream in the upright. You and I need to do some rearranging. You kids, you'll form an assembly line, but give me and Mom a few minutes to get organized."

"But where did this come from?" Mom asked.

"I bought it for two dollars," said Dad. "Let's get it into the freezer. Then I'll tell you all about it."

"Can we have one of these while we wait?" Sarah was being brave. Mom never let us have sweets before supper. Mom shrugged. "Just one," she said. "I guess we're eating dessert first tonight."

Our meal was later than usual: Sloppy Joes on buns dry from warming in the oven too long. Mom told us to let the sloppy part soak into the bun for a while, and she was right; they softened up some. Since I'd already had an Eskimo Pie, I was content to eat slowly, enjoying our good fortune and listening to Dad tell the story.

First, he told us what happened at Hopper's and about how it was eating away at him the whole way home in the car, that someone was throwing away all that perfectly good food. It infuriated him that, while so many people rarely had access to ice cream, some "bigwigs" were allowing perfectly good ice cream to be thrown away. "These kinds of hare-brained policies make no sense!" He banged the handle of his fork on the table. "Do these corporations have any idea of how many people are struggling while they fill their pockets?" He paused to look at us. "So I decided to go to the distribution centre and find out who was in charge of this nonsense."

Dad found the distribution centre, "big brick building, lots of loading platforms, big metal doors with handles that open by pulling down like on a fridge." He sat in the car and watched two guys wearing parkas and fur-lined boots loading boxes into a truck. When the truck pulled away, he jumped out and told the guys that he was interested in purchasing some of the damaged ice cream.

"We don't sell anything here. This is a distribution centre."

"I'm looking for the damaged stuff, the stuff that gets returned. I want to buy that."

"We don't sell it."

"Then can I have some?"

"We're not allowed to give it away."

"Then what do you do with it?"

"It's taken to a landfill."

"When will you be throwing it away?"

"Why do you want to know?"

"So I can be here."

One guy shook his head like Dad was a bit crazy and went inside, but the other guy stayed around and they talked for a bit. Dad told him he was the director of the Welcome Inn and suggested he show some kindness by donating some of the damaged ice cream "to the less fortunate". He told the guy that many of the North End residents could not afford to buy ice cream. He described the voluntary service workers, living unselfishly amongst "underprivileged families" on only a small stipend. He opined that we all had a responsibility to use God's resources wisely and throwing away perfectly good food was a sin when people were hungry. The guy told him to wait a minute and went inside. A few minutes later, he came back out and told Dad to come in.

"All right, we'll let you buy some."

"How much will it cost?"

"How about one dollar for a box?"

"What size of box are we talking about?"

"Any size. You supply the boxes." Dad told them he'd be right back and returned with two large boxes. They showed him the corner where the damaged stuff was. Dad was "flabbergasted," he said, at the size of the pile, and torn between being livid about the waste and thrilled about the haul. He filled the two large boxes, and one of the guys, the nice one, found him another smaller box and told me to go ahead and fill that one, too, for free.

Dad paid him two dollars and they worked out an arrangement. Dad could come pick up ice cream near the end of each month, as long as these two same guys were on shift and no trucks were loading at the time and Dad made it quick. They said that under no circumstances, should he allow anyone else to come and expect the same treatment. This was quiet and private, between Dad and the two of them.

From that momentous day on, the upright freezer was strictly reserved for ice cream. We had a never-ending, heavenly assortment, literally hundreds of bars, cups, cones, sandwiches, most of which were just fine, although some were a little squashed. It was a fantasy come to life to open the freezer door and stare at rows and rows of ice cream treats, free for the taking. Everything tasted better with ice cream: pancakes, day-old donuts, unfrosted cake, banana loaf, bread pudding, and overripe fruit. Because those five gallon drums were replaced each month, ice cream became a dessert staple. It was rare that someone didn't say, "How about some ice cream with this pie/cake/cookie?", and inevitably a tub would come out. The crystallized ice cream around the gashes was scraped away and discarded. Sometimes Mom got out the blender to throw in ice cream with a dash of milk to make it creamy, Dairy Queen-style.

I was not the only one delighted by the ice cream phenomenon. Many of our neighbours who came for food donations began to request that ice cream be included. Mom cheerfully doled it out to families, often referencing Elijah's jug, the one that never ran out of oil. Casually or blatantly, kids would talk about how hot it was, or how hungry they were, or how long it had been since their parents had taken them out for ice cream. Sometimes, they were ignored, other times, a box of Popsicles or Drumsticks appeared. Attendance at clubs and organized activities improved.

There were a few rules around the ice cream. One: ask first. Two: not before dinner. Three: all distribution of ice cream to kids was to be done with an adult present. Other than that, nothing was said about how often or how many or to whom. When it came to ice cream, there was no sense of shortage and no need to be stingy.

I wasn't good at following the first rule. If I had been, I would have saved myself much heartache. But I was young and not overly concerned with nutrition and healthy eating habits. And I learned how easy it was to cut through the alley and sneak into the back porch door to grab a Revel or Eskimo pie out of the freezer to eat in the alley or sneak into my room hidden among school books. With the freezer so abundantly full, my daily pillaging wasn't noticed and my weight gain was steady. Mom and Dad made occasional comments about wise and healthy eating, but they were preoccupied with issues more important than a gradually thickening daughter. I continued my daily foraging through grades four, five and six.

It was hard to resist. Making it even harder was the "can you get me an ice cream?" request during television commercials, which translated into a round for the whole group. If it was my turn to fetch, I usually brought an extra in case "someone might like one of these instead", and often ended up with two for myself, so this gift of ice cream was a dream come true and a nightmare. I developed "rolls". Each spring I dreaded the hauling out of the box of summer clothes, staring at my fleshy thighs, suffering the humiliation of Mom's sighs while I attempted to squeeze into last year's elastic-waisted shorts sets, listening to her mutter about "more sewing" and "how nice it would be if things fit for more than one year."

And that is how it was that Dad was "called" to salvage ice cream, and how it was that I was "led", far too often, to the freezer. I continued to ponder and fret over what it meant to be "called", and how one could be "led" when the leader was silent and invisible, struggling to formulate an idea of how exactly I was supposed to "go ye into all the world and preach the gospel" without being ridiculed for that. Or for being chubby.

TELEVISION

Our first television was a black and white model, donated to our family by a church member who, after an exceptional crop year, invested in a more up-to-date, bigger and better, black and white television. That was during our second year in Oklahoma, where the wind came sweeping down the plains and the television reception was next to nil. We had one channel to choose from, one-and-a-half, if you wanted to spend countless minutes fiddling with the rabbit ears in order to imagine blurry dramas or guess at game shows in the midst of a snowstorm.

The one good channel was reasonably clear when the rabbit ears were in a certain precise position that was difficult to replicate if changed. Not that we were free to manipulate the television any time it struck our fancy. Television watching was strictly monitored in our household. It was an entirely new entertainment concept for our God-fearing family, and shows with violence, drinking, "and such" were simply not allowed.

The older siblings easily memorized the television schedule, since we really had only one channel. I was just learning to read, so I relied on them to plan our viewing. But first, we had to consult our parent's feelings on each and every television show before we were allowed to tune in. Their vigilance in this matter slackened somewhat after we moved to Hamilton. There, the television was upstairs, removed enough to shield us from constant scrutiny. But our "vegetating", a word Mom used to describe TV-watching, was limited. Too much television bred ineptitude and sloth.

Mom kept trying to get us away from that TV. Her comments were a constant refrain: "Go outside and play. Get some fresh air. Turn that noise box off," or "You have a half hour, and then your television watching time is over." This one didn't often stick. She was awful busy downstairs with things. "Staring at that confounded thing will turn your brain to mush," was another of her favourite sayings, unless, of course, it was Dick Van Dyke or something that had Jimmy Stewart in it. Then she'd join us. "When I was young, I had chores to do. I didn't have the privilege to sit on my bottom for hours being frivolous," she'd say. That one had a stinger attached. "Such silliness. Those people aren't real. Why don't you get a book?"

Mom was the chief censor for all television shows. When she was uncertain about whether to allow or deny, she called in Dad for consultation and previewing or asked her church friends for their advice. She and Dad developed the following 'Television Guidelines':

The Good Ones: (endorsed as "good family entertainment", not listed in any particular order).

1. *I Love Lucy*: This show epitomized all that was good and wholesome on television. All of us loved Lucy. Mom laughed so hard she cried watching Lucy and Ethel stuffing chocolates from the conveyor belt into their mouths and down their bras. Lucy's antics not only entertained, but seemed to help make all the other stay-at-home wives feel competent and well-adjusted.

2. *Hymn Sing*: The name pretty much describes the entire show. A choir either stood on tiered dais and sang hymns or were arranged in standing and seated positions in a living room setting with a fireplace in the background and sang hymns. Period. Sometimes there was a solo. Watching Hymn Sing every Sunday at 5:30 was not optional. The good part was that we could have faspa while we watched, as long as we only filled our plates or went for seconds during commercial breaks.

3. *The Dick Van Dyke Show*: He was the male actor who could do no wrong. Mom loved Rob Petrie's stuttering moments and clumsy spells. I envisioned my future, married self like Laura in her little black pants, always smiling in her spotless kitchen. Her wavering voice when she said, "Ohhhh…Robbbbb…" was so touching.

4. *Tiny Talent Time*: A program on local television station CHCH Channel 11."Uncle" Bill Lawrence interviewed the kids for a few minutes before they played their instrument, tap-danced or sang a Broadway show tune. The whole family enjoyed the show, sometimes making "spotte" about a pianist or accordion player, even though none of us, except Dad with his wonderful singing voice, had any kind of talent suitable for television.

5.   *Flipper*: The theme song and Flipper's clicky chatter made Mom, respectively, hum along and smile. Flipper saved people from harm, a natural superhero. And all without talk. How could we resist? Mom said dolphins were smart.

6.   *The Andy Griffith Show*: Any show that started with a whistling theme song and a father and son duo setting out on a fishing trip would melt Mom's heart. We all liked Opie better than the Beaver, and loved to watch Barney Fife getting upset enough to make the veins in his neck pop out.

7.   *High Q:* The local version on Channel 11 showcased smart high school students from one high school trying to answer more questions than smart high school students from another school. Ruth got to be on the show once, looking the whole time as though she wished she were somewhere else.

8.   *Walt Disney's Wonderful World of Color*: A new adventure every week; Pollyanna, Dumbo, Davy Crocket, Old Yeller, shipwrecks, raccoons messing up kitchens... We all loved this one.

Okay, but not fully endorsed: (Translated, this meant we could watch these shows if the weather was too poor outside to play, or it was dark and our homework was done, or Mom wasn't paying attention.)

1.   *Gomer Pyle USMC:* The military context and the amount of yelling done by Sergeant Carter caused Mom concern. It was tolerated because Gomer was innocent and naïve; and came from Mayberry.

2.   *Green Acres*: Mom didn't approve of Lisa Douglas' twisted values about city living, or the fancy outfits she wore around the farm, or her constant whining about giving up her penthouse apartment in New York City. But the show was acceptable because of Oliver's determination to succeed at farm living despite constant trials and tribulations. And Mom liked Arnold the pig.

3.   *Sea Hunt*: Lloyd Bridges as Mike Nelson, rescuing people with his high-powered speed boat and deep-sea-diving equipment. Mom didn't like references to Nelson's past life as a Marine and the fact that some episodes involved the recovery of stolen weapons, but the show gained points because he helped people without being paid to do so, out of the goodness of his heart. My brother Mark loved the show, so we got to watch sometimes because his preferences carried more

weight, he being the only boy. If Mom was watching, Mark talked about how much Mike Nelson had in common with Jacques Cousteau. Mom loved Jacques Cousteau.

4. *Mr. Ed:* Mom thought a show about a talking horse was plain dumb. She didn't believe there was anything that could be gained by taking advice from an old horse, but she let it go since it seemed harmless.

5. *Petticoat Junction:* There was some minor concern about the girls bathing in the hotel's supply of drinking water and showing their underwear, but Mom loved the close-knit family, the daughters with two first names, and Uncle Joe.

6. *My Favorite Martian:* The subject matter involved the controversial issue of extra- terrestrial life. Mom may have had some concerns over the possibility that the show might give us nightmares or put strange ideas in our heads.

7. *The Beverly Hillbillies:* Hollywood glitz, fancy houses, and too much concern by Mr. Drysdale over the Clampetts' assets. Things not to admire or aspire to: Jethro's lack of education and Granny's backyard still and her hunting rifle. Good points: the fact that the Clampetts continued to wear their hillbilly garb, thereby not conforming to shallow Hollywood fashion ideals, and Granny's commitment to home-style cooking, especially squirrel pie and possum stew.

Borderline and sometimes negotiable: (These shows required negotiations, since they sometimes contained violence or adult content. Sometimes we were allowed to watch and sometimes we weren't, and reasons were not always consistent. Circumstances or conditions, like the phase of the moon, the quality of our recent schoolwork, or whether a day's work had been particularly hard, could tip the scales in either direction. Not listed in any particular order.)

1. *The Ed Sullivan Show:* Depended totally on who was on. Russian circus acts: yes. Dog shows or Sherri Lewis and her puppets: yes. Comedians and ventriloquists: yes. Rock and Roll bands: no, especially Elvis: NO. Simple. Sometimes we watched partial shows.

2. *Sonny and Cher:* Usually yes, but due to some sexual innuendos this one could be turned off suddenly at any given moment. Mom liked minority groups being represented on television and she thought it was cute that Sonny was shorter than Cher.

3.   *Rowan and Martin's Laugh In*: Lots of innocent humour, but Goldie Hawn and Judy Carne, painted with flower power and dancing in bikinis, was a bit much. This one was pushing the limits.

4.   *Hogan's Heroes*: Mom was not impressed by the idea that one could joke about concentration camps and prison life. We tried to convince her with a "good triumphing over evil" argument. Another hit and miss.

5.   *The Munsters*: Too much make up on Herman's lips and eyes and general creepiness, but not particularly offensive or harmful. Mom liked Herman's laugh but not the bolts in his neck. Nor was she fussy about werewolf Eddy or Lillian Munster's skin-tight dresses.

6.   *Gilligan's Island*: Its redeeming qualities were goofy Gilligan and the jovial skipper but the moral content was questionable in light of Ginger's seductive wardrobe and the Howells' obsession with wealth. The smart professor and country girl Mary Ann added some credibility.

7.   *Bonanza*: This one was the most controversial show and invited the most discussion. We all loved Little Joe and Ben Cartwright. Even Mom and Dad couldn't argue with that. They, too, loved these characters. And who could resist Hoss and his dimples. The Cartwright family did so many good things, but there were guns. And the use of guns was strictly not acceptable in Mom and Dad's life theology. So the family reached a compromise of sorts. We were allowed to watch... until a gun came out of the holster and was fired. Regardless of whether 50 minutes remained in an episode or just four, if a gun was fired, the channel was changed. That is just the way it was. The outcome of many Bonanza episodes remains a mystery to me.

Forbidden: (These shows were not permitted. No arguments.)

1.   Wrestling: Fighting was wrong. End of conversation.

2.   *F-Troop*: Big mistake letting Mom and Dad tune into this one for the first time at the beginning of the show. A water tower is blown up and a guy has to jump to safety. Bad first impression. Too violent.

3.   *Batman*: Way too many bad characters, fast cars, gargoyles perched on buildings, evil laughter and tight clothing. Never mind all the ooomps and bams, and bonks and bashes in those little talking bubbles.

4. *Roller Derby*: Fast paced, aggressive and mean. And what was the point?

5. *The Monkees*: Long hair. Rock and roll. On par with The Beatles. Absolutely not.

6. *Get Smart*: Way too much high tech spy equipment and emphasis on the evil organization KAOS. And all the automated metal doors Max had to get through at the beginning of each episode, was too reminiscent of prison life. She didn't even like us saying, 'Sorry about that, Chief".

7. *The Honeymooners*: Ralph was a loudmouth who kept yelling at Alice, "One of these days, one of these days...pow, right in the kisser," threatening violence with a feigned punch. Mom said Ralph was a bully.

As a special treat, we would go to the movies, since Mom saw good value in the lower-priced afternoon matinees. She loved any movie by Walt Disney and anything about animals, like *The Incredible Journey* and *That Darn Cat*. She loved *Chitty Chitty Bang Bang* (Dick Van Dyke!) and *The Love Bug* and *The Sound of Music*. Mom even took us to see *Dr. Zhivago*, whispering down the row to us about Bolsheviks and other Russian stuff.

Sometimes, we were allowed to go by ourselves, walking uptown to the Tivoli Theatre on a Saturday afternoon. We had our own money to spend: we each got five dollars in our birthday cards from a dear family friend. We saw some racy movies like *Barbarella* and *Cactus Flower* and excellent movies like *The Great Escape* and *Butch Cassidy and The Sundance Kid*.

Mom and Dad learned a "kill two birds with one stone" trick one family vacation. Take the car and trailer into a drive-in movie and park in the back row. At the end of the movie, just don't leave. Spend the night without paying for a campsite. Mom made sure we all used the washrooms when the final credits were running. There were always at least two movies. Often, the first was a family film, followed by a more adult feature. We got to stay through *The Russians are Coming* and *The Magnificent Seven*, because there was no way Dad would try to exit the crowded lot with the trailer in the dark, even if there were guns and shooting.

MY NEW PANTS

My most exciting clothing "find" happened on the same day a record was set for the fastest donation delivery. It happened in the spring of the year I was in grade four. Let it be noted that it took almost two years of gleaning through donation boxes to find one true gem.

That day, the boxes were delivered in a Cadillac. When the fin-backed, silver-chromed beauty pulled in front of the Welcome Inn, I happened to be next door in the entrance of the Grocery Store, watching little Bernadine, who often sat inside the window, playing with the apples. Shiny and sleek, the Cadillac was the type of car that leggy, high-heeled "gold-diggers" stepped out from in TV ads. I knew something about cars from listening to Mark and Dad who liked to comment on unusual or vintage cars on family vacations, speculating on the year, make and model. Once in a while, I, too, might comment on a particular "beauty" spied on one of these road trips, usually out of sheer boredom.

I'd never seen a car anything like this Caddy in the North End neighbourhood. I watched as the car sat at the curb, idling, its occupants most likely considering whether they should risk getting out. Then, three doors opened simultaneously. Two men in suits emerged and moved efficiently toward the trunk, while a fancy-looking lady stepped out carefully, as though she were looking for a safe place to land. She stood, looking troubled, her gaze moving up and down the street, her eyes lingering for a moment at the Majeska House on the corner. Next, she busied herself by smoothing her camel hair coat and adjusting her matching hat while the men lifted boxes out of the trunk. I was witnessing a real live "Smart Lady" in our neighbourhood, so close I could smell her perfume. I got up to find Dad. He was already watching from the storefront door.

"It looks like a Cadillac," I said, opening the door.

"Oh yeah," he said flatly. "It's a Cadillac."

Carrying two boxes each, the men followed the lady toward the open door.

"We've brought you some boxes of clothing," said the lady, smiling tightly, clutching a purse under her arm. She sashayed past us into the storefront, barely glancing sideways. I looked at her shoes, hoping to see snake or lizard skin as they click, click, clicked along the floor, but they were just a tan colour that matched her purse. It was a typical day in the storefront, a group of kids piled on one of the couches, three women talking in library chairs, some older boys leaning against the wall on one side of the room, whispering and snickering, probably telling dirty jokes while two teenaged girls across the room pretended to ignore them.

The Smart Lady marched past the girls, reached the end of the ping pong table and paused, seeming unsure where to go next. She made a sudden pivot to the right, as though she were preparing to pick up a paddle and start a game. But she froze at the head of the table, eyes darting back and forth with a look of desperation that said, "Get me out of here!"

"We sure hope you can find some use for them." She spoke to the room in a pinched voice, as though the air was too thin. I noticed something then that I had gotten used to: a particular smell about the place that lingered, a subtle mix of unwashed clothing, body odour and nicotine. I wondered if she was worried that the smell might infuse her clothing. I stared at her; I couldn't help it, taking in her peach lipstick, a floral silk scarf, and the finely stitched collar of her satin blouse. I wished Lily were here to see it.

The lady's panicked eyes finally settled on Dad, who was still standing by the door. "We hear you are doing such wonderful work with the community and we want to support your project." She kept going in a louder voice, talking about the work we did, like she was giving a speech. By now the room had quieted, all eyes on her, a few mouths open. The two men continued stacking boxes close to the entrance, neither saying a word, while the Smart Lady chattered anxiously. "We are so sorry, we can't stay. We're on our way to…" She paused for a moment, casting her eyes toward the boxes stacked by the door, as though counting. The instant she was certain all boxes were inside, Mrs. Smart Lady resumed her circuit of the ping pong table, her steps increasingly jubilant as she approached the door, stopping for about one second to extend her gloved hand to Dad.

The kitchen door opened and Mom stood in the doorway, wiping her hands on her apron while Dad thanked the back of the Smart Lady's head.

"Who was that?" Mom asked, coming to the door.

"Some rich people dropped off some boxes," Dad walked slowly to the sidewalk, staring after the car with a strange look on his face. Then he shook his head, as though stumped by a difficult problem.

I found my pants in one of these boxes: a pair of blue, purple and pink plaid bell bottom pants with solid purple patch pockets and a brass button fly. To my mind, they were stunning; they had excellent colours, were almost new and fit me perfectly. Okay, maybe they were a bit too short. Mom thought she should sew a trim of rickrack around the hems, but I wanted no part of that, refusing to compromise the integrity of their design or delay wearing them.

She helped me hand-wash them and pull on the wet legs to try and add length. They hung in the bathroom, and three times during the night, I tiptoed downstairs to pull on the legs, praying they'd be dry in time for school.

In the morning, the pants were dry, but the legs weren't any longer. I wore them anyway, walking confidently down the hall, receiving compliments and reassurances from Sophie and Rita. I felt cool and groovy in my first pair of bell bottoms, my spirits high until recess that day, when Erica followed me into the washroom.

I had been working on a "look", to use on the playground. It was modeled after Lily's "clamming up" look. It was an "I don't really care what you think about my elastic-waisted skirt" look, and could be used with all of my outfits. The "look" was a combination of boredom and mild distain, which I accomplished by titling my head ever so slightly, narrowing my eyes and keeping them deliberately unfocussed while looking at my tormentor with one eye and just past their face with the other, keeping my mouth neutral. I was going for a look of irritated nonchalance to convey a message that spoke, "I don't have time for this nonsense." I'd been working on perfecting this look in the mirror, ready to use it on occasions where my clothing was the subject of derogatory commentary. But on the day I wore my new bell bottoms, I wasn't prepared.

Erica joined me at the sink, her snake eyes narrowed, "Nice pants, are they new?"

I felt my face turning red as I nodded.

"Why did you buy them so short?"

Her eyes blazed into me while I thought, "None of your beeswax, Miss Snotface", and the only thing I could think to say came out, "They shrunk in the dryer."

She responded with a smile that said, "You don't fool me". I never wore them to school again.

SMELTING

Sardine sized smelts follow a migration pattern through the Great Lakes to their spawning destination, and apparently, there were smelts in Hamilton's harbour. I don't know who alerted my parents to this newsflash but Mom and Dad were suddenly keen to tap into swarms of free fish.

"We snuck out last night," said Mom at breakfast, talking like she and Dad had had their first date, "while you were sleeping."

"You wouldn't believe the net loads they were hauling in. It was amazing! People were filling up buckets and tubs with fish," said Dad, slapping the table with his palms.

"Some of the ladies were frying them up right on the pier," Mom beamed, the activity including all of her favourite things: fishing, campfire cooking and anything free.

"I can't sit here and let all those fish swim by," said Dad, shaking his head. "I just can't do it." His face took on a faraway look as he quietly finished his breakfast.

Fishing held a special place in my parent's hearts. So much so, they'd gone fishing on their honeymoon. For me, it was hard to imagine anything less romantic. They loved Bible stories about fish, like the one where Jesus fed five thousand people with five loaves and two fishes, and the one where the doubting disciples pulled up full nets of fish after Jesus told them to move them to the other side of the boat. That catchy tune, "I will make you fishers of men", loved by Sunday school teachers everywhere, was one of their favourites. No family vacation was complete unless there were numerous fishing stops. Mom loved to "mosey along", appreciating God's beauty and abundance, and spontaneous fishing fit right into this agenda. Dad, growing up on a farm, transformed his inborn need to reap and sow into a love of fishing, seeing his catch as a harvest borne of labour:

instead of bringing forth food from the land, he pulled it out of the water. Fishing satisfied their common desire to be resourceful and feed a large family on a small budget. Both frowned on laziness, so fishing provided a perfect opportunity to relax while being productive at the same time.

On family holidays, we transported our fifteen-foot bamboo fishing rods on the outside of the station wagon because they were too long to fit inside the car. The poles needed to be easily accessible when a good river or lake crossed our paths. Whenever the eight poles were attached to the passenger side, using ropes and twine and the door handles for support, we all had to get in and out of the car on the driver's side. It also required that Dad take extra caution when parking because the poles extended far beyond the front and the back of the car. Fortunately, they were flexible, proving on several occasions they could bend like rubber.

My older sisters were embarrassed by the attention we drew driving around with the fishing poles, taking up too much space when parking, and piling out of the same side of the car. I was bothered more by the actual fishing.

"Oh please Lord, let them not notice that lake ahead. Let us pass by without stopping. Oh please, let it not be a potential fishing spot," I silently pleaded from the back seat. But usually, well before I was even aware that a lake or river loomed, the car would slow and I would hear Mom or Dad say, "This looks like a good spot". Within seconds, we were pulled over, often on the wrong side of the road, to examine the accessibility and possibility of fish in whatever lake or river had caught their attention.

With the motor idling, Mom and Dad, along with Mark, who was almost always sandwiched between them in the front seat, hauled themselves out of the driver's door. They'd gaze and deliberate, weighing variables that included time of day in relation to the time fish were thought to feed, depth and current of the river or lake, and logistics of transporting and situating eight long poles along the water's edge, during which I rolled my eyes in the back seat. More often than not, they came back to the car and Dad reached in to turn off the ignition.

The rest went pretty much the same way each time. Dad untied the poles while Mom hauled the shovel out of the back of the car and began to dig. Three or four shovels of dirt usually exposed enough worms to get us started. Dad handed out poles and we untangled the hooks and chipped off any previous petrified worm matter, after which, we formed a line in front of Mom, who ripped the newly dug worms into halves or thirds depending on their quantity and plumpness, and re-baited our hooks. We rarely received a whole worm, unless by some miracle Mom had dug into a squirming jackpot.

With hooks baited we followed Dad to the water, angling our poles steeply upward to avoid gouging the dirt, losing our worm, or poking the person ahead or behind. We chose our spots, carefully to keep enough distance between us to prevent any poking or grossing each other out with wormy hook contact while casting our lines. No one, it seemed, was overly excited about these stops, but dilly-dallying meant longer stops, and Mom got cranky if we distracted her and cut into her fishing time.

The bamboo rods were not equipped with reels; rather, the fishing line was wrapped around and around and around and around the pole, ending with a hook exposed and dangling off the end. Unwinding the line to get the hook in the water could take several minutes, presenting the only honest opportunity to stall, though doing this could provoke a lecture on doing one's share to help catch dinner. Once the hooks were in the water, there was no point in resisting.

When I was really young and didn't know any better, I sat in my spot with my pole and a scowl, squirming, slapping at bugs and mosquitoes, both real and imaginary, and feeling completely sorry for myself. Over many years of reluctant participation in family fishing ventures, I perfected the art of daydreaming, imagining myself stunningly beautiful and pursued by extraordinarily handsome boys. Most of my daydream productions became quite elaborate, considering all the fishing and driving we did on our holidays. In my mental dramas, I looked like Liz or Marcia Brady, went on trips to foreign countries, and was fluent in Spanish. When I finished high school, I would look like Nancy Sinatra and wear a baby blue mini-dress with arm fringes and white go-go boots. My boyfriend, whose identity changed depending on my current TV obsession, was undyingly devoted and could not live without me. He refused to eat when we had an argument or when I turned down a diamond ring because it would cramp my style when mountain trekking or swimming in tropical waterfalls in my bikini.

But during my early fishing years, I sat staring at the bobber, bored out of my mind, thinking about running away and joining a non-fishing family. Generally, we gave each place twenty to thirty minutes. If no one pulled in a fish or got a nibble, we packed up and left. The worst thing was when we did catch fish, or got enough bites to keep Mom and Dad hopeful, because then we might stay for hours. Successful fishing stops were followed by a fish dinner at the evening's campsite.

Witnessing the cleaning of the fish was almost worse than catching them; the sound of our dull camping knife grinding through the cartilage and gills, the glassy bug eyes staring from severed heads, slicing up the fat fleshy belly that discharged blackish red blood and jelly-like guts, the slimy scales, and the fishy stink on the picnic table, even if Dad laid out newspaper first. Watching the fish get rinsed in a bucket of water quickly gone cloudy and then thrown into a plastic bag with flour, all globby after the first shake. The sizzling popping sounds from the frying pan, the fish in the middle burning and sticking in the smoking oil.

Then we had to eat them. The whole time I feared that I might get fish bones caught in my throat, and when that did happen, I would panic, feeling like my throat would swell up and I might choke to death. If we caught fish, we ate them…not as a side dish, not as an optional, have some if you want some addition to the meal. Fish was the meal.

Fishing for smelt was different. It wasn't even called fishing. They called it smelting and it was done in the middle of the night.

Dad had come out of his early morning reverie and was talking about smelting again when we sat down at lunchtime. We fired questions.

"They don't use poles," he said with a mouthful of bologna sandwich.

"Then where do you put the worm?"

"They don't use worms. They don't use any bait."

"Then how do you catch the fish?" I wanted to know.

"With a net," he said.

"A dip net," said Mom. "A huge square net with a pole attached."

"How huge?" Tina asked.

Mom walked around some tiles in the kitchen floor to give us an idea of the size of the net. "It is about five feet on each side," she said.

"Wow, that's big!"

"Each corner has a chain attached to it and they are pulled together in the middle of the square," she continued.

"How do you hold the net?"

"There's a long pole attached that hooks onto the knot in the centre," she said.

"How long is the pole? Is it as long as our fishing poles?"

"Longer," Mom said.

We were impressed.

The first hurdle was finding a net. If it were humanly possible, Dad would have created a net out of materials from his gulch pile. Dad was a master at scrounging and collecting, and the gulch pile was his source of spare parts; his stockpile of nails, screws, metal or wood scraps, pieces of tiles, pipes, assorted parts of machines, vehicles or appliances; in short, anything that had potential for building something or fixing anything.

Even with his well-stocked inventory, Dad lacked netting material that was fine enough to catch small fish and strong enough at the same time to hold a heavy load and withstand the pull of the water. He also needed a pole long enough to support the net. A bamboo fishing pole wasn't sturdy or long enough, he figured. He spent a few minutes thinking out loud about where he could acquire a strong but light metal pole that was long enough.

The fact that he couldn't make his own dip net had him mighty frustrated. Never a fan of paying retail for anything, Dad visibly struggled, weighing his reluctance to spend against all those free fish. Finally, he threw up his hands. "I guess I have to go back and talk to those guys... find out where to get a net." We gathered outside on the sidewalk when Mom and Dad arrived home the next afternoon with a dip net attached to the roof of the car and a long pole tied against the side, its tip dangling inches from the ground. It was exciting, something new, that big.

"We're going tonight," Dad announced.

"We'll all have a nap after supper since we'll be up most of the night," Mom said.

Before we were sent to bed after supper, Trudy asked what we should wear.

"You'll get fishy and wet," Mom said, "so dress warm, but wear something old. You can look for some boots in the basement. Make sure you have everything ready before you go to bed."

I went to bed wondering how I would be able to get to sleep so early, but the next thing I knew the lights flicked on and Mom was standing in our room. She was wearing one of Dad's sweatshirts under a full-length apron with big pockets, her stretchy denim pants tucked into a pair of yellow rubber boots I'd not seen before, and her straw bonnet tied under her chin.

"What are we supposed to do if there is only one net?" I asked groggily, wondering if I really wanted to get dressed and go along.

"You sit on the pier and wait for the net to come out of the water," she said. "Your job is to gather the fish after they dump the net and put them into pails."

Dad was loading plastic ice cream buckets and the cooler into the back of the station wagon, which already contained the camping stove, a fry pan, the Coleman lantern and a pile of blankets.

"What is that for?" I pointed to the stove.

"A midnight fish fry," he said with a grin.

"What will we have?"

"Fish," he said.

"Smelt fish?"

"Yes. Smelts."

"Is that all we'll have?" I asked.

"Mom might've thrown in a loaf of bread. I'm not sure," he answered and moved away to pull on the ropes that secured the net to the roof.

The tires scrunched on the crumbling shoulder as we pulled in behind a long line of cars and trucks parked on the dark side of Burlington Street. The sound of traffic going up the ramp onto the bridge echoed as we got out of the car. Down the street, Stelco and Dofasco were on night shift, muffled industrial sounds of humming and churning and blasts of air emanating from the buildings. Bursts of glow from darkened windows cast eerie light above the streetlights and clouds of smoke spewed upward, painting streaks in the night sky.

The shoulder of the road behind us filled up with cars as Mom and Dad divvied up the load for the walk to the pier. I was given a stack of empty ice cream buckets and an old wool blanket. We formed a single line, staying close to the line of parked cars and following Dad, who carried the net by the pole-handle like the flag-bearer leading a parade, the net up high, bobbing in rhythm with his footsteps. I kept my eyes in front of me, walking closely behind Mark. Mom and Ruth brought up the rear, carrying the cooler between them. During lulls in the traffic noise, I heard laughter and voices from the pier, amplified by the water and growing louder as we approached.

A dim streetlight flickered above us as we turned and moved onto the pier, which stretched like a runway into the darkness of the bay. Our procession passed small groups of smelters, mostly adults warmly dressed in camping gear. Some sat on canvas stools, huddled around lanterns, laughing, talking and smoking. Pole holders faced the water, spaced apart; others stood beside them, staring into the depths.

Ahead of us, a grey-bearded fisherman wearing a yellow slicker and rubber boots leaned forward, bracing his legs while holding the pole with one arm in front of his body and one behind. We stopped to watch as he began lifting with his forward arm, pushing with the arm behind, pulling his chest upward in small increments. A thick-bellied fellow wearing hunting clothes like Elmer Fudd, put his cigarette on the concrete and got up from his stool.

"Looks like this one's pretty full," he said, as he took hold of the pole from the other side.

"Yah… this…. is a good… one," replied the man with the pole.

As they lifted in unison, the tip of the pole strained toward the water, bending like a bow.

"I think that pole's going to snap," I said, looking for Dad's eyes, but he was obviously not concerned. The man in the hunting clothes turned in our direction, chuckling. "It ain't gonna break," he said, going back to his task.

Breathing heavily, they continued lifting, slowly, pausing to let the net hover just above the surface to let the water drain and the fish slide into the centre of the net. We backed out of their way as they pulled upward, staring at the net teeming and rippling with silver. We gathered closer as they tilted and dumped the net, amazed by the squirming mass of tiny silver fish flipping and bouncing like popcorn on the concrete. Two women dressed in aprons, overcoats and kerchiefs holding back their hair, moved in with plastic gloves and buckets, looking like Lucy Ricardo and Ethel Mertz on a winter camping trip. We made exclamatory and congratulatory sounds while they scooped up handfuls of fish. We continued on our way, full of hope and eager to get started.

Dad passed several available spaces. He stopped when he was almost directly under the bridge, sniffing the air and looking up, maybe to check for roosting pigeons and the possibility of falling poop, then nodded, indicating this was the spot.

We spread blankets on the concrete and set up the canvas stool for Mom. I sat on a steel girder used for tying up boats. The other fishermen lowered their nets gently, allowing them to sink once they touched the surface. Dad took his net to the edge and let it plop down. I watched as the water swallowed up the big square.

"How long before we pull it up?" asked Tina, hopping up and down.

"We'll give her five or ten minutes," he replied.

Dad stood holding the net, completely still except for his right leg, his heel moving to some silent rhythm. He must be singing a song in his head I thought and tried to figure out which of his favourite hymns matched his moving foot. I was grateful he wasn't singing out loud, something he tended to do in public places, often bursting into the middle of a hymn, as though some great impulse compelled him to suddenly sing at top volume to any available audience. Sometimes it scared people. I liked to hear him sing, but joined Ruth and the twins when they rolled their eyes and shushed him in restaurants and grocery store line-ups.

I joined Mom and the others sitting on the blanket. She had the Coleman stove ready to light. The fry pan sat ready on one burner, black except for one yellow plop of margarine.

"Grab a hold," Dad hollered. We jumped up to grab a piece of the pole. Mom watched from her chair, her face lit with a big smile.

"Whoa, this is heavy."

"Feels like we caught an elephant."

"Good for the leg muscles."

"Volga boat men, humph."

"Heave ho, heave men, humph,"

The commentary continued as we strained upwards. The net shuddered as it broke the surface, then lightened quickly. When it reached the height of the pier, we paused, breathing heavily to steady the net.

"Whoa, look at that!"

The net was a live, squirming mass.

"We'll put them down over here," said Dad, as he directed us with his stronger movements.

We laid the net flat on the cement and took a moment to examine the spoils.

"Look at all those eyes!"

"Yuck," said a sister.

"Let's dump the net and get her back in the water," said Dad.

The next morning, we were allowed to sleep in until 9:00. "Time to rise and shine," Mom's favourite wake-up call came up from the living room. "Breakfast is on the table." The smell of fish wafted from the kitchen as I came down the stairs. One sink was brimming with water and smelt. I thought I saw water rippling and I imagined them still alive, then realized that the dripping tap was making the water move. Two buckets of smelt sat on the floor by the sink.

Mom closed the door behind us as the last of my siblings wandered in, blocking out the noise and activities in the storefront. Everybody knew, even the youngest of the Welcome Inn clientele knew, that if that kitchen door was closed, the people inside were not to be disturbed under any circumstances, barring medical emergency. So, without a word spoken, I knew my fate was sealed. Any dreams of Saturday morning fun evaporated.

The fishy smell was enough to put me off eating, but breakfast was ready on the small table, a bowl of hard boiled eggs beside a plate stacked with toast, bananas and the peanut butter jar. A pile of makeshift cutting boards —better known as slabs of plywood, a stack of large bowls, some newspapers and an assortment of knives were set up on the big table.

I had no appetite but I knew once we started cutting fish, the smell would get worse. I lifted an egg onto my saucer like it was a chore. We all took our time eating, stalling and praying for deliverance from the task that lay ahead.

"We've been blessed by such a rich bounty," Mom chirped from the sink. I reflected on this bounty. A wonderful night of staying up late and a midnight fish fry meant a day of penance: blood and guts and fishy stink.

Mom left us alone with our eggs while she swished the fish around in the sink, filling her metal colander then transferring the fish to two large bowls. We ate in silence, plugging our noses and making faces when Mom's back was turned.

"Where are all the VS'ers today?" I asked.

"They've eaten. I told them lunch would be late. They'll look after the storefront." A minute later, as though she heard a starting bell, Mom began whisking away the breakfast items, allowing us a few seconds to shovel in our remaining food before she grabbed our plates. I looked at the crumbs on the table.

"Spread that newspaper to cover the table and roll up your sleeves," she said. "This is going to be messy. Each of you take a cutting board and put on an apron." We spaced ourselves around the big table as Mom plopped the two big bowls of fish down in the middle, making sure we could all reach them. And so began our fish-factory assembly-line training.

"Take about six or seven at a time," Mom put a handful of fish on a cutting board and lined up their heads against the blade of her knife. Separating one from the line up, she placed the tip of her knife under the tiny gills. "This is where you cut." With a quick jab, she cut off its head. Drops of liquid, thick as jelly, pooled on the cutting board. "There isn't much blood, is there?" I said to no one in particular. Mom pushed the head away with the knife blade.

"Now, hold the fish close to the cut," she said, squeezing the smelt where its neck would be if it had one. "Then cut along the belly. Cut away from your fingers, so you don't slice yourselves," She demonstrated the technique.

"Now you hold the tail end and clean out its insides," Pinning the tail to the cutting board with her thumb and using the tip of the knife, she ran the blade from tail to neck inside the belly, scraping out some slimy stuff. "You can use the knife to clean the guts, or you can use your thumb." She picked up the first tiny fillet, holding it up for examination before laying it back down. "Now, you try it." She slid the guts onto the newspaper toward the discarded head. "I'll get another bowl for the finished ones."

The first few were tricky, but Mom stood by, demonstrating a few more times and telling us we were catching on just fine. "I'll collect these and rinse them again in the other sink, then pack them in plastic bags for the freezer. With all of us working together, we will get the job done in a snap." she said, sounding like Mary Poppins organizing the playroom cleanup.

We cut off heads one after another, slit bellies, ran our fingers through inner organs and threw the tiny fish into the bowls on the table, pushing severed heads and guts onto the newspaper. Slime ran down my arms, making them sticky. We forged ahead, knowing that resistance was futile and that stalling would bring on a lecture about appreciating God's generous gifts.

I wiped my arms along the newspaper, which added black smudges of smeared ink to the sticky slime that covered them. Guts and heads grew thick on the table. Soggy newspapers were replaced several times.

Elbows deep in mire, we tried to amuse ourselves with a running commentary: "I wonder how many cats will be prowling around here tonight? ...Maybe we can make cat food with the heads and get rich.... We could call it Smelty Good Cat Food... How about Smelty Goobers?... We can bake them and call it Krispy Smelt Bites... Smelt Brain Kibbles...Purina Smelt Chow...Smelt Head Meatloaf...Kitty Spaghetti with Smeltballs...Smelt Head Chip cookies..." and on and on and on.

Next came the fish songs; "A smelting we will go, a smelting we will go, high ho the Derry oh, a smelting we will go... There were three jolly fishermen, fisher, fisher, men, men, men, fisher, fisher, men, men, men..." And rhymes: fish in a dish, fish make a wish, fish I want to squish, smelts in leather belts, smelts give me welts, smelt have the cards dealt, smelts in beaver pelts, smelts in bed with quilts, that doesn't rhyme, it's close enough, smelts wearing felt."

"Smelt failed school 'cause they couldn't spelt," This was Dad's contribution as he brought in fresh buckets of fish for processing. "Gee, it smelts pretty bad in here." He grabbed the bagged smelt and took them out to the freezer. Mark called through the back door, "I'll bet we've done more than fifty baggies."

"Oh that sounds a bit fishy to me," Dad yelled back.

We worked for the better part of three hours, getting through the cooler and several of the ice cream pails. Mom was helping with cutting between swishing, rinsing and bagging. She could clean three fish to my one.

When Dad placed the last two pails of fish in the middle of the kitchen floor and exited, our movements were slowing. We were giving each other "the look", that desperate look that said, "Somebody do something!" And despite the smell and the guts, I was getting hungry. I sensed Ruth preparing herself to speak, and gave her my best pleading look of encouragement.

"Mom, maybe we could freeze some of these just as they are and then clean them when they're thawed out," Ruth spoke carefully.

I held my breath. Mom closed her eyes in response, leaning against the sink, completely still. The rest of us slowed our movements, shoulders tensed. It was a few seconds before she responded. "Well..." she sighed. Opening her eyes, she looked at us and the mess on the table. My eyes returned to the victim on my cutting board. I resumed cutting, but my movements were awkward.

"I suppose... that might be okay..." she said slowly, looking tired. She continued with building enthusiasm, "I think we have more than enough in the freezer. We can give some away, just the way they are. I'll tell them how to clean them!"

"Oh, I'm sure Mrs. Davies would love some of these fish for supper, tonight," said Ruth.

"And Mrs. Bishop, too."

"Go get Dad," said Mom. Mark jumped up, bumping the table, and ran out of the kitchen, leaving smelt slime on the doorknob.

A few minutes later, Dad appeared. He opened the kitchen door to the storefront and whistled, drawing the kids closer. Blocking the door, he announced in a loud voice, "I want all you to run home and tell your parents they can come and get some fish. Tell them to bring a bowl or a bag. The sooner, the better. First come, first served." As he spoke, he moved into the storefront, like a dog herding sheep, directing them to the front door. "It's time for lunch anyway. Tell them to come around 1:30. Off you go."

Within minutes, the storefront was empty and we began the cleanup, a process that thrilled me, since it meant it was really over. Mom told us to put the cutting boards on the porch and Dad would clean them with the hose. The leftover smelts were thrown back into the cooler. We washed bowls and knives, balled up the yucky newspaper and wiped the table.

Mom thanked us for all the hard work and told us to go play outside for a bit while she fixed some lunch. At lunch, she announced there was an ice cold jug of root beer waiting at the A&W and we could all walk up there together this evening. Frosty A&W root beer was well worth a walk uptown and across the tracks.

Soon after lunch, the sewing group ladies began to arrive. "What's this I hear about free fish?" Mom filled up their containers while explaining the cleaning process. "Dip them in egg and flour and fry them in margarine. You can do a dozen at a time," Mom said to each new arrival.

And so smelt were distributed, feeding a multitude, like a story in the Bible — a North End version of the loaves and the fishes.

THE FAIR

There were times I thought about running away to join the circus. It didn't seem to matter that I had none of the skills; no trapeze or tightrope or acrobatic experience, nor the glamorous figure required for pony parades or for being tied neatly to a spinning wheel for knife throwers to aim at. Nor did it seem to matter that spinning or swinging made me nauseous, or that I feared large animals. The appeal of the circus was "being away", the gypsy caravan, carefree lifestyle, the promise of travel, the stories told at campfires, eating canned food... and the clowns.

One night at supper, Herman, a new VS'er, said something that got my attention because it brought to my mind *The Three Stooges*, who always made me laugh. Herman was a tall, lanky small-town Nebraska farm boy in his early twenties. He dressed in Wrangler jeans, pointy-toed cowboy boots and plaid shirts, ironed and neatly tucked in. His oval brass belt buckle depicted a rodeo cowboy twirling a lasso while riding a bucking bull. Mom said his face had good bone structure, and that his sky blue eyes dazzled the ladies. He had an "aw shucks" grin, complete with dimples. I had been harbouring a crush since his arrival and had to remind myself often not to stare.

"Last night, Larry Wilson fell flat on his belly. Boom!" Herman said, clapping his hands together. "Just like that. But before I knew it, he was up again."

Larry Wilson was a local drinker, an older, friendly one —always smiling as he bumped into furniture. I pictured him stumbling along James Street in scuffed up shoes, his prominent beer-belly hitting the ground first and bouncing him back up again like a Weeble, the momentum propelling him unsteadily forward. Larry and his fall focused everyone at the table on one conversation.

"With a curly wig and rubber ball nose he'd make a great clown."

"If he had the coordination required to juggle he could entertain here at the Welcome Inn."

"I wonder if he'd be able to remember any jokes."

I tensed, anticipating a speech from Mom or Dad about appropriate dinner conversations, specifically the one about showing respect for all of God's children, even clumsy drunks. But Dad was chuckling while Mom's eyes followed the gravy boat, seemingly worried it wouldn't last a full round of the table.

The topic of Larry's fall led into a jovial stream of circus and carnival tales, with the usual competition for airtime. When Mom asked for a count on who wanted apple pie or peach, Abe grabbed the floor.

Abe hailed from a small town in Ohio, this one just outside of Cincinnati. He bragged that he was more "cultured" than Herman since the town he came from was close to a big city. Abe was tall with longish black hair, parted at the side and slicked back. He wore black rimmed glasses and black boots that he said he needed for riding his motorcycle back home.

"I got busted when I was ten," he drawled. "I snuck around to the back of the fortune teller's tent to find out what went on behind the curtain. I's on my hands and knees, just got my head inside and I got grabbed from behind. That about made me wet myself." He paused, just long enough for effect, but not long enough for someone to start a new story. "Two fellas in uniform hauled me onto my feet... marched me back to the entrance... called for my Mom and Dad to come git me over the loudspeaker."

"How big a fair was it, to have guards?" Mark wanted to know.

"That whole fair would've fit into the vacant lot," he said, pointing to the south wall.

We never found out about young Abe's punishment because at that instant, Dad sprang out of his chair and yelled into the air, "Let's us have a fair!"

It was momentarily quiet. Dad stood staring ahead as though seeing a vision.

"A fair here?" asked Mom.

"In the vacant lot," Dad said, coming to and sitting down. "We can have our own fair!"

"You mean with booths and games?" Mom asked.

"Yes, we can do it here," he said.

And with building momentum, we shouted out ideas —hit the balloon with a dart, ring the bottle, wheelbarrow race, hot dogs, balloons, dunk tank, on and on we went.

"How about a basketball toss?"

"A white elephant table."

"We'll have a jail," Dad pronounced suddenly, waving his fork like a sceptre. "Put your friends in jail. Keep them in for a penny a minute."

"Put people in jail. What jail?" Jacob, one of the less talkative VS'ers, seemed alarmed. I too, was surprised.

"We'll build one," Dad said, narrowing his eyes, picturing it. "I'll bang some boards together. They can be taken apart when the fair's over."

"Don't you think people might get mad about being put in jail?" asked Ruth.

"We'll make the maximum stay ten minutes or so. That shouldn't upset anybody too much," Dad's eyes were sparkling, as they did whenever he was planning a building project; this provided justification for collecting broken furniture and a reason to take some good whacks with his hammer. "It'll be a money maker."

"How many will it hold?"

"I'll make it about eight feet long, six feet wide," he said. "That should hold around five or six at a time. There's no need to add a roof."

"How will you keep them in there?"

"We'll use a chain and padlock," he said.

I watched my sister's faces, wondering if they were believing this.

"What if it rains?"

"It won't," Dad said with military assuredness.

"Who's going to be the warden?" asked Mark. "Who does the locking up?"

"Oh we'll figure that out," Dad said with a wave of his hand. "But I guess someone will have to keep time and collect money."

The sisters and I volunteered to look for suitable warden attire in the basement. And while we still had the floor, I asked, "What are we going to give out for prizes?"

That caused a brief quiet, the obvious concern being how to give prizes without actually buying anything. Mom broke the silence. "Milkshakes!" she yelled. sitting up like someone poked her with a pin.

"We'll give milkshakes for prizes! That way I can clean out the ice cream freezer! And then I can defrost it! And shortcake! Strawberry shortcake!" I hadn't seen such enthusiasm since Dad pulled in his first load of smelts. "That way we aren't selling ice cream. We're giving it away!"

She continued, drumming her fingers beside her plate, "We'll need to get our hands on another blender or two."

"How about a cake walk?" someone asked.

This was getting better by the minute. I'd been a winner at a cake walk at the State Fair back in Oklahoma, and that day ranked as one of my best days, ever. I picked a perfect chocolate fudge layer cake rimmed with swirls and roses. When Mom sliced it after dinner, we crooned over the thick icing, sighing over how the edges hung over our saucers. Mom said there was enough icing on that cake for three cakes and called it decadent. I wasn't sure what she meant but I thought it was the finest cake I had ever tasted, though I didn't say it out loud, so as not to sound ungrateful for our regular desserts. Mom didn't give out seconds that night, saying it would keep us awake, but she did let us lick our plates.

"The sewing group ladies can bake the cakes," Mom was saying to Anita's raised eyebrows. "I guess that will be our next demonstration," said Anita. "I can't imagine that many of those gals know much about baking cakes."

"We'll teach them," Mom said.

"Will they know how to make frosting? What about decorating the cakes?" Anita had a queasy look on her face.

"We'll teach them," Mom said again.

After supper, the siblings and I gathered in the lot.

"How are we going to hang up all the signs?" I asked.

We looked back and forth between the two brick walls that formed the north and south borders of the lot." Maybe we can put them on posts and stick them into the ground," Mark suggested. "The ground's pretty hard," Ruth said, kicking with her heel. The ground was shiny and had the consistency of cement.

I knew that from trying to dig a hole the previous summer for a robin we found dead in the yard. I was sorry about the bird, since Mom said robins were one of God's magnificent creatures, calling them "a breath of fresh air" when they happened into our yard amongst the mangy pigeons and crows. The dead robin reminded me of the rabbits that had been trampled to death in Oklahoma and I thought it right to give it a proper burial.

I asked the siblings to help me prepare and attend a funeral for the bird, begging Ruth to do the sermon since she had the most experience with church things. She didn't want to, but agreed when I mentioned the magazines under her mattress. I planned to end the service by covering the burial plot with dandelion flowers, a miniature cardboard headstone I had made with "Blessed are the Meek" printed on it, and a cross made with Popsicle sticks.

At the agreed-upon time, we gathered in the lot with the usual impromptu crowd of kids, forming a circle around the dead bird. Ruth said, "Dearly beloved, we are gathered here to …" Then she gave me the nod to go ahead with the digging. I got down on my knees and started chipping away at the ground and in less than a minute, my red beach shovel was broken into two pieces. That made me want to cry since it was my last year's birthday present and had a matching pail. I knew I had been pushing too hard on it but kept going because of the funeral schedule and the seriousness of the situation.

Then I was sent to go find Mom's garden spade, which really wasn't fair since I'd already suffered the loss of my shovel, but they reminded me the funeral was my idea. Mom said she didn't know where the spade was since she had neither the time nor the place to plant a garden, and then she asked me what I wanted it for. I told her it was for burying the robin and she said I shouldn't be touching dead birds. I told her Mark had carried it by the feet. I had to search around in the shed and by the time I got back with the spade, most of the mourners had dispersed, including Ruth.

Even using the garden spade it was next to impossible to dig deep enough to bury the bird. I couldn't even scrape the surface enough to mound up enough dirt to cover it on top of the ground. Sarah said that was a bad idea anyway since a cat could easily get at it. By then, nobody cared about the funeral and it was hot, so I wrapped the robin in newspaper and three of us took it down to the Bay where we weren't allowed to swim due to the lack of supervision and the concern about toxic waste pollution from the steel factories. We buried the robin in the mud close to the shore without the sermon or the cross or the cardboard headstone.

"Where's the jail gonna go?" asked Tina, bringing me back to plans for the fair.

"Maybe there," Mark said, pointing to the shadier side of the lot. "We don't want the prisoners to bake."

"Would we give them stale bread and water?" Trudy asked.

"That's not a bad idea," said Sarah. "We'll have to ask Mom."

"The basketball hoop should probably go over there," Mark said, pointing to a spot on the Welcome Inn side wall where the ground was relatively level and freer of weeds.

"Where should the darts and balloons game go?"

"How are we going to attach the balloons?"

"We can't be throwing darts at the brick wall. They won't stick" We decided to leave that problem to the adults.

"The white elephant sale should go in the middle," said Ruth. "Then people can go around the tables." I wondered where we were going to get white elephants, and Sarah explained that "white elephant sale" was when people sold used stuff or stuff they didn't need any more. "But aren't we having races and stuff?" I asked. "Shouldn't we leave room for the races?"

"Oh yeah," said Ruth, rolling her eyes. "The races."

Mom decided the date for the fair should coincide with strawberry season since it was clear that her heart was set on strawberry shortcake. We had plenty to do in preparation; signs and posters were made and hung, tickets were mimeographed and cut, phone calls were made to canvass the church ladies for additional cakes, delegations recruited the appropriate person to man each booth, a search was made for a dunk tank. There were items to be priced for the white elephant table, and books to be checked for appropriate content. Mom was adamant that reading material coming through our hands should not contain un-Christian ideas, so any covers with lustful scenes or cleavage or guns were ousted. The "jail" idea was rehashed, and concerns were raised that it could be seen as promoting or making light of jail sentences. Dad stuck to his guns saying yes this, and yes that, but wouldn't it be fun, and he'd handle any "jail" concerns on fair day.

Another issue that came up for discussion repeatedly was where to hold the cake walk, the difficulty being that electricity was needed to play recorded music. Otherwise, when would the contestants know when to stop walking? The storefront wasn't good because that's where the ladies were selling food and Mom said it would be too loud and rambunctious. Running an extension cord to the vacant lot was not an option; it was just too far, and potentially dangerous. And the cakes might get covered in dirt or flies or get droopy and melt in the sun.

Holding the cake walk in the back yard behind the Welcome Inn was not a great option because it was so small and access was difficult, but in the end, that was the best option we had. We decided it could be done if we had one person, an adult of course, directing participants and spectators through the storefront, kitchen and rickety back porch and out the back door. After this debate was settled, we had to decide on the type of music required. We didn't think church music would suit the event or be a big draw, but Mom and Dad would not allow rock and roll. In the end, it was decided we would play records by The Irish Rovers and Peter, Paul and Mary and the soundtrack from Mary Poppins.

"What flavours of milkshakes will you make for prizes? I asked Mom one day leading up to the fair.

"Chocolate," Mom said without hesitation. "And tooty-fruity."

I should have known. These were Mom's specialty milkshakes. Her personal favourite, tooty-fruity, she described as "tropical" and "exotic". Her recipe for tooty-fruity shakes: blend any combination of fruit-flavoured ice creams, like strawberry or raspberry ripple, and/or sherbets together with an unspecific amount of overripe or "subject to freezer burn" frozen fruit, instant milk powder and water. It was rarely clear what fruit flavours you were actually getting when the shake was handed to you, but it was always fruity and sometimes came in a pleasant pastel colour. Any requests for specific flavours, like strawberry, were met with, "Try this, you'll like it better".

Here is Mom's recipe for chocolate milkshakes: blend any non-fruit-flavoured ice cream or combinations of ice cream with homemade chocolate syrup, instant milk powder and water. Eligible flavours included chocolate and vanilla of course, as well as English Toffee, Butter Pecan, Maple Walnut, Butterscotch Ripple and Rum 'n Raisin. Usually, they tasted good, and even if they didn't taste anything like chocolate, their brownish tones produced a convincing illusion. Many were delicious, but, like grandma throwing in a pinch of this and a handful of that, the truly great ones were rarely replicated. If you were really lucky, your chocolate shake might actually contain chocolate ice cream.

Mom's least appealing shake concoctions came from her need to use up bits of this and that, sometimes using combinations like Neapolitan added to Butterscotch Ripple. The absolute worst chocolate milkshakes were made with Rum 'n Raisin; the one flavour on this planet that I absolutely hated. I cringed when I saw a Rum' n Raisin barrel beside the blender, praying that mercy might come in the form of some new method or addition of a magic ingredient, something, anything, to disguise that taste. But regardless of what Mom added, the pungent essence of rum permeated the mixture, seeping into every frothy molecule, invading the milky substance, saturating its creamy essence and the surrounding air. No amount of chocolate syrup could mask the rum flavour; like fermented syrup, repulsively sweet, slimy raisins concentrating a sharp, unpleasant tang. No amount of blending could dissolve those raisins, and lumpy remnants muddied and clogged our drinking straws, making it difficult to suck in or blow out, neither choice a good one. Blowing hard got you bubbles and messy splotches on clothes or the table, and sucking till your cheeks hollowed to dislodge the raisin clog, unleashed an explosive stream, like a dam of the foul stuff bursting into your mouth. Better to drink right out of the cup. But what fun was there in that?

Like the biblical jug that never ran out of oil, our freezer never seemed to run out of Rum' n Raisin. Perhaps, the Dairy Rich delivery people shared my dislike for this flavour, taking out their aggressions by stabbing or bashing the tubs around, kicking them like soccer balls in the warehouse, rendering them unsellable. Or maybe nobody bought them and eventually they were returned, old and stale. Dad loved the flavour and ate bowls of the stuff, delighting in smacking the raisins around in his mouth, his face euphoric when he swallowed. I later wondered if this was a latent form of rebellion, an inadvertent way to consume trace amounts of alcohol after his strict alcohol-free Mennonite upbringing.

So Mom's milkshakes were anticipated with varying degrees of enthusiasm. And once the blender was out, we were committed to consuming whatever she whirled up. In her own quiet way, Mom made it clear she did not go to all the trouble of fixing milkshakes for ungrateful children who were picky about flavours and troubled about bits of raisin residue in their straws.

The Wednesday before the fair, the ladies group, having supposedly mastered the basic skills of cake baking and decorating, made biscuits for the strawberry shortcakes. Mom and Anita decided the ladies should bake the cake walk cakes at home, and recommended they work in pairs for support. If absolutely necessary, they could come and pick up a Betty Crocker cake mix. While the ladies rolled and stamped out the biscuits on the kitchen table with flour rimmed water glasses, Dad went on his monthly ice cream run, instructed by Mom to "get all the vanilla you can find", and to "be picky and bring home only prime stuff".

Mom wanted to keep the menu for the fair uncomplicated and economical, so the North End residents would get the most for their money. She decided that hot dogs, chili dogs, milkshakes and strawberry shortcake would be the main staples for the day. The shortcake topping would be "Dairy Queen" ice cream, made by throwing vanilla ice cream into a blender with a small dash of milk to give it that extra creamy, swirly look.

In order to get the required strawberries for the shortcake, Dad did his Dad thing, and arranged a morning of free strawberry picking with a nearby Mennonite grower.

"You can pick in certain rows that have been picked fairly recently," the grower told him. "You'll get the berries the pickers missed. You can keep all you pick, but you have to stay in your designated rows. And bring your own boxes."

The sisters and I begged to go but Mom said it wasn't worth missing school for.

Early Thursday morning, Mom drove a vanload of ladies to the strawberry fields, the ones that she could "drag out of bed".

On Friday, the Welcome Inn closed early. A crew was blowing up balloons for the dart toss, tacking them by the nub to a sheet of plywood, Dad and Herman and Abe joking about who had the most hot air. The entrance was crowded with kids pressing their noses and hands against the glass, as they always did when they weren't allowed in. Dad usually ignored them until it looked like someone might actually pass out from being smothered in the crush against the glass. Then he'd move toward the door and the kids would back away, but within minutes, they'd be back, squashing and smudging.

I wasn't good at blowing up the balloons, and so was not making "productive use of my time." Mom called me and the sisters into the kitchen to cull and cut strawberries. Then she brought out the biscuits. "We'll slice each one in half. At the fair, we'll serve shortcake with one biscuit layer for the kids."

"Why do the kids only get half?" I asked timidly, worried about not getting a large enough portion.

"Because lots of them will want just the strawberries and ice cream. I don't want to see a whole bunch of biscuits in the garbage," she said. "We'll give them half… minimize the waste."

"Maybe we should just leave out the biscuit," Trudy suggested.

"No. The biscuits are necessary filler," Mom was stern. "Without the biscuit, they'll want a larger portion of ice cream and more strawberries. Besides, we need the biscuit or it won't be strawberry shortcake." She continued, infusing each word with guilt, "The ladies group went to all kinds of trouble to make these." Then, more lightly, "They're proud of them. So...half a biscuit for the kids and both halves for the adults and growing boys like Russell Green. Slice them carefully, so they're even." She lined up the knife with the middle of the biscuit in her hand. "Like this."

Early Saturday morning, the dunk tank was set up and the hose turned on. Dad had said "no way" to setting it up the night before. "You never know what might end up in that tank," he said. "Better wait till morning. Even if it's not full, whoever's getting dunked will get wet."

"And the hose gets turned off before the fair starts. We don't need any mischief with spraying water," he said at breakfast. After that and a few other instructions, he got to work connecting the walls of the jail cell, the faces of the kids he recruited to hold them upright fearful and apprehensive as he whacked away with his hammer.

Dad's basketball hoop contraption was already up, installed soon after we moved into the neighbourhood. It was a free-standing movable structure, the hoop and backdrop supported with a tall post wired to a rusty metal stand he'd found in the alley. A rubber tire encircled the base as a protective barrier cushion so we wouldn't have to rush anyone to the hospital for tetanus shots if they misjudged their jump shots. The whole hoop unit wasn't very stable: dunking the ball and grabbing the hoop could turn out to be fatal, what with the rock solid dirt, broken glass, and possibility of being squashed under the structure if it happened to topple over. We often found the basketball hoop contraption lying on its side in the lot. It was fairly easy to stand back up, though too heavy for me to lift by myself.

Occasionally, Dad hauled his beloved basketball net into the garage for a week or two if he felt it was being mistreated. Sometimes it wasn't in use simply because none of our basketballs bounced, casualties of the rocks and glass that littered the ground. Dad bought a brand new basketball for the fair, saying the fair was an event worthy of such a purchase. "And," he said, "The clean shiny ball might attract customers".

Cakes arrived throughout the morning from the ladies sewing group, carried in ceremoniously at chest level like offerings to a king. Apparently decorating supplies had been given out, as all sewing group cakes, without exception, came frosted in a pale shade of blue, pink, green or yellow, and were decorated with sliced jujubes or the kind of coloured sprinkles you find on iced donuts. A few were embellished with attempts at swirls. Most were squat, some misshapen. Some looked good, but even those that didn't, at least had some candy to pick off.

Around 11:00, Mrs. Schmidt arrived with a dozen cakes donated by the Hamilton Mennonite Church ladies. Once all the cakes were assembled on the kitchen counter it was obvious which ones had been baked by which group. The Mennonite ladies' cakes were perfectly shaped, neatly iced and simply decorated. Some were made in bundt-cake pans and drizzled with a clear or creamy white glaze. Each one of the church ladies' cakes was covered in plastic wrap, toothpicks poking out strategically to protect the icing. None of the cakes from either group came close in quality, in my estimation, to my Oklahoma cake, but I figured I'd take a few turns around the Cake Walk just the same.

Trudy, Sarah and Ruth were in charge of the Dart Toss and the Ring-a-Pop booths. Between the three of them, they could take turns spelling each other off. I helped the twins put the pop cans in straight lines. We practiced tossing the rings, but I missed every time. Sarah ringed two but we said she couldn't take the pop.

The twins started to argue over where to place the skipping rope to mark the tossing line, so I left to look at the Hockey Shoot Station where Mark was taking practice shots with a rubber ball. Two large cardboard boxes stood in front of the net to serve as goalie. If the ball made it past the boxes, it was considered a goal...win a milkshake. The rationale for having a cardboard box goalie was that cardboard would be impartial to the person shooting, and not subject to serious injury. Two substitute boxes sat close to the net, in case someone dented or destroyed one or both of the goalie boxes, Mark told me, "with a wicked slap shot".

By 11:50, the dunk tank was full enough to cover my thighs, Pastor Heibert was entering the lot in his bath robe, the balloon covered board had been brought out and was being guarded by Jacob and a line-up was forming at the ticket table.

Dad got on the bullhorn and declared the ticket booth open. Mom sat at the ticket table collecting money and slipping extra tickets to the poor families and those with lots of children, which was just about everybody. Tickets were five cents each or 25 for one dollar. All events were priced in tickets, as were the white elephant items. The only cash item was the jail. Mom gave us each 20 tickets for all our helping, saying, "don't spend it all in one place, and don't buy back the same stuff we gave away" and "have fun".

Many of our neighbours headed directly to storefront, where food was exchanged for tickets, perhaps in order to be sure they'd have full stomachs before squandering their remaining tickets. Chewing on hot dogs and sipping from Dixie cups, they wandered back to the lot, some hanging back and investigating the booths from a distance, as though formulating a plan.

The jail was an instant hit, but it backfired a bit. Dad was a good sport during his first two jail terms. During the third sentence, he paced the four-step cell, making jokes with the other inmates through gritted teeth and yelling out new rules about "maximum number of jail sentences per person". In spite of his attempts to impose these rules, he was locked up again every time he was released, rounded up posse-style by the teenage "pool table rats". They clearly got a kick out of seeing his face between the jail boards and probably only hung around for that reason, and for the Basketball Shoot.

Herman was running the Basketball Shoot. Participants got three shots per ticket. Shooting two out of three baskets won a milkshake voucher. After locking up Dad for the second time, the pool table boys sauntered toward the Basketball Shoot, pushing at each other with attitudes of being way too cool to participate but wanting to be the first in line. Herman stood with one foot on the rubber tire base, firing the basketball from one hand to the other, a big grin on his face.

"From the looks of it, nobody in this crowd has a hope of winning a milkshake," he taunted them. "If you fellas want to see true NBA action, step back and I'll demonstrate."

"Hand over the ball," Tom Fletcher was standing at the front of the line, gesturing with both hands, his tone suggesting he had far better things to do with his time. "I'll show you how to shoot." Tom was sixteen, the oldest of the assembled. He had hair and sideburns like Mike Nesbitt from the Monkees and despite the heat, wore a denim jacket with too-short sleeves, the cuffs turned up to disguise this. A purple tie-dyed shirt, baggy cut-off jean shorts that reached his knees, black ankle socks and well worn sneakers completed his attire.

Herman faked three passes before he bulleted the ball into Tom's gut, making Tom double over, to which Herman laughed, mimicking a chimpanzee with some "oooh, oooh, ooohs" and scratching himself. While the other boys hooted and guffawed, Tom positioned himself, tilting his head to get his hair out of his eyes. I stood by the jail, focusing on Tom's pale legs so he couldn't accuse me of staring, like he did when we first came to Welcome Inn. I'd been the fool elected to try to deter Tom and his girlfriend from necking on the hood of the derelict car in the neighbour's back yard by staring at them out the kitchen window. The older siblings thought it would compel them to find another kissing spot, but all it had done was earn me the nickname "Eyes".

Tom got only one out of three shots, but seemed unruffled despite continued heckling. He gave Herman another ticket. "Technically, you should go to the back of the line, but since you're the first shooter of the day, I'll let you go again," Herman said. "The rest of you…one turn, then go to the back of the line."

Tom missed the first shot, claiming he got dirt in his eye, but made the next two baskets, smiling as he fired the ball back at Herman's stomach, cannonball style. Herman was caught off guard, which got the boys doing monkey imitations while Tom strode off to collect his milkshake.

Next in line was Tom's younger brother, Brian, a "real doll" in the looks department, with blue eyes and wavy blond hair parted at the side. He knew it too, judging by the amount of time he spent staring at his reflection in the storefront windows combing his hair. He kept a rat-tail comb in his back pocket and a pack of cigarettes that I never saw him smoke tucked in the sleeve of his T-shirt. Brian never said much; whenever we discussed the merits of the various boys we knew, we couldn't decide whether or not he had a "good personality".

Tom was a talker, but the biggest mouth in the group belonged to Glen Davidson, who stood behind Brian in line. Glen liked to sing when he wasn't talking, and his favourite song was his version of *You're Just Too Good to be True,* which began "I'm just too good to be true, can't take my eyes off of me," and continued in the same vein. Glen carried a white comb, brown between the teeth, which he whipped out flamboyantly beside Brian at the windows to comb his mouse brown hair, usually greasy with visible dandruff flakes. Glen was sort of cute but had acne and a paunchy waist. He was funny at least, and didn't mind when we watched the boys play pool in the basement, probably since we were an audience for his incessant chatter.

Bogdan and Marco stood behind Tom in the line-up, skinny twin brothers with a last name I couldn't pronounce. They made out okay with the rest of the group since they stuck up for each other and made snide comments to each other in Yugoslavian, which no one else understood. Another set of brothers, with crew cuts and prominent ears, Barry and Colin Gregg, brought up the rear. The Gregg brothers were accustomed to following in the wake of the other five, and were rarely given a pool cue in the basement, relegated instead to watch from the lumpy sidelines. In good weather, they played sidewalk hockey with Mark, talking "breakaways and slap shots" during the timeouts when they moved the net to let drunks or strollers go by.

Brian scored one basket out of three and went to the back of the line. Glen missed all three baskets. Likewise, the twins and the Greggs missed but seemed content to try again, returning to the back of the line. Tom strutted back with his milkshake.

I'd watched these boys shoot before and Tom was not one of the regular stars. Both Glen and Brian, usually accomplished shooters, were missing more than scoring, perhaps distracted, checking to see if girls were watching, wondering how their hair looked. The twins, too, missed most of their shots, claiming basketball isn't popular in Yugoslavia, and if there were a soccer net set up, they'd score some big points. The Gregg brothers were lucky if they hit the rim. Thus the boys monopolized the Basketball Shoot for the first half hour or so, stopping only to put Dad back in jail. Tom was having a stellar day, slurping down his third milkshake, perhaps motivated by Herman's goading.

After four unsuccessful attempts, Glen handed over his ticket to take another turn, then stepped aside to let Tom take his place. Tom, all smiles and fired up on chocolate, accepted the offer and won his fourth milkshake voucher, which he handed to Glen. One by one, the boys let Tom take their place in line, paying his ticket and letting him shoot. Tom, puffed up like a peacock, smiled as each boy returned, flaunting their milkshakes like Dean Martin with a martini.

Dad flagged me down from his cell as this was going on, his passion for principles clearly creating angst as he watched the boys fudging the rules. With his face pushed between the boards, he implored me to go round up some other kids to get into the Basketball Shoot line-up. I pointed out that kids were already congregating there; and they were, their noses slightly lifted as though drawn by the smell of success or chocolate. I sauntered back toward the hoop, not the least bit interested in doing his bidding, but by then, each of the boys had gotten a milkshake, and Herman told Tom to step back.

Herman drew another line in the dirt, about two feet further back. As though it were a dare, Tom got back in line, but the extra distance got him ruffled, and after missing a third consecutive turn he led the boys to the Dart Toss. Herman smudged out the new line with his boot and recruited the younger spectators.

Nobody interesting was shooting anymore, so I rounded up Tina and Carol to check out the Cake Walk. Peter, Paul and Mary were singing *Puff the Magic Dragon*, and it made me nostalgic for Mom's stories in the sewing room back in Oklahoma. The storefront was buzzing with activity, the ping pong table set up with hot dogs and condiments, a crock pot of chili and two rows of milkshakes. Mrs. Schmidt from the church and Mrs. Davis from the sewing group were aproned up, collecting tickets and supervising the food. We walked by into the kitchen, where Mrs. Bagley stood at the stove stirring a pot of chili next to a pot of boiling wieners. Mom stood at the table, pouring a fruity liquid into one blender with sticky-looking hands while Mrs. Bishop filled Dixie cups with the peachy coloured contents of the other blender.

"How is it going out there?" Mom asked in our direction.

"Good," I said. "Dad's in jail again."

She shook her head and pushed a button on the blender, creating a sound like a chainsaw.

"We're going to the Cake Walk," I yelled at her but she looked mesmerized by the whirling.

In the backyard, a walk was in session. Larry Wilson was in the game, tottering from one numbered plate to the next, a concentrated smile on his face, the other participants moving robot-like in a circle, some hop-stepping to the next spot as though crossing a stream. The circle was flowing around six-year-old Annabelle Bishop, who was crouched on circle number two, her arms circling her knees. When Puff the Magic Dragon was ceasing his fearless roar the music stopped and Abe yelled, "Stand on your circle!" even though everyone already was. "And the winner of this lovely chocolate cake is standing on circle number." Abe reached into the bucket to remove a numbered ping pong ball. "The winner of this beautiful cake is standing on circle number four!" It was Angelika, sister to Bogdan and Marco. She yelped and went running to claim her cake.

Most of the participants stayed for another round, Abe walking around collecting tickets. "We have four empty circles," he announced, so the three of us moved to occupy one of the vacancies. Annabelle stayed put.

We played two rounds of Cake Walk, both times stepping around Annabelle Bishop. When Abe announced the winning number, all participants' eyes turned toward the winner, which happened to be Carol. Carol's reaction was contrary to the usual excited and gleeful standard that most winners exhibited. She looked alarmed, as though she had been caught stealing. Her eyes grew wide, her body stiff. Abe had to coax her off her circle to collect the cake. She continued to look completely stunned until she was actually holding one of the

Mennonite church ladies bundt cakes. It appeared to be lemon, bits of yellow peel in the glaze. She stared at it for a moment, smiled, then quickly turned and left the yard, scurrying through the kitchen with her cake. I followed, curious to see where she was going with it, wondering if she would show anyone. I followed as she bee-lined through the storefront, holding the cake in front of her chest, and watched her take it in the direction of her home without once stopping or turning her head. She came back a while later with glaze on her chin.

The Dart Toss booth was popular with the younger set. Balloons were tacked to a board, with coupons stuck behind about a third of them. If you threw a dart that broke a balloon and exposed a coupon, you won a strawberry shortcake. I took three turns and won a shortcake, which I had for lunch before getting a chili dog. Sarah told me to bring the shortcake back to the Dart Toss booth in order to encourage others to participate. The shortcake was scrumptious, the combination of strawberries in their prime and the swirly vanilla ice cream absolutely delicious. Even the biscuit was good, though I was glad not to have to eat two halves.

Beside us was the Ring-a-Pop booth where the objective was to loop a can of pop, which in those days, were way smaller, with the kind of rubber ring used to seal preserving jars. The prize was the can of pop. Dad had picked up three cases of the bargain brands; Cola and Bubble Up and Root Beer. Ring-a-Pop proved harder than it looked because the ring had to slide down the can to rest on the ground, so the tossing angle was strategic. For the most part, the rings got caught between the cans, and no one was eager to throw rings for nothing. Nor did it seem that anyone was eager to win a can of bargain brand, solar-heated pop. So Ring-a Pop turned out to be one of the less popular stations.

The Dunk Tank wasn't as popular as anticipated either. There was no great drama or splashing to witness since the water wasn't very deep. It was fun to see about once. Reverend Hiebert was in there for the first hour, wearing an odd looking bathing suit, knee length and fitted. He was an excellent sport, waving from his seat on the bench, gesturing to entice people to take some shots with the baseball, and making an effort to splash around in the less-than-waist-deep water for a few extra seconds each time he was dunked, sort of like a Mer-man.

Jacob took the second shift in the tank. He sat completely still on the bench with his hands under his thighs. Whenever he was dunked, he bounced straight up onto the bench with little fanfare. We all wanted Dad to take a turn sitting on the bench, but he insisted he was needed for overall supervision, and to deal with problems around the jail. And to his credit, he did end up spending a great deal of time supervising the jail—from the inside. When Jacob's shift was over, the booth pretty much closed down. There weren't any line-ups and too many boys were bothering Dad by asking if they could take a turn in the tank.

The races were scheduled to start at 2 p.m. Mom and Dad figured this was about midway through the fair and kids might be getting rambunctious. Dad finally got out of jail. Freeing the other two inmates, he padlocked the door and pocketed the key. The races were strongly endorsed by Mom —something free and fun for everyone, a way for kids to run off some energy and get some much-needed exercise. I figured I might have a shadow of a hope of winning a race since most of the kids didn't have running shoes, and if they did, they were usually the wrong size or had no laces.

I didn't win any races, nor did I come close. Amazing how many kids can run fast without proper shoes. The VS'ers tried to encourage the adults to race, but the only responses were sarcastic comments from some of the men, the women hiding behind spouses or fleeing to the storefront.

Somebody, I never really found out who, decided to sell shaving cream pies in disposable aluminum pie plates for the purpose of shoving into faces. That was popular for about three minutes, and was shut down after a few nasty incidents. The white elephant items were all dispersed; sold or given away. Cuts and bruises incurred from the races were tended to with Band-Aids, rubbing alcohol and mini-sized milkshakes.

Dad dismantled his jail cell without much comment. Mom was able to defrost the freezers. I don't know how much money was made; maybe none. I don't think it mattered. I didn't hear about the money, but that fair was talked about for some time. The event somehow christened the vacant lot, giving it legitimacy. From that day, the lot stayed cleaner and became a gathering spot, as though the ghosts of the booths and jail were there, drawing people together.

GOODBYE SUGAR FACTORY

One day, a team of public workers put up boards along the sidewalk across the street, completely enclosing the old sugar factory. Not long after that the demolition crews arrived with their giant wrecking ball. Over the next few days, Dad stared from the street or the second storey windows, his arms firmly crossed, shaking his head in frustration, "They're smashing up perfectly good windows. All that lumber going to waste! The things I could do with those building materials. The absolute waste and senseless destruction!"

My blood pressure, too, was elevated, but not for that reason. I had visions of that gigantic ball breaking free and crashing through one of our windows like a catapulted bowling ball, then collapsing the floor to crush anyone below. But that didn't stop me from watching, amazed by the operator's ability to swing and aim that ball in the right direction. I was mesmerized by the slow-motion flow of events; the initial smash of contact, the shudder of walls cracking and splintering, sometimes remaining erect while waiting a second hit, the cascading down of massive hunks of brick and concrete into a heap of rubble, emitting giant white billows of dust.

My sisters, Mark and I watched from the street or the upstairs windows, and if no adults were present, one of us performed the "Death Scene". At the precise moment when the wrecking ball hit a wall, the performer clasped their chest as if they'd been shot, like they do in a wild-west shootout. The eyes shot open wide, facial expression becoming one of horror; gazing downward in mock disbelief at blood-soaked hands while strength drained from the body. Hands moved back to clutch the heart while the shoulders and knees swayed, the performer making a gallant effort to remain standing as long as the still-standing, shuddering concrete across the street. Then, to coincide with the fall of the building... the crumple. The buckling knees, the eyes closing and breath escaping in moans of agony, then a final gasp and careful fall onto the couch as the walls collapsed. Followed by a round of applause for the prone player while the dust settled across the street.

It was more comfortable performing the Death Scene upstairs where the player could collapse onto a couch or chair, but not as much fun, as it attracted only the siblings who were in the vicinity. In the vacant lot, however, we could stand back behind the player and get a better view of the collapsing building and the Death Scene which, when performed well, was spectacular. But falling on the hard-packed litter-strewn ground was not fun. Falling dramatically also attracted neighbour kids, who sometimes participated but were apt to tell, and that was bad because Mom and Dad didn't approve of this activity. They'd witnessed one episode and told us not to repeat this game, so we had to be very careful. We knew that if they caught us, their knowledge of our actions would support their theory that watching *Bonanza* and movies like *The Magnificent Seven* was influencing us in a negative way, encouraging us to participate in games they deemed violent, even if we were only pretending.

Eventually, the wrecking crew was gone, leaving a space across the street like a crater and a gap in the sky. I was relieved, having been somewhat unsettled by the constant noise and destruction. On the other hand, I enjoyed watching that creepy wreck of a building meet its cruel fate; retribution for causing me nightmares. The workers moved to the next block and then the next, tearing down houses to open up an additional area of two city blocks. After that, the whole thing was boarded up and sat idle for some time.

"They're building a housing development over there," Mom said one day. "Low income housing. We've applied for a spot." I gave her a questioning look but she ignored it.

I thought about sleeping in the place where the sugar factory stood and wondered if those nightmares might come back.

FILM NIGHTS AND GO-KARTS

One of Dad's many "special arrangements" was with the Hamilton Board of Education. Once a month, Dad was able to borrow films from the School Board office, et voilà: "Film Night" was born, a tradition begun, with an old reel-to reel-projector showing movies on a pinned up sheet.

On Film Nights, the ping pong table was folded up and all available couches and chairs, even from the kitchen, were moved into the storefront facing the sheet in a movie theatre arrangement. The unwritten rule was that age determined who sat where. The older you were, the better your choice of seats. Us youngsters, sat on the floor. Movie nights were generally quite fun and took the residents of the North End to places they would otherwise never see. Due to the large numbers of people there, heckling and peanut-gallery comments during the movies were not uncommon. As long as people weren't obnoxious or inappropriate, things just carried on.

Once in a while, an individual or small group was asked to leave. It was more apt to happen when teenage boys were in the audience. If one was being a smart-aleck and was asked to leave, depending upon his place in the hierarchy of said group, he might exit taking the whole herd with him, which was fine. They'd already paid their ten cents, and that left more of the popcorn for the rest of us, except as a rule, they didn't eat the popcorn. That would mean they'd have to uncross their arms or take their hands out of their pockets.

The admission fee included a paper lunch bag of popcorn. In those days popcorn was made on top of the stove and popped in vegetable oil. Due to the large crowds and the vast amounts of popcorn required, the popcorn was made in a huge stock pot that ended up burning on the bottom. Try as whoever happened to be popping the corn might, the popcorn always had a tinge of scorch-taste about it. The pot ended up permanently blackened on the inside and would never quite come clean despite numerous efforts, and there was always the smell of burnt popcorn in the air.

Movies were approved by the Board of Education, so we never saw anything too racy or thrilling, mostly documentaries and Canadian films, National Audubon Society and the like. There were lots of films about birds and pond life, that I thought were boring and had to be careful not to "spotte", lest I be asked to leave. Now and then we saw something really good, like *Paddle Me Home* and *Cosmic Zoom*. Sometimes we even got half-naked tribes dancing around fires or cartoons. Since there was no movie theatre in our neighbourhood, these nights were popular, if not for the movies, then for the in-between times, when the films were being rewound onto their original reels, times for people to chat and visit and just enjoy being out on a Friday night.

One night, several boys left midway through a film and stood outside the storefront making all kinds of racket. Dad was still stewing the next morning at breakfast. "Those boys need something to do," he said. "They need a project that interests them...I'm thinking of trying something out, but we'll need to do it on Saturdays during the day because we need to be able to work outside." Mom's expression was a mixture of curiosity and trepidation. "What are you thinking of?" she asked.

"Go-karts," he said.

"Go-karts?" she replied.

"Yes, go-karts," he said. "We'll build them." With that he began eating his porridge with fervour, his face taking on a look of creative zeal while he swallowed and chewed.

"I'll go have a look in the shed," he said, scraping his bowl. "See what I've got in wheels and piping material for axels."

"Can I make one, too?" asked Mark.

"Sure," Dad said. "You can help me make a prototype."

"What's that?" I asked.

"Oh, it just means we'll build one so they know what we're talking about," he said. "Then we can test it out, too. See how she runs."

Dad and Mark spent the better part of that day in the garage. First, they needed to do an inventory...look for what was available to build the things. Just before supper, we were allowed in to look at their progress on the prototype.

I was rather disappointed, actually. All they had was a long thick piece of wood with a shorter piece nailed on midway back for the seat. There were little wheels on the front and two bigger ones on the back.

"How does it go?" I asked.

"Someone has to push it," Dad said. "One guy sits on the seat to steer and another runs behind with a pole. Pushes him along."

Dad was smiling, "It's not finished yet, needs a place for the feet, and a rope to steer from the front, and the front wheels need to pivot." He was obviously pleased with the strange contraption, a word Mom used to refer to most of Dad's gulch-pile projects.

I didn't say any more, wondering why anyone would want to do that, especially the pushing part. "Nice," I said, then went back inside. I was also thinking "I hope Dad isn't too disappointed when the boys sneer and turn up their noses."Little did I know the effect some junky wheels and lumber scraps can have on a group of boys.

Dad brought the thing into the storefront the following week. He might as well have brought in a Stingray convertible with the attention it drew. Within minutes, the prototype was at the centre of a ring of boys, all standing around as though watching Ford unveil the first Model T. Dad stood quietly, holding onto an old broom handle like Moses with his staff. The boys "oohed" and "ahhhed", making boy-comments about how the thing was built. The timing of the unveiling was perfect, after school on a Thursday. When two boys asked to try it out, and then several of the boys asked if they could build one, Dad said, like it had just occurred to him, "How about coming Saturday morning and we'll see what we can do," and without having to suggest any "club", since some of the older boys hadn't joined Boys' Club simply because it was called one, a different club was born. Dad seemed to know not to give it a name. It was called "just come on Saturday morning," and only boys were allowed.

I think Dad was just as excited as the boys were. Perhaps more so, since it gave him reason to go scouting for more wheels, pipe and other appropriate go-kart material. "I'll need to scrounge," he said, like he was off to a gold rush. "Old baby carriages, wagons, lawnmowers... for the wheels... Maybe I'll try the dump. I bet they have all kinds of stuff there."

Building go-karts turned out to be a hit with the neighbourhood boys. It was so popular that Dad split them into a morning and afternoon group. The older ones wanted to come in the mornings, maybe to get first dibs on good wheels. Many of the afternoon boys were young and needed help, and it just happened that several older boys volunteered to help in the afternoons. That worked out well, because no one was standing around with their hands in their pockets, making snide remarks and snickering. Except Dad now and again, but only in fun, since he was letting the boys do the work, supervising and assisting only when necessary.

As work on the speed machines progressed, boys started to bring stuff to embellish their go-karts; license plates from old cars, pieces of chrome, emblems and the like. Carol and Jeanie came around from time-to-time, and we lingered on the sidelines watching. The karts-in-progress were looking much more impressive than the original prototype, which ended up being a piece of lumber with four wheels and a rope attached to the front wheels in a loop to steer. One of the boys built his kart with a front end in the shape of a barn to cover his legs and attached a steering wheel from an old car. Another kart had the seat built up so that it looked like a wheelchair, with larger wheels in the back. That one looked dangerous. Another sat low on the ground with a box to sit in, open at the front. I would have chosen to ride in that one had anyone asked, which they didn't.

As the boys hammered and painted, they began to talk about how they would race the karts when they were finished; who would push whom and with what kind of pole. They test- drove them in the vacant lot, but the distance was short and the ground surface uneven. They wanted to race on the street, but Dad told them "no way". They tried the sidewalks but cracks and curbs cramped their style. Sidewalk racing simply didn't satisfy their thirst for speed, and it frightened pedestrians, many of whom had choice words for the cruising boys. Dad had to intervene. He told them he'd do some thinking.

A few days later, Dad reported back to the boys that he'd organized a go kart race at one of the parks. And apparently there was such an event, but it seems I didn't go. Mark told me later about the winners and losers, the thrills and disappointments and some of the malfunctions under stress, karts crashing together and getting jammed, wheels falling off, and one veering off in the wrong direction. "It was great!" he said.

The following Sunday, the phone rang. A very distraught woman claimed a group of boys were racing go-karts down the hill past her house to the park by the bay. Apparently, they were not only disrupting traffic, but causing a situation that looked very likely to result in serious injury to themselves or others in the vicinity. I knew this hill, having walked up and down it many times to play down by the bay. It was long and steep. While I pictured the go-karts careening downward, crashing into cars or plunging into the murky bay with a giant splash, Dad got in the van and drove off. When he returned, he said the go-kart project was over and he'd get the boys involved with some other tasks, like building bird houses.

GRADE FIVE

I had a new teacher for grade five, fresh out of Teachers College. Mr. Carlisle was tall and stocky with a scar across his chin that made his handsome face look rugged. He greeted us with a scowl that would have made him look like a buccaneer, had he not been wearing a short sleeved plaid shirt, red tie, and green corduroy pants that were a little too long. He sat us in alphabetical order and glared and/or yelled if someone talked during lessons or in a line-up. He unsettled me to such a point that I would not speak about him at home, fearing Mom would prod for details and phone the principal. One good thing about the situation was that he also scared Darlene and Tammy; they hadn't yet found a way to harass me in the grade five classroom. Another good thing was that our class was really big, so his yelling and glares were diluted amongst the many bodies.

I dared not talk about Darlene or Tammy at home either. I knew exactly how that would be managed. Dad would quote some inspirational scripture about "loving thy neighbour and doing good to those who persecute". Beyond that, I imagined Mom arranging a meeting with each set of parents, showing up with a plate of squares and an invitation to Bible study, so their families would become Christians and we'd all like each other. Instead, I counted on my "look" of distain and nonchalance and kept out of their way, certain that at some point, the venom would spew.

So once again, I was both nervous and thrilled about going to school. Thrilled that Liz Harrison was in my class. And Joe Arcangelo. The two most beautiful people in the school. My guardian angels Rita and Sophie were also in my class, and that was a huge relief to me. Patricia and Beverley were there, too, and that was good. We stood together in a circle each recess, and soon Faye and Karen joined us. We were finished with skipping and Jumpsies. Standing in circles worked well for me, since while I was looking into the circle I could avoid the challenging glares of the witch hags.

In class, I could watch and dream about what life would be like if I could be Liz or if I could speak to Joe Arcangelo. Joe was taller than the other boys, with sleek, shoulder-length black hair, deep brown eyes with lashes like Bambi, and extraordinary cheekbones. I could've just stared at either Joe or Liz all day and been perfectly content.

During the second week of school, Mr. Carlisle gave us our first big homework assignment: to colour and label a map of Canada. "Use pencil crayons," Mr. Carlisle almost shouted, startling several of the girls, "A different colour for each province... but not black or brown or blue. He paused. "Blue," he paused again, scanning the room for attentiveness, "is only used for large bodies of water." He glared, giving us time to grasp that idea.

"Label each of the provinces neatly on horizontal lines. Name the two oceans and the Great Lakes." He began to pace, barking like a drill sergeant. "You will use a pencil and a ruler, and colour with pencil crayons. Ensure correct spelling and use of capital letters. See that your pencil crayons are sharp, and colour neatly. Marks will be deducted for incorrect spelling. Marks will be deducted for incorrect labelling or incorrect use of colour. Marks will be deducted for incompleteness, messiness or handing your map in late." He faced us, hands on his hip.

"You may take an atlas home," he said in a tone implying privilege of the utmost magnitude. "Which, I expect you will take proper care to return in its present condition. You have until Friday to complete this assignment." He crossed his arms, "Any questions?"

I don't know what possessed me. Suddenly, my hand was up.

He nodded at me. "Will there be marks deducted for that, sir?" I asked.

"Excuse me?" he asked.

I was momentarily stunned, realizing I had spoken out loud. He gazed intently at me, leaning slightly forward. I forced my most polite voice and stammered a bit, "For...for returning the atlas in a worse condition." I made myself breathe. "Will there be marks deducted for that?"

His mouth started to open slowly. Then he made an abrupt turn to face the chalkboard. Grabbing a piece of chalk he began to write, jabbing so forcefully his chalk broke and a piece went rolling along the floor. As he continued to write with the broken piece, a few kids laughed. He wheeled around, his face reddening.

"The first person in each row, step forward and get enough maps for your row. Last person, hand out atlases. You can get started," he said more quietly. He sat down at his desk and began writing.

I worked on the map when I got home from school, thinking that not starting it might induce a nightmare. But I couldn't find a way to label the four tiny East Coast provinces or to get the word "Saskatchewan" to fit inside its borders. I called Sophie. She said she'd call Rita. Then I asked the twins but their suggestions didn't sound right. So I coloured all the water blue.

The next morning, five of us huddled on the playground. After everyone said, "I don't know," regarding the labelling question, Sophie started breathing heavily and said, "Erica's looking at us." I kept my eyes down and made a wish that Erica's father would be fired from his job and have to move to one of those tiny East Coast provinces. And then I hoped the wish would not be recorded as a sin.

After another night of phone calls and no answers, we decided the only course of action, other than risk failing grade five, was to talk to Mr. Carlisle. The girls said I had to ask. I made Rita go with me. We approached Mr. Carlisle just before lunch.

"Sir," I said. "May I ask you a question?" He nodded, his expression not changing.

"Some of us are wondering how you would like us to label the small provinces on the East Coast. None of us can print the names that small." I paused. "Should we use abbreviations?"

"Have a seat," he said, getting up. He cleared his throat to get the attention of the rest of the class. "Some of you are wondering how to label correctly," he said, actually speaking nicely. "This is how you manage the small provinces." He rolled down the map of Canada. Taking his yardstick he drew a horizontal line on the chalkboard beside the map, and printed Nova Scotia neatly on the line. He turned to face the class. "Now, use your ruler to connect the name to the province, using an arrow." He showed the class by holding the yardstick in front of the map, pretending to draw along the edge with the chalk. He looked at me. I nodded and smiled. He smiled back.

I was pleased with my map until I saw some of the others. Beverley had outlined and shaded each province a different colour, with a box around each label. When placed beside hers, mine looked "amateur", a word Mark often used when he watched hockey or talked about some of his classmates. I caught a glimpse of Liz's map as she handed it in. It was hard to see details in such a short moment, but it looked perfect.

Mr. Carlisle collected the maps and announced that we would be learning about Canada. "Now that you have completed the assignment, you should be familiar with the names of the provinces and territories that make up our country. Can anyone name the capital of Canada?" He stood with his arms crossed, angled toward the map as though talking to it, then turned back to face us, perhaps because of the silence. No hands were raised. He gazed at us as he might gaze at a troubled sea. No one moved.

After a long uncomfortable silence, I raised my hand and he looked at me. "Ottawa, sir."

"That is correct," he said, pointing to Ottawa on the map. "Has anyone ever been to Ottawa?" he asked in a way that suggested his belief that the answer would be no. I hesitated, but raised my hand again.

"And what did you see there?" he asked.

"We watched the changing of the guards at the Parliament Buildings," I said. "We didn't go inside because of the line-ups."

"Did you take any pictures?" he asked. It sounded like he wanted some verification.

"Yes sir. We have a picture of one of the guards on a stretcher." There was laughter from the class. Mr. Carlisle was looking at me with some interest, so I continued. "The guards were dressed in red coats and fur hats and leather boots. One of them fell over. There was an ambulance right there, and the attendants walked right by us with the stretcher. Dad said it was probably heat stroke. I think Dad took a picture of the buildings, too, sir."

Mr. Carlisle stood in the stance that was becoming quite familiar to us, one hand holding his chin, the other hand nesting an elbow. He was quiet.

"Can anyone name the largest city in Canada?" he asked suddenly.

Eric put up his hand, "Ottawa, sir?"

"Ottawa is the nation's capital, but is not the largest city," he said.

He looked around. No hands. I put my hand up.

"I believe it is Montreal," I said.

"That is correct," he said. "Has anyone been to Montreal?

No hands. Mine went up slowly.

"It was on the same trip as when we went to Ottawa," I said. We were actually going to Expo, sir."

"And what impressed you about Expo?" he asked, sounding genuinely interested.

"The kangaroos," I said. Some kids laughed but he didn't seem to mind. "They were in a pen outside the Australia pavilion. One of the mother kangaroos had two roos in her pouch. And we all liked the Man and His World Pavilion."

He smiled then. "I was there, too," he said. "I saw those kangaroos."

"I am curious," he said, surveying the room. "Have any of you been to the West Coast?" He touched British Columbia with his pointer stick. Seeing no hands, he returned his attention to the map, relaxing his posture.

"I was just there," he said in a dreamy drone. He began to speak, not in choppy barks, but in a voice full of awe and wonder, gathering momentum like Dad did when he was getting into the meat of a parable. He spoke of snow covered mountain ranges extending as far as the eye could see, of trains that snaked along mountain ledges in and out of tunnels blasted through rock, of ferries transporting a parking lot of cars, of miles of sandy beaches, of surfers, of orcas travelling in pods, their dorsal fins emerging in smooth arcs, of salmon the length of his arm, totem poles the height of buildings, canoes the length of transport trucks, and cedars so thick in circumference, it took more than ten people joining hands to circle them.

"I met people who liked to go skiing in the morning and play golf in the afternoon," Mr. Carlisle said excitedly, though he didn't strike me as the golfer type. At that point, he paused as though waking up and pointed to Alberta so suddenly, Sophie gasped. "Has anyone been to Alberta?" he asked.

Liz slowly raised her hand.

"What did you see in Alberta, Liz?" he asked.

"The Calgary Stampede, sir," she said. Her voice was gentle and sweet.

"What did you think about the Stampede?" he asked, clearly thrilled to have some fresh participation. The sound of Liz's voice drew Joe Arcangelo's head upward to look at the map, a change from his typical defiant slouch.

"I liked the chuck wagon races... and the barrel races," she paused, but he seemed to be waiting for more information. She continued. "My mom didn't like the calf roping. She said it was cruel. And I covered my eyes when the cowboys got thrown off the bucking bulls". A few laughs. He moved the pointer to Saskatchewan, looking for any acknowledgment of travel there. Liz's hand went up. Then Manitoba. Liz's hand went up again.

"We were driving, sir," she said. I laughed and took the opportunity to look around. Joe was smiling in Liz's direction.

Mr. Carlisle lifted the pointer and plopped it onto Newfoundland. No hands went up. Then Nova Scotia. My hand went up. He pointed to Prince Edward Island and I kept my hand up as he continued to New Brunswick. "We were driving, sir," I said and everyone laughed including Mr. Carlisle as he looked at the clock. I looked at Liz. She smiled at me.

"Was this all on the same trip as Montreal and Ottawa?" he asked.

"No, sir," I said, caught unaware and blushing. "When we were at Expo, my parents got excited about going to see the Atlantic Ocean, so we went last summer."

"What did you like about the Maritimes?" he asked.

I didn't want to say how I loved the *Anne of Green Gables* play and the tour of her house, which would have been a sure invitation to Darlene or Tammy to comment on Anne's sucky house and her stupid freckles and braids, so I quickly blurted, "I watched my mom eat a lobster in Prince Edward Island. She told us it was one of her dreams to eat a whole lobster."

"Did you have one, too?" he asked.

The bell rang for lunch.

"No sir, Dad said we could only get one. The rest of us had French fries. Mom offered us each a bite, but we all agreed ahead of time she should eat the whole thing, so her dream would come true."

Mr. Carlisle smiled and dismissed us with a wave of his hand.

MY NEW KILT

By the time I got to grade five, I could feel extra rolls here and there due to excessive consumption of Eskimo pies and various ice cream desserts, but, wishing to remain in denial, I avoided the scale and silently promised to cut down on my secret forages to the freezer. I wasn't exactly fat. "Chubby" was the word I overheard when Mom was catching up with old friends on the telephone.

It was around this time that I developed a major aversion to kilts— the current fashion rage. My sisters all wanted one. And so did I, at first. We showed Mom pictures from the Eaton's catalogue, knowing she'd balk, calling the prices "ridiculous", which meant buying them was simply out of the question. Our tactic was to convince her to sew us each a kilt. She sewed our outfits anyway—she might as well make us something we would actually want to wear. The oldest three started our offensive by pointing out that kilts were "respectable" (one of Mom's favourite words) garments, worn at an acceptable length—just hitting the knee. In addition to that important consideration, kilts were made of "durable" (another favourite word) fabric. And because kilts were the cultural uniform of Scotland, they were unlikely to ever go out of fashion.

"And we can wear them at Christmas," said Ruth. "Then we won't need new Christmas dresses." We hadn't had new Christmas dresses for three years, but Mom seemed to take this as a valid point.

"Lining up plaids is tricky," Mom said, pursing her lips. "Especially, with all these pleats. And I'm not sure how to sew this fringe along the front panel. Or whether or not it's just frayed fabric."

"And we can wear them to school," added Trudy. "You like it when we wear skirts to school. And they're warm for the winter."

"Wool is expensive, and tricky to wash," Mom said. "And it shrinks."

It wasn't looking good. "Expensive" and "shrinks" were two major strikes against our campaign. "And if they're not lined, they'll be itchy. And that's a lot of extra work. I never line your skirts," she said.

"You don't need to line them," I said. "We'll wear them with leotards so they don't itch."

"Well," she said finally, looking at our downcast faces. "I'll look at a pattern, to see whether I think I can manage. If it's a lot of extra work, I won't. But if we do go ahead with this, I don't want to hear any complaints about being itchy...or hot."

I heard no more about it until later that week when I came home to find Mom leaning on the windowsill in the kitchen, seemingly mesmerized by something in her hand. At first, I thought it was a book, but when I realized what it was, I had to stop myself from grabbing the pattern envelope out of her hand. I gazed enviously at the pencil-drawn girl standing tall and slim in a white blouse, green and navy kilt, and matching tam.

"How does it look?" I asked, already envisioning myself slim in my new kilt outfit, made with the same blue and green plaid fabric as the model.

"It's not as bad as I thought," she said.

"May I look at the back?" I asked, after about three seconds, momentarily deluded into thinking that holding the pattern might transform me into that model. Liz had a kilt. She was even prettier than the model. I wanted to know how long it might be before I'd be wearing my new kilt. I was thinking that the number of pattern pieces required might give an indication, but I didn't want to ask and risk irritating Mom while she was still "mulling it over".

As I took the pattern from Mom, my eyes scanned the tiny diagrams. The shapes of the pieces were fairly straight-forward; mostly rectangular panels. That shouldn't be too hard, I thought. But then my eyes were drawn upward, and suddenly my elation was sucked from my body as though an invisible vacuum had been turned on. Standing by the kitchen window, sunlight shining on the pattern, I read and reread five words, bolded and in capital letters, running across the top of the pattern: "NOT SUITABLE FOR CHUBBY GIRLS". I couldn't move, the five words echoing inside my head like a gong.

Immediately, I felt the words fly off the pattern and into the airwaves; the message floating out and broadcast to the world, KILTS ARE NOT SUITABLE FOR CHUBBY GIRLS, KILTS ARE NOT SUITABLE FOR CHUBBY GIRLS... these same words running across billboards where slogans disappear at the other end to return again like a dog chasing its tail, appearing on buildings, in shopping malls, and across the front pages of the newspaper. It became quite clear in that moment. I knew that if I wore a kilt, people would laugh, point fingers at me, and whisper behind cupped hands, "See that chubby girl over there —the one wearing the kilt? Doesn't she know better???"

The three vile hags were going to make mincemeat of me. Despite the protection of the Circle, one or two, and sometimes all three of my tormenters, still found me or caught my eye, when I was alone in the washroom, the hallway, the library. It didn't happen often, but when it did, it still got me right in the gut. The looks. The comments. Usually, related to my attire. And for the life of me, I could NEVER think of and deliver a response that would make me appear anything but lame and spineless.

Mom was pulling the pattern out of my hand, interpreting my numb unresponsiveness as an indication that I was finished with my perusal. "This really isn't so very difficult," her voice sounding faint and far away. "It's really just one long piece of fabric that you wrap around and fasten with just a simple button and this huge safely pin, here." She was pointing at the picture. "Looks just like a diaper pin. And the fringe doesn't look too complicated. I think I can manage."

She looked at me. My mouth opened and closed.

I was now faced with a new and desperate mission—to find a way for Mom *not* to sew me a kilt. I needed to proceed with caution because I knew Mom would think the reason ridiculous if she knew it. Mom didn't conform to the opinions of so-called fashion experts. She didn't give two hoots about current fashion trends or fashion etiquette. She wouldn't let five words stop her from sewing a kilt for a chubby girl.

No. Mom would do it to prove them all wrong. "NO," she would say, "My chubby daughter looks wonderful in her kilt. And it doesn't matter what her clothes are like... she's beautiful on the inside." I would become the centre of a human rights issue: "Everyone should

have the right to wear a kilt, regardless of race, religion, gender, size..."
which would draw even more attention to me being chubby in a kilt,
since she might feel compelled to defend me openly, without
provocation, on any occasion I might choose to wear it.

Over the next few days, I began to make comments about not
needing a kilt after all; that the material *was* awfully expensive... that a
kilt really wasn't practical for summer, that kilts were really meant to
be worn by men. I even said kilts might not be as popular by the time
she was finished, a remark Mom took as an insult, thinking I was
questioning her ability to sew efficiently and motivating her to steam-
roll ahead with plans for our fabric shopping-spree.

After that, I knew there was no hope. So I pretended to be happy in
the fabric store, smiling as we browsed the plaid section, nodding as
my sisters made their selections. It didn't take me long to decide. I
chose the least conspicuous and darkest plaid I could find.

Mom started making the kilts. I watched her progress and prayed for
diversions, any emergency situation that might distract her during
sewing time, but it seemed as though the more I watched and the harder
I concentrated on her not working, the more her proficiency improved. I
prayed she would make a mistake when cutting mine, so the plaids
wouldn't line up. I prayed the scissors would slip and she would cut a
gash that would ruin the entire piece of fabric. I prayed that a plague of
moths would come and eat holes in mine during the night.

One day, they were finished. Mom assembled us girls in the living
room, where the kilts were ordered in a pile from oldest to youngest. I was
glad she hadn't piled them from largest to smallest, in which case mine
would have appeared sooner in the handing-out ceremony. Mom held
each of them up, waiting for the recipient to step forward. Not that this
was some sort of unveiling; we'd all had turns trying them on as she was
working, but Mom wanted to make this a special event, and rightly so. She
had worked hard, and all her daughters had a brand new kilt. And truly
the atmosphere was jubilant, since everyone was excited. Except me.

I put mine on with a forced smile, knowing I must look hideous. The
others looked great, especially Tina, who looked cute in anything, and
the twins, with their white knee socks and penny loafers. But they were

slim. Kilts obviously were suitable for SLIM girls. I pretended to be happy and endured the silent humiliation, for surely they knew. They had to know. Those words had yet to be spoken out loud, but I knew they all knew. Surely, they were looking at me in my kilt with pity.

Yet no one seemed concerned that I was breaking a very important fashion rule. They were more interested in who would get to wear their kilt first. We couldn't all wear our new kilts on the same day in case we might be mistaken for the Lennon Sisters, so they were pleased when I volunteered to go last. That would give me more time to diet.

I ironed the kilt carefully and thoroughly, thinking that might help flatten and alleviate any extra bulk. I mentally rehearsed comebacks to the barrage of insults I would certainly have to endure on the playground. I practiced my "look". I prepared statements like, "Yah, I didn't really want this kilt, but my Mom wanted me to have one." And "My sisters all wanted one, so I had to get one, too." And "It probably doesn't look that great, but I have to wear it once in a while." I looked in the basement for a long dark cardigan that might hide my chubby hips, but found only pilly, grandma sweaters that emphasized my bulgy parts.

When it was my turn to wear my kilt, I passed, announcing I would wear it to church instead of school so I could show my friend Dorothy. The others kind of took me for "stupid" on that one, since Church was open territory, meaning it wouldn't have mattered if we all wore them at once. Mennonite moms were familiar with sewing bulk quantities for their families, and sisters often arrived in matching outfits that sometimes included mother/daughter variations. As it turned out, that Sunday we all wore the kilts.

I pretended to be excited as I showed off my kilt to the church ladies who'd all been sharing kilt-making tips during the past weeks. Mom received kudos in the vestibule on her sewing prowess and I was grateful I could wear it here, where I didn't have to worry about being openly mocked.

I told Dorothy about the "not suitable for chubby girls" thing.

"Where did it say that?" she asked.

"On the back of the pattern."

"You shouldn't worry about that anyway," said Dorothy. "Because you're not that chubby."

"Does it make me look fatter?" I asked.

"No, it doesn't make you look any fatter," she said.

"But I still look fat," I said.

"You don't look fat," she said.

"But I look chubby," I said.

"You look fine," she said.

I wasn't sure whether to believe her because she was my friend. And I knew she was way nicer than some of the girls at school. After that, on two occasions, I wore my kilt down for breakfast on a school day, and then, as though suddenly remembering that it was a gym day, dashed upstairs to change, timing my departure with care and running out the door so as to make it to school right on time in an outfit that was suitable for chubby girls.

I managed to avoid wearing it to school until a day in mid November, when I arrived at school in my kilt just as the bell was ringing. I walked up the stairs looking straight ahead, praying no-one would notice. Keeping my eyes down as I hung my jacket on a hook outside the classroom, I saw two pairs of familiar, dread-inducing shoes step into my viewing range.

"Hi Mary," Darlene said to the side of my head. "I see you got a new skirt."

"Oh why, why, why," kept going through my head. "Why do they torment me?"

"Yah, I see you got a new skirt, Mary," Liz's wonderful voice came from behind me. I turned around with a relief that suddenly turned to worry. Liz might think my kilt was all wrong. My bowels felt liquid.

"It looks really good," Liz's voice was kind and sweet. "Did your Mom make it?"

I nodded at her. Hagitha and Bagitha stood watching, tongue-tied. "She did a great job," Liz said, smiling. "I like the colours. I think I like your kilt better than mine." I smiled, not able to speak.

"Hey," she said. "Can you wear it again on Monday? I'll wear mine, too. Then we can look alike." She walked beside me into the classroom, asking me if I had blue knee-socks to wear on Monday. It felt like one of my fantasy dreams.

On Monday, I wore my kilt. I even borrowed, well, kind of borrowed without asking, some blue knee-socks. I was praying Liz had been sincere in her request and that she would arrive in hers, since as per usual, Mom was right with respect to the itchiness, a condition not so noticeable with leotards. But the discomfort would be worth it if Liz thought it was a good idea. And so would the repercussions of my taking Sarah's only good pair of knee-socks, possibly stretching them out so they'd be baggy and slide down her slimmer calves. On Monday, Liz arrived in her kilt and she stood beside me in the Circle on the playground. She whispered in my ear that she'd ask her mom if I could come to her house for lunch.

During the time that I was fixated on the kilt problem, Mr. Carlisle began to "let down his hair". Literally. His hair was growing. You could no longer see his ears or the back of his neck. Perhaps the short cut he'd sported in September was for the benefit of the job interview and general first impressions.

The growth of Mr. Carlisle's hair seemed to be coinciding with a general mellowing in the classroom. He still maintained discipline in a rather militaristic fashion, but the atmosphere was more relaxed. He told us excellent stories and we laughed a lot, but no one gave him any guff. Anything he didn't want to handle resulted in a visit to the principal's office and three visits resulted in "the strap". That happened two times I knew about in grade five. And we knew. Everybody knew when someone got the strap, the news reports and updates sweeping through the student population like a swarm of bees.

All it took to solve most classroom issues was a long stern glare from Mr. Carlisle, always delivered with his familiar crossed-arms stance. That pretty much took care of fights, arguments, inappropriate behaviour or laziness.

It wasn't hard to distract Mr. Carlisle from a lesson so he would tell us a story. He even told us about the scar on his face, saying it happened during a hockey game, when he got hit with a slap shot that knocked him off his feet and left a red spot on the ice. Growing up, he said, his mother had all kinds of dreams for him to play for the Maple Leafs, but she wasn't so keen on that after picking him up at the hospital with stitches across his chin. He laughed after he told us this. I wasn't sure which part of the story was funny, but I loved any diversion from spelling or math.

Mr. Carlisle brought in artifacts to accompany his lessons; a rattlesnake skin, a chicken skeleton, rocks that sparkled, arrowheads. He even brought in a bunch of eggs to hatch in an incubator. I was loving school again despite the kilt and the three hags. He'd show us slides of old European cathedrals, then put on a Rolling Stones record while we painted or drew. He seemed to recognize my enthusiasm for art, but, since my talent did not equal my exuberance, rather than comment on my mediocre creations he would choose mine from the eagerly waving hands responding to his call for volunteers to wash paintbrushes and baby food jars.

I loved being able to tell some new tidbit at supper that Mr. Carlisle shared with us, since none of my siblings had him for a teacher, but it was frustrating that I could not brag about listening to the Rolling Stones. If I mentioned that, Mom would have been on the phone with Mr. Becker before dessert was served.

My revelations had to wait until bedtime." Guess what music we listened to in art today?" I asked into the air after Mom said good night from the bottom of the stairs.

"*The Sound of Music*," said Sarah.

"No," I said.

"*Chitty Chitty Bang Bang*," said Tina.

"No."

"Just tell us," said Trudy. "I'm not guessing all night."

"*The Mennonite Children's Choir*," said Ruth in a zombie voice.

"No, someone good," I said.

"Just tell," said Ruth. "Or we'll be up till midnight."

"Just one more guess," I said, trying not to beg.

"Okay, the Beatles," said Sarah all sarcastic.

"No. Mr. Carlisle says the Beatles are overrated. We listened to the Rolling Stones." I was trying to contain my delight.

"No you didn't," said Ruth. "You don't even know who the Rolling Stones are."

"Yes I do," I said, now almost bursting with pride.

"Okay, name a song," she said.

"Jumpin' Jack Flash," I said. I almost said, "Don't tell Mom" but I didn't. Since I'd stopped joining them on their late night excursions over the roof to watch the drunks, I had that as leverage. Of course their hidden stash of reading material also came in handy.

There was no response, which I took as a compliment.

LUNCH AT LIZ'S

Occasionally at recess, I thought about Lily, looking with nostalgia at the hopscotch courts. When Lily moved, I gave up reading as a pastime. I just decided I wouldn't do it anymore, which may have been my subconscious reaction to her leaving. The only things I was moderately interested in reading at home were the magazines my older sisters kept hidden. I could decipher the text, but couldn't comprehend the meaning. When I asked Ruth about words like "rape" and "lesbian" she said to ask Mom, or wait until I was older. At school during "quiet reading time", I stared at the page of the book I was supposed to be reading and fabricated stories in my head. I did the same at home.

Liz was now a regular in our Circle, and she always stood beside me. Liz also stood beside me in the line-ups and whispered things in my ear, but she never said the words "book" or "library". I'd noticed none of the Circle girls talked about books or reading. But one day at recess, my attitude toward reading changed. Very quickly, I might add. Sophie pulled a magazine from underneath her jacket. "Who do you think is cuter?" she asked, opening the magazine at hip level. "Bobby Sherman or Jack Wild?"

The girls crowded in while Sophie displayed the centre poster, oohing and ahhing over the two full-page glossy, colour pictures. I was quiet, feeling stunned, never having seen a magazine like that. I'd seen both of the boys on television, so I knew who they were. Bobby Sherman was the hunky, stuttering, younger brother on *Here Come the Brides*. Jack Wild had a dumb show with a big puppet, but he was also starring as the Artful Dodger in the movie *Oliver*. Bobby looked adorable in his photo, smiling with his crinkled eyes and dimples. The vote was swinging in his favour. "What magazine is that?" I asked.

"*Tiger Beat*," Sophie said and added, "I like Jack Wild. Look how his hair falls over his eyes!" Sophie started turning pages, pausing at a picture of a singing group.

"That's *The Cowsills*. The cute one is Barry," said Patricia. I thought all of them were cute. "Where did you get the magazine?" I asked.

"It's my sister's," said Sophie.

"Here comes Mrs. Blackburn," hissed Rita. Sophie immediately shoved the magazine inside her jacket. At the same time, the Circle appeared to inflate as we all stood upright in unison.

"Hi girls," Mrs. Blackburn said, leaning over Sophie's head, briefly examining each of our faces. "Are you talking about boys?" Patricia began to bounce on the spot, so we followed suit, hugging ourselves as though we were cold, but really to distract attention from the bulge in Sophie's jacket. Rita started to giggle, which set off a chorus of nervous laughter. Mrs. Blackburn appeared to take this as an affirmative answer to her question, and seeing no cause for concern, turned to leave. "Keep it clean," she said over her shoulder.

"What would she do if she saw the magazine?" I whispered.

"Oh, she'd take it away and my sister would kill me," said Sophie.

"How much is that magazine?" I asked.

"I don't know, but I better not look now," she answered.

"No, better wait till later," said Rita.

On the way home from school, I bombarded Sophie with questions. Among the answers were; thirty cents, the Portuguese grocery store up the street, once a month, another magazine called *16*, and no, she'd never seen the Beatles in one, and no, to my request to borrow it. "Come over to my house tomorrow," she said. "Then we can read it." And thus began my new passion for reading, though it was limited to *16* and *Tiger Beat*. From that day on, my life had new meaning and purpose: I needed to find funds to buy these magazines and a way to get them into the house.

In Monday's line-up, Liz told me her mom said I could come for lunch sometime that week. I felt like the heavens were smiling on me. "I'll ask my mom," I said, trying not to gush.

Mom questioned me about where Liz lived and her background, of which I said little in the two days leading up to the day I was to go to her house. She must have sensed my eagerness and delight and she might have wondered why I was suddenly so anxious to go to school and wear my kilt.

Liz lived in the opposite direction from the school on the fourth floor of an apartment building with neatly mowed grass. We took the elevator. Liz used a key to unlock the door to a small hallway next to the living room and took off her shoes. As I bent down to untie my laces, I saw her mother lounging on a sofa, wearing a frilly housecoat trimmed with pink fur. Her hair was teased at the back and flipped up around her shoulders. She was reaching toward a tray on the coffee table, holding a fancy little knife.

"Hi sweetie, how was school?" she called out, slicing into a wedge of cheese. Before Liz could answer, she said, "You must be Mary," and placed a cheese slice on her tongue. I nodded and smiled, feeling like I was in the presence of Cleopatra or someone equally majestic, taking in her red polished nails and elegant chewing. In our house, eating cheese like that, without bread or a cracker, was almost a sin.

"Make yourselves some lunch," she said, looking back toward the television.

"*Another World,*" whispered Liz, as we moved down the hallway. "She only talks to me during commercials when *General Hospital* is on." When we reached the kitchen, she asked, "What would you like for lunch?"

I shrugged, not knowing what to suggest. Liz smiled and said, "We can have soup and crackers... or..." while she opened a cupboard laden with cans, several with the famous label *Chef Boyardee*. I tried not to look as though I'd just stumbled upon a gold mine. I dreamed of tasting *Chef Boyardee* every time that bell tolled on TV, envying that lucky Italian kid shovelling spaghetti and meatballs into his mouth. "Would it be okay to have some *Beefaroni*?" I asked.

"Sure," she said. "I like that, too."

"You can sit down," she said gesturing toward the table. "I'll fix it."

I sat down and looked at the kitchen, tidy and modern, white cupboards, grey and black tiled floor, silver chrome canisters lined up from large to small. I watched Liz pulling out a pot, working the electric can opener, going about her tasks with confident and efficient movements in her navy stirrup stretch pants and white sailor boy blouse.

"I make tea every day for my mother," she said. "Would you like some, too?"

"Sure," I said.

When we sat down to eat, Liz asked. "Do you like any boys in our class?"

"Not really," I said. "But I think Joe Arcangelo likes you."

"Yah. He asked me to go steady," she said.

"At school?" I asked, and when she looked confused I said, "Did he ask you to go steady at school?"

"No. He phoned me," she said.

"Wow," I thought. A boy phoning. And not just any boy. Joe Arcangelo.

"What did you say when he asked?" I was absolutely floored by this revelation; excited to be in the presence of a budding romance AND eating *Beefaroni*, which had to be one of the best things I'd ever tasted. I was using all the restraint I could muster not to gobble, and to show neither envy nor shock at the idea of "going steady" in grade five.

"I told him I'm not sure," she said. "I said I would think about it."

"Does he want you to go out on a date?" I asked, completely unsure what going steady meant, wondering if there might be kissing. Imagining Dad's reaction to a boy phoning and asking me to go steady. Or Mom's.

"Not really a date," she said. "He phones some nights."

"WOULD you be allowed to go out with him if he asked you?" I asked.

"I'm allowed to meet him at the park on Friday," she said, "as long as Karen comes with me." Karen was her friend in the apartment downstairs, and two years older. "But I have to be home at 8:30."

I decided not to ask any more questions. I had as much information as I could digest.

"Who do you like?" she asked.

Obviously, I couldn't say "Joe Arcangelo". I looked toward the window.

"Who?" she asked, eagerly. "Come on Mary...I told you."

"But I'm not going steady," I said.

"But who do you like?"

"Okay... I like Donny Osmond."

"That doesn't count," she laughed. "Everybody likes him."

And I wanted to say, "And every girl likes Joe Arcangelo," but I didn't.

"What about Kevin Matters, or Jeff Hillier?" she asked.

"I dunno," I said, feeling privileged for this rather intimate conversation, yet uncomfortable, too. "I don't think my parents would let me go steady."

"Oh," she said.

"Is the tea ready?" Liz's mother called. "Thank you Lord," I thought as Liz stood up.

"One minute," Liz called back. "Do you want biscuits today?"

"Two, please," her mother yelled back. "No, make it three."

"Have some biscuits," Liz said and put a small plate of biscuits on the table. She poured me a cup of tea.

"Cream and sugar?" she asked.

"No thank you," I said, not wanting to delay the delivery.

"I like mine plain, too," she said and turned to assemble the tray with the teacup, saucer, spoon, sugar cubes, tiny cream pitcher and three biscuits. She lifted the tray and left the room looking like a miniature airline stewardess.

I dipped my biscuit in the tea and tried to imagine a different kind of life...phone calls from a boy like Joe Arcangelo...clothes from Eaton's...a mom who watched television during the day...fancy store-bought biscuits...*Chef Boyardee* in the cupboard.

DRAMA CLUB

Ever since I was very young, I dreamed of becoming a famous artist, but no talent was evident in my paintings or drawings. I did not, however, work at it very hard, perhaps believing that talent should develop without effort and that fate would make it happen. By the time I was in grade five though, I was beginning to face facts: when it came to artistic ability I was average, if not slightly below.

So, just after Christmas, when announcements started coming over the P.A. about "exciting opportunities to join the Drama Club", I felt a stirring inside. Maybe *this* was where my artistic talents lay. I decided to give the dramatic arts a try, thinking I might actually be quite good, what with all the practice I had acting brave and confident at school. My decision may also have been an attempt to delude myself into thinking I'd look ravishing in the spotlight. And it was influenced by the fact that I'd been totally enthralled with a play I'd seen in grade four. I'd seen plays before, but that one, a musical production at the Junior High School, was, by far, my favourite. Leading up to it, my sisters had been coming home, singing the songs so often I knew some of them by heart.

"It's about a boys' school and a girls' school that are side-by-side," Ruth said. "But there's a massive hedge between them so they can't see each other. And it's against the rules for the boys and girls to talk to each other, so they never do...because the headmaster and head mistress are strict about the rules."

"Then, one day, a boy gets in trouble and cuts a hole through the hedge because he's mad at the headmaster," added Trudy. "And, of course, he sees the prettiest girl from the girls' school. And, of course, he falls head over heels in love with her."

"Don't tell her," Sarah said.

"Yes, tell me," I pleaded.

"Well, he tells the other boys and then they look, too," Trudy continued.

"Stop telling her," Sarah said. "You'll spoil it."

"I won't tell her the good parts," Trudy said.

"What good parts?" I almost shrieked.

"And the ending," she continued in her taunting voice.

"What happens at the end? Tell me!"

"There's kissing," Trudy grinned.

"Trudy, stop it!" said Sarah.

I kept begging for more details, which just made them laugh.

"What's all this nonsense about kissing?" Mom asked one evening. No response.

"Ruth, what is all this business about kissing?" her voice was becoming a bit shrill. "It's the play, Mom. In the play, there's a bit of kissing," she said. "It's just a play."

"I'm not sure students should be doing a play with kissing," Mom said. "How old are these kids?"

"My grade. And there's not that much, just a bit," Ruth said.

"I've seen kissing, Mom," I said. "Tom and Rhonda kiss in the back yard all the time. And there was kissing in *The Sound of Music*." That seemed to throw her off balance.

"Just don't get any silly ideas in your heads about kissing," she said. "Kissing is for grown-ups."

In the weeks before the performance, I asked countless questions... when Mom wasn't around.

In the auditorium on performance night, I sat on my feet, trying to make myself taller, nervous Mom might suddenly decide to take us home at intermission if there was too much kissing. Throughout the first half, I tried to contain myself, fearing my zealous attention might get Mom into a flap. I sang along quietly, wanting the play to go on and on but dying to see the ending. At intermission, I tried not to look too star-struck or excited about the romance, and most importantly, not ask too many questions lest Mom drag me home.

I was so grateful when she led us back to our seats for the second half of the show, I almost cried. I sang along some more, loving every minute. And then came then the final scene. I'd thought of all kinds of possible endings, but I didn't see this one coming. The prim headmistress and the gruff headmaster enter the stage from opposite sides, seemingly on solitary evening strolls. Upon seeing each other, they turn away all huffy, and in doing so, discover two of their students kissing in the background. Their huffiness escalates to rage.

Fists clenched, they advance on each other, looking ready to throw punches, meeting at centre stage, eyes blazing. They remain face-to-face for several seconds, chests heaving. And then their breathing slows and deepens. Their shoulders relax. His jaw slowly drops as she raises one hand to unbind the tight bun at the back of her head while removing her glasses with her other hand. As she tosses her head, her hair cascades around her shoulders and his arms reach toward her, suddenly circling her waist as though a giant magnet were drawing them to her. Their lips connect and they are kissing. I slap my hands on the arms of my chair, holding my breath, disbelieving. The kissing continues while I let the air out of my lungs and the entire cast comes onstage for the finale. My hands sting from clapping.

Before school on the morning of the first Drama Club meeting, I joined the Circle on the playground. "Guess who else is going?" Patricia said. This question was directed to me.

'Who?" I asked.

"Darlene," Beverley said and immediately looked down.

"No way," I said. I simply could not imagine anything so ridiculous. Darlene was not the type to take directions and follow the lines in a school play. I just couldn't see it. It finally occurred to me that they were kidding. "Oh, very funny," I added.

Mr. Becker, our principal, was also in charge of the Drama Club. He stood in front of the rows of benches that were set up on the gym floor in front of the stage, looking a bit like Dad did when he was ready to preach. "I want to congratulate you all for having the courage to join the Drama Club. It takes a special kind of person to get up on stage," he said.

I sat on the third bench feeling content for having taken this step in spite of the fact that none of my friends had come along, and was raising my apple to take a bite, when I saw Darlene. I stopped moving, the apple taking on the weight of a lead ball. I brought it down to my lap while she sashayed forward in a blue flared mini skirt that emphasized her long, lean legs. I felt the world sway as she approached the front bench, where she did a half spin that lifted her skirt enough to billow as she sat down.

A wave of nausea passed through me as I focused on Mr. Becker, who was giving a synopsis of the play, *Heidi*. I felt like I was breathing underwater. "Why, why, why", kept going through my head. "Why does she have to be here? Why would she think she might like this? Why does she think she can act?"

Mr. Becker was talking about how hard he expected us to work. "Good," I thought. Darlene didn't strike me as a hard worker. "Make her go away," I prayed. "Go away, go away," I said over and over again. "Auditions and play rehearsals will begin this Thursday at lunchtime," Mr. Becker continued. "On Wednesday, I will tell you more about the characters and their roles. Yes Brenda?"

"Can I be Heidi?"

"We will have auditions to find out who will get what role," said Mr. Becker.

"What's an audition?" was called out from the back. Mr. Becker demonstrated his annoyance by exhaling at the ceiling.

"An audition is when you try out for a part," he said, after staring briefly upward.

More hands shot up. Darlene was leaning forward. I prayed she was thinking this was a complete waste of time and wasn't about to return. But I knew that whatever happened, I would suffer. If she came back, I'd have to prepare for a weekly onslaught of nastiness. If she didn't, she'd torment me about the stupid boring waste-of-time Drama Club play for idiots.

"If you want to audition, bring your lunch on Thursday. Please pick up a permission form on your way out." We were dismissed.

Thursday morning at recess, I was starting to get a headache. I had seen Darlene's lunch bag. I considered not going to the lunch meeting, but, on par with my fear of Darlene, was my fear of Mom's reaction to the news of my quitting before I even started. If I showed up at home for lunch, she'd march me right back to school, and who knows what she'd say in front of everyone. Mom was delighted by my announcement that I was joining the Drama Club. Now, I regretted my enthusiasm.

At lunchtime, I walked to the gym as though gravity were pulling at my body. I walked with Cathy, a classmate whose mother attended sewing class at the Welcome Inn. I didn't hang around with her because she needed to watch over her many younger siblings and step-siblings on the playground. I couldn't quite figure out the reason for Cathy's interest in being in a play: maybe it was to postpone going home once a week, but I was grateful for her company. She was chunky, too.

We sat on a bench midway back, facing each other, our lunch bags between us. I busied my hands, setting up like a picnic, anticipating *her* arrival. I stared at the "real chocolate chips" Mom had used for baking the cookies she packed, splurging to celebrate my Drama Club debut. Happily, the benches around us were filling up. "Darlene must be in the bathroom," I thought, "adjusting her plastic barrettes." She finally waltzed in and took a seat at the front.

Mr. Becker poked his head in several times, leaving his office to make sure we weren't playing cootie tag or throwing garbage through the basketball hoops. After we had time to eat he came in, walked to the front, and began. "Drama Club," he said, "is for students who know to behave." He continued his spiel with a pep talk on proper behaviour that went on for a while.

Just as my patience was wearing thin, Mr. Becker began to talk about each of the characters in the play, after which he announced, "Those of you who wish to play one of the lead characters will need to audition. The auditions will be on Friday at recess. Only the students who are auditioning will be allowed to attend."

I wanted to play the part of Heidi's friend Clara who was in a wheelchair, partly because she was the co-star, but mainly because she'd be sitting for most of the production. I liked the idea of performing from a seated position because then the audience wouldn't see my thighs. I even figured that, due to the Swiss Alps being cold, I might be allowed to wear a flannel blanket over my chubby legs and hide them completely.

"How many of you will be trying out for the lead roles?" he asked.

My hand went up hesitantly. I looked around. About half the kids had their hands up, including Darlene. "Good," said Mr. Becker. "This should work out well. You can find a partner and practice reading together."

During afternoon recess, Darlene caught me at the washroom sink, appearing behind me suddenly. "Which part are you going to audition for?"

"I'm not sure yet," I answered. Darlene's eyes narrowed, clearly doubting me.

"What about you?" I asked, since she was still there and I didn't want to answer any more questions and get tangled up in more lies.

"Heidi's friend," said Darlene.

That hit like a slam. Despite my first thought, " like they are going to pick you, the Queen of Snotheads, I don't think so," her announcement made my stomach clench. For the millionth time I wanted her to go away. To disappear.

After school, on the stairs going down, I heard Tammy's voice right behind me. "I hear you're in Drama Club," she said, in her sweet-as-syrup-voice. "Have you decided who you're trying out for yet?"

"Go away, go away, go away," was all I could think.

"Are you going to try out for the lead role, or girl in the wheelchair?" she asked, beside me now.

"I might," I answered, turning my head without looking into her eyes.

"Really," she answered coolly. "I think they'll pick slim girls for those roles."

My hand gripped the rail while my pace slowed. Tammy flounced past me down the stairs.

At supper the next evening, Mom asked if I was ready for the audition. My throat had a lump and I'd been seriously thinking about not going for a lead role. Maybe it was true. Maybe they would only pick slim girls. "I think so," I answered quietly.

"You should practice some more tonight," said Mom.

"I will," I went to my room after supper, supposedly to practice, but I lay on the bed dreaming about being Julie on Mod Squad, first wearing a mini dress, then changing into stirrup pants for a slim walk-around.

My voice was shaky during my audition. Darlene tried out after me. After the auditions, I tried not to think about the play and avoided any talk about it. None of the neighbourhood kids cared one iota about the play or had anything to do with it. Some of them could barely read, and many would have trouble getting their moms to sign a permission form for anything at all.

On Tuesday, a meeting was called at recess to announce the roles. Of course, Jennifer Kelly got the role of Heidi; everybody expected that. I sat, ready to nod and smile when I accepted the co-starring role, so I was completely floored when they announced that Darlene got the part of Clara. All of the energy left my body and a lump formed in my throat. The rest of the too-long meeting was thick and blurry.

On the way out, Mr. Becker stepped in front of me and quietly asked me to come to his office. I racked my brain to figure out what I had done to deserve not getting the part and being summoned to the principal's office.

When we were both sitting in his office, Mr. Becker said he wanted me to be the understudy for Darlene's part. It meant that if anything should happen to Darlene, if for example she got the flu on performance night, I would need to step in to play her role. I would also get the role of the housekeeper, which had about eight lines.

"We chose you for the understudy because we know you can handle it," he continued. "If you would like to have the role of the girl's mother, you can have that role instead. Think about it and tell me tomorrow. Being an understudy is a very important job."

"Is there an understudy for the role of Heidi?" I managed to ask.

"Actually no," Mr Becker said. "But that is because Jennifer is in grade six and has experience with being in plays and in a choir. And she has had almost perfect attendance since she started school."

I almost expected him to add, "And Jennifer can yodel."

He smiled at me. I was dismissed.

Math was well under way when I returned to class. As soon as I sat down, Liz passed me a note. "Meet me at lunchtime by the tree." She always dotted the "i" in Liz with a heart.

Kids were looking at me when we were dismissed for lunch, so word must have gotten around. I kept my face indifferent, asking questions to avoid having to answer any. When I got downstairs, Liz was waiting. "What happened?" she wanted to know. I told her about my conversation with Mr. Becker.

"What are you going to do?" she asked.

"What would you do?" I asked her.

"I don't know," she said. "I'm too scared to be in a play. I couldn't learn all those lines."

"Sure you could. You'd be great," I said, just because I admired her so. "I have to tell him tomorrow."

"Tell me before you tell him," she said. "See you this afternoon."

I was thrilled. This time I could pass her a note.

I knew I would take the role of the housekeeper and be the understudy. If I played Darlene's mother, I'd have to spend a lot of time with her, and I needed that like I needed fleas in my hair. I wrote a note to Liz during Science. She turned and smiled at me after she read it.

At our first rehearsal, Mr. Becker announced that I was to be Darlene's understudy, going on about how important a job it was. Hands began waving, all eager to know about who else would be an understudy. "I need people who can memorize quickly," he said. "I'll keep my eyes and ears open."

I got a few admiring looks, so I didn't have to hang my head in complete humiliation for only getting the cranky old housekeeper role. Darlene looked concerned, as though she were wondering whether being an understudy was better than having the real role. I could feel her glaring eyes while I looked nonchalantly elsewhere.

I didn't have much to do at rehearsals. Mostly, I watched and listened to Darlene, who was doing a much better job of memorizing her lines than I was. Since she was so busy playing opposite Jennifer, she didn't bother much with me, and for that, I was grateful. She hadn't been saying much to me in class either, probably because Liz was usually close by. But she still made me tense anytime she was within speaking distance. I avoided eye contact and, at recess, I kept myself surrounded.

It was at a rehearsal in early March that my life took one of those significant turns. I was taking the first bite of my sandwich when I felt Darlene's presence. I always knew when she was swooping in; a wave of unsettled atmosphere would suddenly surround my being, making my muscles tense and sending a chill up my spine, even in summer heat.

I looked up to see Darlene on the next bench. Cathy and I locked eyes in disbelief while Darlene settled in. I struggled to swallow, looking at my lunch; salami sandwich, an apple and a homemade, lightly charred cookie, thinking it might be the target of her nastiness. Darlene placed her lunch bag on the bench and smoothed her skirt, clearly planning to stay awhile.

My mind began swirling, then snagged on a memory from a recent Sunday School class. We were learning the Golden Rule; "Do unto others as you would have them do unto you." I suddenly realized that I had little to lose, since no matter what I said or did, I would inevitably be insulted. Maybe it was a deep burning need to be a martyr, or maybe a vision of David fighting Goliath inspired me. I don't know why or how I managed, but I spoke before she did.

"You're doing a really good job," I said, looking directly at her.

"Thanks," she said. "My mom's helping me learn the lines."

She pulled a sandwich out of her lunch bag and started to peel off the plastic wrap. Cathy watched warily, expecting a pounce.

"Is that a salami sandwich?" Darlene asked, nodding toward my sandwich.

Ah, there it was. Yes, she would begin by ridiculing my food. I imagined she'd start with the stinky salami and move on to the crispy dried up cookie.

"It is," I said. There was no way to deny it. It looked like salami and smelled like salami. It was salami.

"I wish I could have a salami sandwich," she said. I paused to ask myself if I had really heard those words. She wished for something that I had? Maybe, she was luring me into a trap. "I love salami," she said with emphasis on love.

"Why don't you ask your mother to buy some?" I asked, not knowing what else to say without reeling myself in.

"My dad won't let her. We're not allowed to have it in the house," she said.

"Why not?" I asked, racking my brain for potential reasons.

"He says it's Wop food," she said, taking a bite of her sandwich. "And he hates Wops." I glanced around to see if anyone nearby had heard this. And since I wasn't sure where this was going, I asked, "What kind of sandwich are you eating?"

"Ham and cheese," she said, opening her sandwich to show me. It looked delicious.

"That looks really good," I said. "Did you make it?"

"No, my mom did," she said. "Do you want a bite?" I thought about a prank toy we had at home that someone got at a souvenir shop; a fake package of chewing gum with a hidden spring that slammed on your thumb like a mousetrap when you tried to pull out a stick of gum. Rather than answer, I asked, "Do you want a bite of mine?"

"Sure," she said.

What was happening didn't seem real. Darlene, who'd been making my life hell for over two years, was reaching for my sandwich, taking a bite. "This is so good," she almost moaned.

"Do you want to trade half?" I asked her. She nodded, her eyes excited, like Winnie the Pooh with his honey jar. We exchanged unbitten halves while Cathy sat mute. I took a bite of the ham and cheese with lettuce, perhaps one of the best sandwiches I had ever eaten. It was the kind of ham that came in slices, the kind we never got.

Something significant was occurring, and I felt uncertain. So I chattered nervously about seeing the movie *Oliver* on the weekend.

"I'd love to see *Oliver*!" Darlene said. "Mark Lester is soooo cute," she continued, then asked how much it cost. I told her Dad paid $32.00 to take the whole family to the Saturday afternoon matinee.

"I thought you were poor," she said.

"I don't think we're poor," I said. "Mom and Dad take us to plays and movies. Mom says we save our money for travels. And last spring, we saw the *Harlem Globetrotters*." Dad had said it was likely the only time we'd ever get to see live professional basketball in Canada, but I didn't tell her that.

"Wow! I've only seen them on television. They're so funny!" she said. "Did you see Soupy Sales?"

"Yah, he was there," I said, trying to sound casual. "But I like Meadowlark Lemon."

"Yah, he's funny," she said.

We chewed for a few moments, my body feeling almost tingly.

"Do you want to trade the other half?" she asked as she was taking her last bite of salami.

"Mine's got a bite in it," I said.

"So does mine. Wanna trade anyway?"

She asked what other movies I had seen and seemed impressed with the list I rattled off. She said she'd never been anywhere. Only Niagara Falls. So we talked about the boat stuck at the top of the Falls and the wax museum. Then we talked more about Mark Lester, since she seemed to love him. He didn't really interest me, but Ruth had been grinding at me to respect others' opinions when conversing if I wanted to keep my friends. When we finished eating, Darlene asked, "Can we trade again next week?"

"Probably," I said.

"Can you bring salami?" she asked.

"Can you bring ham and cheese with lettuce?

"Sure," she said.

"Do you like mustard or mayonnaise?" I asked.

"Both," she said. Then she reached over and touched my arm. She leaned her face toward mine, her eyes narrowing, holding me like that for a few seconds while my heart almost stopped. "Can you smell salami on my breath?"

I could hardly breathe. "A little bit," I said, coughing to cover the fact that for a second, I thought I might burst into tears. "Get some gum," I continued, half in shock, "That should take care of it."

It was well into March before I began to accept that Darlene was no longer tormenting me. She just completely stopped being mean to me, and I really didn't know why. Even Tammy wasn't sure what to make of it and seemed to recoil when I caught her eye. I made sure we had salami for my lunches. Darlene and I traded sandwiches three more times, though I didn't tell Mom. I didn't think she'd like the idea, even if it was promoting peace.

The play was performed on the Wednesday before Easter holidays. Darlene was healthy and strong. It was unlikely I would need to play her role.

The performance started well. Darlene was speaking her lines just like she'd practiced. Everyone was doing exactly as they had during rehearsals. I was backstage, nervous, but excited. I heard my cue and made my entrance onto the stage with my tray. And I made a mistake. I looked out at the audience.

I shouldn't have done that. I looked right at Mom and Dad. And in that instant, I became fully aware that my class was out there. The whole class. Liz and Joe Arcangelo and everyone. My mind went blank.

The room was dead silent as I gaped at the audience. From the sidelines, I heard Mr. Becker's voice, whispering, slow and harsh. Apparently, it was for my benefit. I didn't respond because I couldn't. I heard him again, whispering the same thing over and over like he was talking to a stubborn kid. I stood there, looking at the characters on the stage, completely bewildered. They watched me staring at them with looks of mild shock. Darlene was discretely mouthing some words. Again, I heard Mr. Becker's voice, almost hissing. It dawned on me that he was saying my line, but I still couldn't speak. I saw him then, behind the curtain, eyes imploring, everything but my neck was frozen in place. Mr. Becker practically yelled the line loudly enough for the audience to hear it, and I finally pulled myself together and repeated what he said. The other lines came back to me then and I said them like a robot, humiliated and deflated.

The play went on forever, and I held my tears just behind my eyes for the duration, then let myself cry all the way home and during supper. Mom let me be excused early from the table to go to my room, where I cried some more.

The following morning, I dawdled on my way to school, arriving just in time to line up. Before we started out lessons, Mr. Carlisle congratulated Darlene on her performance and then thanked the rest of us who participated. He asked for comments from the class. The first came from Joe Arcangelo who said, "I liked the part where Mary forgot her lines."

Before I quite knew what was happening, I was running for the door and down the hall to the girl's bathroom. I was sobbing into the circular trough sink when Liz arrived with Sophie. They huddled behind me, cooing things like, "it's okay", and "don't worry". Ten minutes later, I was laughing while tears continued to stream down my face. When we returned to class, the kids were reading quietly at their desks. I imagine they'd been told to lay off the comments on my disastrous performance.

In the afternoon, we had an Easter party, playing *7-up* and *Detective* and listening to music. During *7-up*, I was sure Joe Arcangelo touched my thumb, because I swear I could feel an electrical current run through my body, but when it was my turn to guess there was no way I would say his name for fear that if I was wrong, I would be further humiliated. Joe smiled and winked at me after I guessed "Beverley," so I knew it was him.

I was thankful that there would be no school for several days, so everyone would think about Easter and forget about the play. After school, Liz said she was going to ask her mother if she could have a pyjama party in April. "Ask your mom if you can come," she said.

MOVING ACROSS THE STREET

In the spring of grade five, construction crews started building across the street where the old sugar factory used to be. Rows of houses took shape, connected in groups of six or eight. With wheels they could have been trains parked at uniform distances apart, both perpendicular and parallel. Square, two storey, flat roofed brick homes, identical down to the inside layout: kitchen, hallway and living room on the main floor, four bedrooms and a bathroom on the second, and full basement. If the front and back doors were held open you could throw a ball through the house, or run from the front step to the back yard in less than three seconds. The only variations were the house numbers and the colour of the front door; brown, orange, green and yellow.

In the summer after I finished grade five, we moved into a north-facing end unit with an orange door. The commute time to the Welcome Inn was between forty-five seconds and two minutes, depending on breaks in the traffic on James Street. It was all exciting for us, a brand new house, fresh and sterile, with a new bathroom and kitchen appliances. No nicks or scratches in the paint. No leaky pipes or steamy radiators that spewed and clanked in the night, and no creaky wooden floors. And a brightly lit, smooth, level-floored, clean-smelling basement.

Now our immediate family would have meals together, some quality family time minus the crowd of VS'ers and others. When it actually happened, it took some getting used to. Only the eight of us sitting around having meals together. We were used to meal crowds of up to sixteen on a daily basis. We had to get into the swing of family-only supper conversation with things like, "pass the potatoes" and "do we have any ketchup?" But we soon got the hang of it again. Each of us would be asked to relay some fascinating snippet we had learned at school that day. The move to our new home served to remind me that none of my verbal contributions to the supper conversation were ever as exciting as those of my older siblings, who I was still forever wishing to be as old as. They always got to tell about teachers I didn't have and interesting things they learned in Science or History, names of astronauts and lunar landings, discoveries of insulin and stories about Vietnam War protest marches. None of my news was ever anything they didn't already know. So, they laughed when I rattled on about stuff they learned *ages* ago, a practice they continued throughout my time in high school whenever I talked of my current studies or teachers. Nothing I said was ever fresh or funny since even the jokes were the same, told year after year.

After the new housing units went up, the neighbourhood was even more kid-dense. Kids were everywhere. A family with four very young kids lived next door to us. Often two or three of them would be standing on our doorstep staring in through the front door, pressing into the screen with their grubby hands, foreheads and snotty noses. One of them wore a diaper that always looked soiled and sucked on a soother that left wet indentation marks in the screen. At first, we were kind, telling them nicely to go away, but when this became a daily routine we said, "Go home" and if that didn't work, we shut the inside door.

I asked Mom why there were so many kids. "It's a requirement to have kids in order to live in this housing complex. That's why all the houses have four bedrooms. It is government assisted living. For people on low incomes," she said. Which is how we qualified; Mom and Dad were raising a family on a volunteer stipend.

Each back yard had forty cement squares to form the back patio, with an eight-by-eight-foot wooden partition to separate one yard from the next. Sitting outside while your neighbours were doing the same, was like being separated by a shower curtain. The mother of the children next door often suntanned on a rusty chaise lounge on her patio squares, so one of us would always check by peeking under the partition, in the same way as one would peek under a bathroom stall, before engaging in conversation or gossip. She wore a lime green bikini with frills across the bottom, a style that did not flatter women of her age and size. She kept a bottle of *Coppertone* tanning oil close by and pulled her blonde hair back with a plastic head band, which emphasized her dark roots. She usually lay on her stomach, her greasy arms crossed under her head with her top undone, parts of her breasts pushed outward.

Behind the partition-separated patios was a communal lawn, covered in sod. A few white concrete-slab sidewalks broke up the monotony of the grass, leading off the main path and branching off, turning again at right angles, like a crossword puzzle, but going nowhere in particular. Some scrawny trees were planted, but it didn't take long for the neighbourhood kids to torment them with jackknives and attempts to climb them, horribly stunting their growth and eventually killing many of them.

Soon after we moved, Dad's attention focussed on a group he called "able-bodied men on welfare". "These men need something to do," he said one morning at breakfast. My first thought was, "Oh no, he's going to get them building go-karts."

But Dad had a better idea.

"I think I'm going to start rounding up some of the men and get them helping out with some projects. The Conrad's fence is falling over, and there's a bunch of junk in their yard that could be hauled away," he spoke with that familiar gleam in his eyes, the one he got when he was thinking up new projects, especially those involving tools and wood, or wheelbarrows and trailers, or making use of anything from one of his many "gulch piles" in the garage.

"I can think of twenty painting projects right now. There's no reason some of these guys can't get themselves out of bed and get to work with a paintbrush. They're getting a pay check from Social Services. Maybe they should do some community work. It'd be good for them". And so began the North End Urban Renewal Project.

Dad decided to start with a small crew. He was smart, the way he planted seeds that grew into the project. Knocking on doors in his quest for able bodied males, he'd begin a conversation with friendly chit chat, then casually make a comment about some kind of repair that might be needed on the fellow's yard, or porch or roof or any number of things. Then he'd say something like, "Hey what do you think of the idea of me bringing some guys around this Thursday and we can give you a hand with that?"

And so it began. When one guy got help, he joined the crew to help someone else, who then joined to help on the next project, and so on and so on. When a project was completed on each of the participating men's properties, Dad suggested they start seeking work at the homes of single parent families and the elderly.

The result was a crew of men that got together several times a week, working together on house and yard improvements. Some of these projects may not have been up to professional standards, but nonetheless, huge improvements were made, not only in the aesthetic look of many properties, but in the energy level and self esteem of the participants as well. They came back to their newly improved homes with a new sense of usefulness in the world, sweat on their brows from what Dad called "honest labour", along with the occasional black fingernail from missing with a hammer.

THE AUCTION

Discussions about fundraising and using resources wisely were often a topic of conversation around the dinner table. Many ideas were talked about over the years. After one of these conversations, we decided to have an auction at the Welcome Inn.

An auction would provide a way to raise money for the programs, including Mom's and Anita's sewing group, Dad's woodworking sessions, or craft nights. It would also, hopefully, encourage and enlighten the North End residents about the concepts of re-using things and spreading resources around; these concepts long-practiced and dear to my parents' hearts.

There was plenty of stuff around the Welcome Inn that was not being used, partly because of Dad's tendency to scrounge and collect things that might be useful. His trips to the dump were often counterproductive; Mom worried; with good reason, that when he set off with a trailer load, he'd return with as much as he dropped off. The garage was getting full. Chairs missing legs or with broken spindles, dressers without handles, one missing a drawer, tires of different sizes and assorted windows were just a few of its contents.

My siblings and I were delegated to make signs advertising the date and time of the auction and hang them around the neighbourhood. I always liked a good art project and we happily busied ourselves at the big kitchen table. Though I wanted my posters to be creative and colourful, I could never think of anything original and exciting, so I watched what my older siblings put on their posters and did my best to copy.

We hung the signs on telephone poles and inside the storefront windows. They attracted immediate attention.

"What's the sign say?" I heard as I tacked one up.

"It says there's going to be an auction," I answered through the tacks between my teeth.

"What's an auction?" A small group had gathered and was staring up at the sign.

My grandparents had held an auction in their barn when they sold their farm, and I had been at a livestock auction with my uncle Curt, so I considered myself a bit of an expert. I let the tack fall into my hand.

"You sell stuff. It's like a sale," I said. "But it's different. You have to bid on the things they sell. The one who bids the highest gets to buy it."

"They bit on it?" said Frannie, looking alarmed. "I don't get it. I don't know what you mean."

Francis Nickerson was two years older than me and lived in the low-income housing across the street. She went to a vocational school for girls since she had had trouble in regular school. Frannie had coarse reddish blond hair, cut in a straight line just below her ears and midway across her forehead for bangs. It was wiry like horse's hair, and thickened out at the ends, almost forming a triangle. One of her blue eyes was lazy, so I wasn't always sure what she was looking at. She always wore the same dingy baby-blue sweat pants, too short and baggy at the knees, and a long-sleeved, fuchsia button-down blouse, worn untucked. She was a head taller than me, slim but with wide hips; the two lowest two buttons on her shirt had to be left unbuttoned. A pair of scuffed Adidas, worn without socks, completed her "look".

I found Frannie downright annoying when she first started coming around, mostly since she breathed loudly through her mouth, sometimes gurgling and spitting as she talked continuously.

"My mom said I'm getting my adenoids out cause I can't breathe through my nose," she proclaimed one day. It impressed me that she knew a word I had never heard of and this gained her some credibility. "I have to go to the hospital for that," she boasted. "Mom says you get ice cream in the hospital." She said this with a big smile on her face. You only get ice cream when you get your tonsils out," I said, and then regretted it, watching her face fall.

It seemed that whenever I turned around Frannie was right behind me, breathing in my ear, talking in raspy blurts. I tried to shake her off at first, but she was not up on social cues. Even when I blatantly ignored her, she didn't go away. Eventually, I gave up. She asked a lot of questions, and though this was irritating at first, it gradually became endearing since she believed everything I said. Frannie was more than a little curious about the auction.

"What will they sell?" she asked and before I had two words out she went on, "Do they sell toys?"

"Yah, there'll be toys," I replied. I knew this since I was helping to gather the stuff together. Mom made us pull everything out from the floors in our closets and under our beds, peering at our progress from behind as we dug through our messes, going on about how other kids could sure use these nice toys and games that we weren't even taking care of anyway. Our "unappreciated" stuff was added to the growing stockpile of goods that were being collected from the garage, the basement, our church, and some of the neighbourhood residents.

"Do they sell food?"

"No food, Frannie."

"Pets?"

'No pets."

"Do they sell records"… and on and on.

A few days before the auction, walking home from school, I saw Frannie fidgeting at the corner by the Majeska House. The way she was pacing back and forth, hands in her pockets, arms and elbows flapping, concerned me. I conjured up possible scenarios as I approached; maybe Eddie got a job, or something not so good. When she saw me she came barrelling at me, grabbing my arm, rasping for breath, and bellowed into my face, "Can I buy a toaster?"

"Jeeze, Frannie, I don't know," I said, relieved that someone hadn't died.

"I need to get a toaster. Eddie says we need a toaster. Mom says I need to get a toaster," she blurted on. Eddie was one of her brothers. She had several, but he was her favourite, judging by how often she talked about him. Eddie this, Eddie that.

Eddie was partially bald, but he still lived at home. I thought he was a bit old to be getting his mom to make him toast. "I'm not sure about a toaster, Frannie," I said, "You'll have to wait and see."

"I'm going to get a toaster, we need a toaster…I am going to buy a toaster," she walked along beside me to the Welcome Inn, repeating various versions of this proclamation. She hung out with me until supper and asked me again at least four times whether there would be a toaster for sale.

On auction night I was inside helping with setting up the chairs. I could see Frannie outside, wedged up against the door, pressing her face and hands all over the glass, smudging and steaming it up, her eyes darting back and forth. The only stationary part of her was her feet. A growing crowd milled around the front door, a few of them taking last drags on cigarettes before opening time.

I had told Mom and Dad that Frannie needed a toaster and they managed to find one. I hadn't told her, since I didn't know if that was allowed and I knew she'd pester me to see it. I tried to make eye contact with Frannie, wanting to communicate that there was a toaster. But her eyes were scanning the items piled up on the tables and around the sides like a desperate mother hen.

When the doors opened, Frannie shot toward me, chattering away, "I'm gonna buy a toaster. My mom and dad want me to buy a toaster." Rasp, rasp. "I have to buy a toaster." "I got 45 cents. I need to get a toaster." I led her to the front and sat her down on the floor, off to one side, leaving a large empty space between us and the chairs.

"We'll sit up here," I said. "That way we won't miss anything." As soon as we sat down, Frannie dug in her pocket and pulled out a quarter and two dimes, which she showed me, smiling proudly.

"I have 45 cents…I'm gonna buy a toaster…"

The space behind us started filling up, children delegated to the floor, adults taking the chairs, the elderly in front. Sulky teenagers leaned against the walls, looking bored. The room was noisy with all kinds of murmuring and laughing, with sounds of kids jostling for spots and jesting amongst the adults.

"Hey Al, are you here to buy yourself a shovel to clean up your yard?"

"No, I'm hoping they'll auction off my kids!"

Dad, looking impressive in his white shirt and tie, was shooing kids away from the auction items and pointing them toward the diminishing free space in front of the chairs. Frannie had quieted, seeming intrigued with watching the other kids sit down behind us. When I figured our seats were established so she wouldn't jump up and make a beeline for the front table, I said, "There is a toaster, Frannie". Immediately, the air was charged like she'd been zapped by lightening. She twitched and leaned forward like an excited poodle, almost levitating, scanning the tables, her commentary off and running:

"I need to buy a toaster, I'm gonna get the toaster. Where is the toaster? When will they sell it? Where is it?"

"Don't worry," I interrupted "We're at the front. We'll see it." I pulled gently on her arm to settle her back into place, "You need to sit down Frannie, or the kids behind us won't be able to see."

Dad planted himself front and centre, standing in his "ready to preach position", feet shoulder-width apart, arms hanging loosely, hands clasped gently in front. His eyes swept the crowd and he loudly cleared his throat. Stragglers scurried to find a seat. When everyone was settled, he paused for a moment, his expression calm.

"Let's bow for a word of prayer," He repositioned his black horned-rimmed glasses and bowed his head. I was startled by this, not expecting a prayer. And it seemed no one else was either. I could feel a collective squirming in the crowd. There was some shuffling, but thankfully, they remained quiet. I took a deep breath, feeling guilty relief that none of my school friends were around.

"... and bless us and help us to use Your resources wisely, remembering those in the world who are not so fortunate, those who suffer. Let us remember that our resources are not ours alone, but ours to share." He said a few more words about blessing the auction and helping our brethren and then, "Amen." I could feel the room exhale in unison as Dad began his welcome and explanation.

"If you make the highest bid, go over to the table," he gestured toward Mom and Anita at a card table set with paper and pens, "and they will record your purchase. You can pay right away, or wait until the end of the auction. They will keep a tally of your purchases. If it is less burdensome for you to pay at the end of the month, you can make those arrangements there," he nodded in Mom's direction.

Dad introduced his two auction assistants. Herman and Abe gave a big wave and smile, and started to punch each other playfully. There was applause. Dad chuckled and said something to the two of them quietly and they laughed.

Dad picked up the first item, a stack of nine or ten mismatched dinner plates. Herman and Abe each took two to display, walking around the audience, presenting to some of the women for a closer look. "We'll start the bidding at twenty five cents. Do I hear twenty five cents?" Dad called. "These are beautiful plates. All unique and different."

There was a muttering drone, but no calls. Abe spoofed using one as a mirror, holding it up to admire himself, then Herman made motion to toss one to Abe like a Frisbee.

There was laughter and finally, someone said twenty cents.

"I hear twenty cents. Do I hear twenty-five?" yelled Dad.

There was murmuring, but no further bids.

"Twenty cents going once. Twenty cents going twice. Sold," announced Dad.

The crowd applauded politely. They were just getting the hang of this.

Frannie's eyes were darting around like a hawk. "Is the toaster next?" she blared.

"Next up folks, is a set of four TV tray tables, just perfect for having a leisurely dinner in front of the television," said Dad.

Herman and Abe grabbed at the set, each trying to get one first while the audience tittered. Abe won and they each held one up to show. While Dad started the bidding, they put them down on the floor and clumsily attempted to set one of them up, racing to be first. Herman won that round. Abe stuck his tongue out at Herman who was holding his TV tray table in the air, pumping it up and down like a world champion weightlifter.

"Let's start the bidding at twenty-five cents!" Dad had to practically yell to compete with the laughter from the audience. The legs on the table were rusty and the paint on the rose-decaled tray tops was chipped in places, but I could feel interest spreading through the crowd. People were sitting up straighter in their chairs, heads leaning forward for a closer look.

"Twenty five cents" someone yelled from the back.

"Thirty!"

"Thirty-five."

I craned my neck toward Mom, searching for her eyes, thinking this could be a good purchase for our family since we were allowed to have Sunday faspa in front of the television to watch Hymn Sing. Mom was busy with her head down, writing and looking up only occasionally. I knew it was pointless when the bid exceeded the amount of money in my pocket. The bidding continued to rise in five-cent increments.

Dad was grinning. Herman and Abe were up at the front like umpires at a baseball game, yelling "yup" and "hep" and stabbing the air in the direction of the last bid, moving around, changing sides, scanning the rows. The bid rose rapidly until it stopped at ninety-five cents. Not a soul in the room seemed willing to part with a dollar just yet.

"Sold," yelled Dad.

The items came up one after another. Herman and Abe carried on with their antics, pretending to fight over things, presenting them to anyone who looked interested, moving to stand beside them like a violinist performing a personal serenade in a gypsy restaurant, trying to entice them. They pointed and posed with flowing hand gestures like Carol Merrill on *Let's Make a Deal*, moving around the room to keep the momentum going while Dad monitored the bidding.

Beside me, Frannie was agitated, like a race horse waiting for the gates to open, flapping her elbows and squirming. I wondered whether she'd wear a hole in the floor. Every time something new came up she asked me what it was.

I patiently answered, "A magazine rack, a planter, a picture frame…" while thinking, what else could it possibly be?

"When will they sell the toaster?" she demanded again and again.

There were three unenthusiastic bids on the picture frame. It lacked the wire you needed to actually hang it on the wall. "This needs fixing," Dad said. "But you can bring it in and I'll rig up a wire across the back." The bidding started at five cents. Then ten.

"Sold for fifteen cents," answered Dad.

"What's that?" Frannie persisted. Dad was taking a lamp from the auction table. I felt like saying, "It's a vacuum cleaner", just to see what her reaction would be. "That is a lamp," I said flatly.

It was a bedside table lamp, short with a rectangular base that was painted with an old west pioneer scene of covered wagons forging through the plains with mountains in the background, a few tiny cowboys riding shotgun. The colours were mostly different shades of brown, with a little yellow and red thrown into the sky and on the cowboys' shirts.

Dad explained that the wiring had recently been fixed. Herman plugged it into the nearest wall socket. Abe took the lamp and held it so that the bulb appeared to be above Herman's head. He turned the switch and the light bulb went on and Herman's face took on the surprised and exhilarated look of someone who'd just discovered a medical cure.

Everybody loved the gag, and even without the lamp shade, the bids came in like popping corn. Dad was having trouble keeping up, the bids indistinguishable from the "yups" and "yehs" from his two assistants. From twenty-five cents, the bidding went up in five-and ten-cent increments, slowing around the dollar-fifty mark. It sold for a dollar seventy-five. There were oohs and ahs of congratulations to the winning bidder of the lamp.

And then came Frannie's moment. The next item was the toaster. Dad held it above his head, showing the attached cord, and handed it to Abe to walk it around and give the audience a closer look. Frannie yelled out, "Is that a toaster?"

"Yes, Frannie," I said but I don't think she heard me because she immediately sat up about a foot taller, put up her hand like she was flagging a taxi, and yelled "FORTY-FIVE CENTS!"

I pulled on her arm. "Wait, Frannie, they're not ready yet," I whispered.

Dad hadn't introduced the item yet, nor had the bidding started.

"Start with twenty cents," I urged.

She may have heard me but she wasn't listening.

"FORTY-FIVE CENTS!" she yelled again.

Dad looked at her and then at me with a question mark on his face and then said, "We'll start the bidding at twenty-five cents." Frannie yelled out, "FORTY-FIVE CENTS!"

Dad took that as the first bid. "I hear forty-five cents. Do I hear fifty?"

"Fifty cents," someone yelled from the back. Frannie looked at me with alarm and yelled, "FORTY-FIVE CENTS!"

I pulled on her violently waving hand and tried to tell her that the price had gone up and she needed to bid more if she wanted the toaster. She wasn't hearing me. Behind me, I could hear the price going higher.

"FORTY-FIVE CENTS!" Frannie yelled louder. Dad halted the bidding and explained to the audience, but mostly he was talking to Frannie, that the price had exceeded forty-five cents. Frannie looked bug-eyed and panic-stricken. "FORTY-FIVE CENTS," she called out again, right in the middle of Dad's explanation. He gave me a look that said "do something or say something to her" and carried on with the bidding despite Frannie's continued calls of "forty-five cents." The bidding rose to almost a dollar.

All the while, I was sitting there knowing that Frannie was going to be crushed and thinking, "how can I help." But I only had forty cents to spend myself. I could help make this work, but I, too, had been anticipating this event for some time and wanted desperately to bid on something. So I was relieved when the bid hit then passed ninety cents and I knew there was no longer anything I could really do. I tried to console Frannie but she was confused by what was happening so quickly. Finally, Dad said "sold for a dollar ten" and Frannie looked at me and her eyes started to well up with tears.

"But I said forty-five cents first," she said in a tone of quiet desperation.

I told her it didn't work that way. "The person who says the highest amount gets to buy it." I tried to say this in a soothing tone. "But I only had forty-five cents," she said, her voice shaky. "Mom and Eddie want a toaster." I felt awful, but was relieved she wasn't actually crying.

While the auction continued, I could hear her talking under her breath about forty-five cents and how her mom and dad would be mad. She refused to look at any of the new items.

"Look, Frannie," I tried to sound excited, "A towel rack! I bet your mom would love that!"

"Mom doesn't want a stupid towel rack," she said tonelessly. "She wants a toaster." I heard her slow, heavy breathing, like she was quietly seething. I tried to entice her to bid on some board games but she wasn't interested in those either.

"I'm supposed to get a toaster." She spat out the words. After that, she was quiet, sitting with her elbows on her knees, her hands covering her face.

I ended up with the winning bid on a shoebox containing some combs, a hairbrush and some plastic hair bands, knowing I probably wouldn't wear them, but needing to buy something. After the auction, I followed Frannie out and offered to give her some of the items in my shoebox, but she just glared at me and walked away with her chin on her chest, kicking at the sidewalk.

When I went back inside, Mom was still busy talking to some of the patrons about when they could pay for their purchases. The crowd eventually dispersed and we started the clean-up. Herman, Abe and Dad were putting stuff to the side that would be picked up the next day. The chairs were all over the place, so my sisters, brother and I were told to stack them.

Tallies and numbers were still being added up and figured out, and a few people were still milling about, so Mom and Dad were occupied. After cleaning up, we were told to go home, make ourselves some peanut butter and banana sandwiches and put ourselves to bed.

Dad found a used toaster about a week later. He showed me and said it would be nice if I got a rag and polished it up. When Frannie came into the storefront that afternoon, Dad called her over to the corner of the reading area where the toaster was sitting in the middle of a card table.

"This is for you, Frannie," he said.

Frannie looked at the toaster like she'd gone into a hypnotic trance, motionless for many seconds. Then, a smile spread across her face and lifted her body. She seemed to inflate and grow taller. She leaped forward suddenly, grabbing the toaster in both hands, embracing it, clutching it against her chest. A swivel turn and she was running for the door, feet pounding the floor, cradling the toaster like a newborn baby. When she got to the front door, she tucked the toaster under one arm while she flung the door open and then ran out, leaving the door ajar.

"Mom, Dad, Eddie, Mom, Dad..." she yelled, even though they were nowhere within earshot. "Mom, Dad, Mom, Dad, Mom..." We could hear her voice fading down the block.

Frannie smiled for days after that, talking non-stop, acting like she'd saved her family from starvation. "We had toast this morning for breakfast. All of us. We all had toast," she rambled. "Mom likes the toaster, Eddie likes the toaster, Dad likes the toaster..."

We never saw the forty-five cents but that was okay. Frannie's family had a toaster.

MY WARDROBE

I only said I had nothing to wear once in Mom's presence. That happened at the beginning of grade seven and I never said it again because right after I said it, Mom made me very sorry for uttering those words.

Within three seconds, she was marching up the stairs behind me, to my room, muttering on about what beautiful clothes I had to choose from. I stood by while she half-disappeared into the closet, rooting to its depths like someone foraging through dense jungle with a machete. Before I could think of something to say that would stop her, she yanked out a garment and turned, raising my poncho like a banner in front of my face. I felt like I'd been socked in the gut.

I stared as though hypnotized, the poncho wavering before my eyes, mesmerizing me with its glowing hues. It was polyester. Plaid lime green and sunset peach in fluorescent shades, with a poorly matching bright-orange dingle-ball fringe. I had made it. Yes, I had chosen the fabric and the fringe that didn't match and sewn it all by myself, thinking it was going to be the coolest poncho in Hamilton. It wasn't. It was hideous. I should have burned or buried it, or cut it into a million pieces, or left it outside to be torn apart by animals, but it was one of those practically indestructible fabrics that even goats can't digest.

"This is so bright and cheerful," she said in her not so bright and cheerful voice, pushing it toward my chest. "I haven't seen you wear this in a long time." She turned toward the closet again, and with a show of great annoyance, yarded through the hangers for a suitable skirt and blouse to go with it. When she was satisfied with her selections, she piled them on top of the poncho in my arm-extended, stupefied stance. "Now get dressed," she ordered. "It's getting late."

I left for school wearing the garish wrap over an off-white blouse that gaped at the chest and my old homemade chocolate-brown crimpline skirt, its dullness intensifying the brilliance of my poncho. I felt like a walking neon sign, as though I should have stepped out and directed traffic, or stood by to mark a dangerous curve.

Mom had sewn our clothing for years, so I was accustomed to wearing homemade clothes, and actually got excited at one point about learning to sew myself, but that only lasted through the completion of one garment, said poncho.

Like other Mennonite mothers, Mom had developed a system for clothing our family efficiently and economically. With one extra large piece of material, she could sew a batch of outfits, one for each of us, using one sewing pattern and a stick of white chalk, adjusting the size for each of her daughters with chalk lines on the laid-out fabric. By carefully arranging the pattern pieces, there might be enough fabric to make each of us a matching bandana.

I was used to the look-alike thing, especially on family holidays where we travelled around in a pack. It must have been one of my older sisters who put her foot down and demanded, begged, pleaded, whined, who knows, but at some point, the spell was broken and a new era in our family fashion evolution began. I cannot say how this decision was reached, but one day, Mom announced we were to get ready to go shopping. Before I really understood what was going on, Mom had us parading uptown along James Street to the fabric store, so each of us could choose a piece of fabric.

Inside the store, she herded us to the stand where the giant pattern books were displayed. "One pattern will do," she said as she slammed closed the *Vogue* pattern book and shoved it aside. "Too posh," she said and reached down to haul up a *Butterick* catalogue. "You can choose from either of these," she said as she hefted another book with *Simplicity* patterns.

We gazed at drawings of tall slim models while she turned the pages in the "coordinates" section, occasionally commenting on something we liked. The criteria for choosing a pattern was that it needed to have the pieces required to make a vest, pants, skirt and shorts. This was an awkward process, with us all trying to peek over each other to see, but we finally found something suitable. Really, the older three chose, seemingly more knowledgeable about fashion. I was starting to get a headache from craning my neck so I just nodded when they said "how about this one?" Tina nodded, too, most likely aware the result of the vote was already a foregone conclusion.

Mom told us to start looking at fabric while she figured out which pattern size to buy. On the way to the store, she had been telling us about a new, state-of-the-art fabric, called crimpline. This new wonder fabric was a synthetic fabric. It was claimed to be highly durable, machine washable and dryable and guaranteed not to wrinkle and never fray. And it was water resistant, thereby being stain resistant, and the kicker... she loved this quality... it didn't shrink. Regardless of whether it was washed in hot or cold water. Mom had heard about it from the church ladies. It was a Mennonite mom's dream.

Mom pointed to the long tables where the crimpline was lined up on cylinder bolts. "We'll get enough so that each of you will have a skirt, vest and slacks. Let me know if you would like a pair of shorts, too. And I need to know whether you want a vest that hangs just to your waist, or covers your hips. That will make a difference in how much fabric we will need."

I walked slowly along the aisle, examining the colours and running my fingers over the fabric. It felt a bit like indoor-outdoor carpet, but there was a good assortment of colours. "I choose the black," I said as soon as Mom rejoined us. "No," Mom said. "Black is morbid and too hot. And dust and hair will show. Choose something else."

"Louella says black is a slimming colour," I said, but Mom didn't respond even though I know she heard me. So I chose chocolate brown. Mom looked sceptical, frowning for a moment at my choice, but then she smiled. "It will go well with your gold blouse," she said.

Ruth chose sky blue to go with her eyes, the twins, navy and dark green, and Tina picked royal purple since she was currently intrigued with kings and queens. "Good," Mom said, "Now we won't get all the outfits mixed up. And we will be able to wash them all together." Yet another endorsement for this amazing fabric. The colours don't run.

Over the next week, Mom was busy working with the new fabric, seemingly thrilled. "Try to see if you can fray this," she said excitedly, handing me a small scrap. "It is just the most amazing thing! I won't even have to double stitch the seams!"

I tried unsuccessfully to secure a string and pull it apart from the rest of the piece. Mom was clearly onto a good thing.

In record time, the outfits were completed. Mom was an advocate for the 'elastic waist', which saved her valuable time because she didn't have to fiddle with zippers or button holes. Finished garments practically flew off the machine. She didn't even have to turn on the iron. We were summoned for the fitting and I hurried upstairs to get my gold blouse. I put on the pants/vest/gold blouse combo for my crimpline debut. My outfit fit perfectly. I noticed the fabric was a bit scratchy against my skin and mentioned this to Mom. "You'll get used to it," she said.

We continued to make annual trips to the fabric store. The instructions on said shopping trips remained constant. We must choose crimpline. Not wool. Wool was expensive, hair stuck to it, and it required special hand-washing or dry-cleaning. Not cotton. Cotton had a shorter life-span, had potential for shrinkage and required ironing. Silk, rayon, anything shimmery...are you kidding?? (Only once did Mom stray from these rules. That was when she made us our kilts.) And one updated pattern was selected for purchase, but never from *Vogue*.

Our previous year's crimpline outfits would still be in exactly the same shape that they were when they fell off the sewing machine, except perhaps for an occasional snag in the fabric. Like suits of armour, they hung in our closets, completely unwrinkled. I continued to marvel over their durability, sometimes wondering how long it would take for a crimpline outfit to decompose. I pictured the inside of a coffin, decaying faded purple plush casing, a corpse laying there, transparent remnants of skin, yellowish along the neck bones and around the eye sockets, leg bones and toes flopped outward, arm and finger bones scattered to the sides, said corpse wearing an almost brand new, coordinated crimpline skirt and vest set, the rust on the chain that fastened the vest together at the front the only indication on the outfit of passing time.

"If you plan right," Mom always said, you can choose a colour that complements your last year's outfit. That way, you can mix and match the vests with the pants and skirts. Think of how many different outfits you will have then!" Because Mom sewed with large seams and hems, she was able to alter them to keep them fitting properly. And since the fabric didn't fade, the alterations were barely noticeable.

Through the years, my enthusiasm on these trips dwindled, but I knew it was pointless to resist. To say, "No, I really do not want another crimpline outfit. I have enough already," would be ineffectual because I knew that Mom really wanted us to be well dressed. I got lots of use out of my outfits by wearing them to church, where all the girls were sporting their own family's version, and the church moms gathered in the vestibule, bubbling over the merits of crimpline.

Mom was right about the itchiness factor. I did get used to it. And I did appreciate the armour-like qualities of the fabric, because bulges and rolls weren't so apparent when wearing the sturdy outfits. The long vests helped to cover imperfections, panty lines, evidence of brassieres, and shirts that weren't ironed. And I did like the mix and match thing. We all got a lot of wear out of our outfits. They did stand up well. So well in fact, that I wondered if this fabric might be bullet-proof.

CHUBBY

At the beginning of grade six, Mom suggested we go shopping for a training bra. I almost cried, shocked and unwilling to face the idea of wearing a bra just yet. I told her that only one girl in my class wore one and the boys made fun of her, snapping her bra straps in line-ups. That gave her pause. Boys poking fun at breasts was not something she could endorse, so we agreed to revisit the subject again after Christmas. In the meantime, I would wear undershirts under my blouses or cardigans over them.

I was never the fattest kid in the class. In grade six, two girls and one boy were heavier. The heaviest girl, Peggy, nicknamed "Piggy" or "The Pig", was conspicuously fat, or "fully developed", as Mom would put it. Peggy wore polyester suits, so tight her seams looked ready to burst, tight enough to reveal underwear outlines of a girdle and a corset-like bra, the kind the TV ads claimed "put an end to midriff bulge". Peggy didn't flop or jiggle, but her legs swished when she walked.

Gretchen, the other fat girl, flopped and jiggled, but carried her weight nonchalantly, seemingly unbothered by her size, and completely unconcerned that she seriously needed a bra. I knew I shouldn't judge or compare, but I only needed a trainer. By grade six, Gretchen was ready for at least a B-cup, and she didn't wear undershirts.

She flopped around the classroom in snug polyester shirts with pointy collars, buttons gaping enough to flash glimpses of boob. The flopping was especially noticeable in gym class, where she took the comments from the boys as compliments, or completely disregarded them, depending on her mood. I was grateful that Peggy and Gretchen were there to jiggle, swish and gasp for breath more than me when the class was forced to run laps. It drew attention away from my flabby thighs.

Roy, the most overweight boy, charged at kids who taunted him, making awful wild animal sounds, behaving the way a cannibal might, as if he were to actually catch them, they would be pummelled and eaten. Roy struggled with school work and had a volatile temper, like a pressure cooker ready to blow. Most of our classmates left him alone. It was the younger kids on the playground that enjoyed watching the screams and chasing game, from a safe distance.

I felt guilty for being happy that most of the "fat jokes" weren't directed at me. I received the odd comment, but there was only so much bullying and teasing per flaw and there were so many provocations for ridicule at school: being too tall, or short, or fat, or skinny or ugly, or dumb, or being on welfare, or having head lice cooties, or buck teeth, or pimples, or wearing homemade/second-hand/hand-me-down clothes, or failing a grade, or having to go to church, or having parents who were alcoholics, or didn't have a car, or a job, or who didn't speak English, or had a dirty house or smelled bad.

Of all these potential triggers for ridicule, I had three. I could control one of them, and I wasn't. The ice cream was too big a temptation. I couldn't seem to stop myself. When we moved across the street, I thought I'd be safe from living with so much ice cream around, but, being economically minded consumers, Mom and Dad required a freezer in the new house to keep bags of smelt and fruit and vegetables. They couldn't discontinue their practice of gleaning. They had made connections with various farmers throughout the Niagara Peninsula, and there was no way they would ignore a "come and dig up all the carrots you want before we plough the field" or "the pickers have finished in the orchards. Come on over. You can have all you want" phone call.

And since Dad loved his homemade-from-gleaned-fruit pies "a-la-mode", we needed a ready supply of ice cream. There was no getting around that. Ice cream ranked as was one of the three absolute staples in our household; I was never sure of the hierarchy, but the other two were ketchup and peanut butter.

It was a matter of developing the willpower and self-control needed to stop my arm from being sucked into the freezer three or four times a day. I adopted the "tomorrow is a good time to start a diet" plan, and I stuck to it pretty much every day. Needless to say, I didn't lose any weight. I may have gained some, but couldn't say for sure because I avoided the scales for fear of three digit numbers. Instead, I relied on the "this outfit doesn't fit anymore" approach to monitoring my weight. I did try a few moderating tactics, like cutting down on water.

For inspiration, I hung pictures of models on the fridge, which Mom tolerated for short periods before she ripped them down. She didn't say anything. I knew her thoughts on fashion models and vanity, and serving the Lord rather than whining about a few extra pounds.

Once I was established with a paper route and with my own disposable income, I tried the *Ayds* diet plan. I'd read testimonials in magazines from obese women who claimed to have gone from a size 22 to a size eight. *Ayds* candies, available in three flavours, were guaranteed to control your appetite if eaten twenty minutes before a meal. I thought it was a brilliant idea. What could be simpler? How many times had Mom insisted we not eat before dinner so as not to spoil our appetites? So simple and so smart —I couldn't wait to get started, eager to be slim and svelte.

My first problem was that the people at the store wouldn't sell them to me, a mere sixth-grader. Ruth helped me with that. She was packing on a few extra pounds too, so she smuggled the first box into the house, aware this was contraband of the worst kind. It would surely get Mom's goat if she ever discovered we were taking "silly and dangerous diet pills". I could just imagine the speech we'd get, having heard her diet pep talk umpteen times—moderation, smaller portions, healthy food, no snacks, no short cuts, exercise. I didn't like any of those suggestions. If we were caught with *Ayds*, I could only imagine the tirade would make her usual diet lecture seem like a day at the beach.

Once the *Ayds* were safely stashed in Ruth's bedroom, we carried our glasses of water upstairs fifteen to twenty minutes before meal times, as per directions, drank it with the square of *Ayds* candy, and waited for all our hungers and cravings to disappear.

I started out with a box of the chocolate flavour, excited my prayers were being answered; I could eat chocolate, I would soon be thin. But the taste, oh my soul, was like the taste of something that was fed to domesticated animals in barns. I stuck to the plan eagerly for the first day, forcing down the vile squares, excited by the prospect of being thin. On the second day, I had to talk myself into putting them into my mouth because the smell put me off. But I was still excited about being thin. By the third and fourth day, I had to plug my nose, but I managed to swallow the squares by chewing as little as possible while contemplating how long it should take to lose fifteen pounds. On the fifth day, I cut the squares into tiny pieces with a steak knife and put them on my tongue two at a time to swallow with a sip of water like pills. By the sixth day, nauseous, I was ready to flush my half of the box down the toilet.

For the record, I did NOT notice a significant decrease in my appetite, even with the nausea. Actually, the whole thing was counterproductive because eating those vile squares made me long for large delicious meals. On the seventh day, I quit the *Ayds* diet.

A few months later, I decided to try again. Surely, I must have exaggerated the unsavoury taste sensation. Surely, nothing so trivial could deter me from sticking to it this time. I would try harder. I would be slim. In my testimonial I would tell the story about how the pounds melted away, and how my big clothes literally fell off my tiny frame, and how my eyes looked big and bright in my new slender face. This time Ruth bought me the caramel flavour. By the fourth day, I could not bring myself to swallow the foul-smelling squares. Even the cost of the box could not get me to continue taking them.

Liz was having a sleepover during my second 'diet" and invited me. I was ecstatic about the invitation, but horrified that my bra might be discovered and discussed. I had to succumb to wearing one after Christmas. There was just no way to hide my budding breasts. Even wearing lots of layers didn't help.

I needn't have worried. The subject of "bras" turned out to be the hot topic of discussion at Liz's sleepover, even before we changed into pyjamas. The girls were all saying things like, "wouldn't it be great to wear a bra" and "I've been begging my Mom to take me shopping for a training bra", and "I just can't wait to get my own bra". Well, wasn't I zapped into the spotlight for the next hour after I confessed and revealed my 30-inch-double A. I was fussed over and questioned and prodded for information. Embarrassed by the extra rolls around my middle, I showed it off, and thankfully, no one commented on my excess bulk. Still, when I saw Liz in her pink baby doll pyjamas and Patricia and Beverley in their short little nighties, I was green with envy, lying on my sleeping bag in a full flannel nightgown like Ma Kettle. So, despite the popularity of the bra, I knew I needed to slim down.

I decided to try the *Ayds* diet one more time. Surely, I thought, the taste wasn't as bad as I remembered. What could be so hard about eating two small squares before supper? I'll be brave, I thought. I'll think of something pleasant while I take them—walking along beaches in a bikini, wearing suede hip huggers, eating ice cream. This time, I tried the vanilla flavour. By the third day, I could not bring myself to swallow those squares. None of the three boxes ever got finished.

I didn't get to write a testimonial.

PAPER ROUTE

Two things motivated me to get a paper route when I was ten. One came from watching my paper boy brother become rich. The other had to do with a crush that took control of my otherwise sensible senses.

Initially, I viewed newspaper delivery as a masculine thing; thoughts about hauling heavy bundles of papers, braving adverse weather conditions, and taking on the responsibility of getting them delivered, made the idea too daunting to take seriously. I watched with mild curiosity and some embarrassment when Mark rattled off on his delivery route, wheeling his homemade jalopy of a wagon. Most of his route was in our housing development, and he had worked out the most efficient way to get it done, following the same daily trail through the maze of attached houses. Sometimes, I happened to be in his vicinity, hanging around one of the communal areas with Sophie and Rita. Mark would pull his cart along the walkways with his helpers, calling out house numbers and giving tips on which lawn was okay to walk over or where to watch for dog poop while the helpers darted or sauntered back and forth between the houses and the wagon, depending on the weather.

What really got my attention was the "after collecting" ritual at the kitchen table. The first time I sat and watched, it almost didn't seem real, all that money and Mark sitting there like a bank official, stacking coins, organizing bills into piles with all the faces in the same direction. I quickly became his loyal audience for these sessions, waiting for the moment he separated the amount owed for the papers from the amount collected.

"This is profit," he announced the first time, running his fingers over the smaller pile.

He counted and recounted, probably showing off a bit. "Three dollars and ninety cents."

"Wow," I exclaimed, "What are you going to buy with all that?"

"I don't know yet," he answered trying to sound nonchalant. "I'll put it in the bank until I decide. Maybe new skates or a stereo."

All I could say was, "Wow, a stereo," amazed it was possible and totally jealous.

I'd been dreaming of having money, and how I'd spend it. My older sisters had money from babysitting, but for me, that wasn't an option since they got all the jobs and all I got for helping them was a snack. And sometimes Mom made them babysit for free. I wanted to buy *Tiger Beat* and *16*, clothes from Eaton's, and bell bottoms that were long enough. I figured Mom might, someday, let me buy new clothes from a store if I had some money. The older sisters had been fighting that battle for a while, and she was now letting them buy sweaters and leotards. My most pressing need for money, however, was for two dollars to join the Donny Osmond Fan Club.

After school one day, I came outside while Mark was negotiating wages with some potential helpers. During a lull, I asked if I could be a helper. They responded collectively by looking at me like I was mentally ill, and then ignored me while I stood there looking hurt. I concluded that helping Mark as a source of income was unlikely to occur.

Mark usually gave us highlights of his daily delivery at supper. I enjoyed listening to his commentary almost as much as watching the money part, and especially liked hearing the stuff that made Mom grimace: updates on which couples were fighting or who was already drunk or which house stunk. It was after one of these conversations that I expressed my wish to have a paper route, too. Dad responded, "Well, why don't you apply for one?" That brought me up short. I had no idea it was even possible, never mind that it could be so simple. Mom looked sceptical and said something to Dad in German and he responded in kind.

Dad made a phone call the next day about the application forms. A week later, they were filled out and sent back and I began pestering Mark about being his helper. Having only sisters, my barging into what had been "boys only" territory may have caused him angst. He wasn't thrilled but Mom insisted, wanting me to get some experience before getting my own route.

"It could be years before she gets a route," Mark said. "Or maybe, she'll never get one."

"But she could. And she needs to be prepared," Mom replied. "Let her be your helper. She could use the exercise." He couldn't argue with that, and he knew anyway that arguing with Mom wasn't wise. He agreed to take me on as a helper. "But only on Saturdays," he said. I would soon find out that Saturdays were the heavy paper days, with inserts, extra sections, and the *Saturday Night* magazine. It was the day when helpers bargained for higher wages.

My first task as a Saturday helper was to wheel the cart down to the branch. Mark acted as though I had to pass some heavy machinery operator's test, telling me I needed to learn how to "handle" it.

The existence of the paper cart was, in itself, a major source of embarrassment for me, due to the fact that it was unlike any other wagon in the world. It was a homemade model, similar in style to the travel tent-trailer and painted bright blue with the leftover paint. The boxy wagon sat low to the ground, with dinner-plate-sized wheels salvaged from a baby carriage at the rear, a single, much smaller swivel wheel at the front, and a very heavy, U-shaped bar for a handle. This bar was about two feet long, and was so heavy it could inflict bruises or worse if it fell against your body or slammed down onto your foot. Awareness of that fact, I learned from subsequent experience, was the most critical aspect in learning to "handle" the cart.

Dad was very proud of that cart. He said it was "ideal"; sturdy, and deep enough to hold a good supply of papers, unlike those "flimsy red models with no depth". He had a point. But on par with having the world's dorkiest looking wagon was the noise caused by the tiny front wheel swivelling every which way as it bounced over stones, garbage scraps and cracks in the sidewalk. As was the metal-on-metal racket of the handle bar jiggling against the loose hinge holders. Heads turned as we rattled along, Mark filling me in on how the bundles were dispersed and tallied by Marcel, the "branch guy" and other vital aspects of newspaper delivery.

"You need two days for collecting," he said. "Sometimes people say come back tomorrow. I don't have the money right now. Or else they just don't answer the door."

I already knew about that, and about the float and metal punch he carried while collecting, and about the ring of cards attached to his belt loop in the style of a custodian with keys. On the cards were lists of calendar dates, which were punched when payment was made. Each customer kept an identical card.

"It's crucial," Mark went on, "that you remember to punch both cards. That way they can't argue or try to cheat. And be real nice to all your customers. Cause you never know who might give you a tip." As we rounded a corner I could see about a dozen boys and wagons in a line of sorts at the entrance of an open garage. "Is that the branch?" I asked. "That's it," he replied in a voice that implied I might be stupid.

We joined the line-up and Mark started chatting with the other boys without introducing me, so I stepped aside to look into the garage. Newspaper bundles were piled high behind a long table. I watched someone, who I presumed was Marcel, grab a bundle of newspapers in each hand and plunk them onto the table, muscles and tattoos bulging beneath his Rolling Stones tank top. He had granny glasses and long hair, most of which was glued against his glistening neck. I thought he looked Italian.

He turned and grabbed two more bundles, lifting them high and placing them directly on top of the two on the table, grinning at the scrawny boy facing him. Turning his head to acknowledge someone I couldn't see, laughing at something I didn't hear, he clipped the strapping from one of the bundles and counted the newspapers. Then he began writing on a clipboard while the scrawny boy struggled to load the bundles onto his wagon.

As we got closer, I could hear some of the exchange between "Marcel" and the person inside. 'Blah,blah,blah... cylinder head," said the guy inside."You wouldn't know a cylinder head from a horse's ass," Marcel was laughing as he spoke, obviously amused by his own wit. The guy inside was laughing, too.

When we were second in line I looked further into the garage, mildly curious to know who couldn't tell a car part from a horse's ass. A guy was sitting on a stack of bundles, leaning against the wall, his arms crossed across his chest.

The next few seconds passed in slow motion as my entire body transformed from a solid to silly putty, starting with my head and working down through my bones. I had to concentrate to keep my balance as I took in a chiselled face, dazzling ice-blue eyes and wavy, perfectly-messed brown hair. He was wearing a white T-shirt that showed off a perfect physique and bronze tan. The noisy interactions around me disappeared into silence. As though sensing my metamorphosis into jelly, the incredible hunk looked at me. My eyes were glued in place. Too stunned to move, I stared at perfection, a person out of a magazine, far cuter than Donny Osmond and anyone else I had ever seen in real life. It took a sheer effort of will to look away.

Mark moved to the head of the line. Somehow I managed to lift one stumpy lead-filled foot and propel myself forward to stand beside him at the table. He began talking to the incredibly gorgeous movie star guy who was alive and breathing, so close I could have reached across the table and touched him. I held onto the table, afraid to open my mouth, afraid an animal sound, like "baaaaa", would escape. I clamped my lips and smiled weakly when Mark introduced me to Marcel and his younger brother, Anthony.

"Tony," said the amazing gorgeous person, grinning at me.

The three of them talked while I stood there with a frozen half smile, watching the world move in slow motion, hearing words from far away. I looked up as we turned to leave. He smiled at me in farewell, his eyes crinkling like he was looking at a puppy.

I walked numbly away beside Mark, who seemed oblivious to the fact that an internal earthquake had dismantled and rerouted my veins. My blood was rocketing through me like electric waves. Keeping my eyes down, practicing in my head so I could sound casual, I asked, "Are those brothers French or Italian?"

"Both," he said. "Their mom's French." I took a deep breath before speaking the next words, "Does that Tony work there, too?"

"No," Mark answered, "but he hangs around sometimes. He's supposed to take over when Marcel gets his mechanics certificate." I desperately wanted to know how long it takes to get a mechanics certificate, but Mark was giving me a look. I changed my line of questioning, asking about where we were delivering and other things I didn't care about.

The actual delivery of papers that day was a blur, so intent was I on my new state of being. Just like that, a clear strong goal had developed.

With absolute clarity, I knew I had to have my own paper route. There was no other option. And I wanted it as soon as possible. Until then, I would take every opportunity to be the helper, for cut wages or free, just so I could go to the branch for a chance to see Tony. And I would be "super helper", the girl for the job, so there would be no reason for Mark to balk or complain about having to drag me around. I vowed to hustle to and fro from the wagon, obey his "whose grass not to walk on" rules, place newspapers fold side down and never let a screen door slam. And never complain about the cold or wet or black ink stains on my sleeves.

From that moment, Tony became my new daydream guy. The guy to make any car ride, Sunday sermon or fishing experience not only tolerable, but enjoyable, as I sat squashed in the back seat, propped on a stacking chair or staring into a nameless river or swampy lake. This beautiful Tony had just slammed Donny Osmond into second place and completely wiped out other part-time daydream contenders like Little Joe Cartwright and The Sundance Kid. I began to pray that my paper route might be given unto me soon, and that Marcel might breeze through mechanic's training.

My prayers were intense and must have been heard, because within four months, the delivery supervisor called. He said a route was available. It may have been Mark's impeccable reputation or Dad's ministerial credentials, and perhaps the supervisor was following the "apple not falling far from the tree" theory of hiring delivery people when he offered me the job, since I was still a bit young. Because this new route was in another neighbourhood, Dad insisted Mark take it. I was to take over Mark's route.

Sadly, I also inherited the paper cart. Mark got to buy a normal red wagon from Canadian Tire. I wanted to buy one, too, claiming I could save the money required. "There's no need to buy another wagon," Dad said when I mentioned the idea. "You already have one. That wagon has ten years left in it." I couldn't argue with that; it probably had at least twenty.

The day came when Mark handed over the cards and the list. "Buy your own punch," he said. "I still need mine." And I became a wage-earning, independent paper girl. By that time, I practically knew the route off by heart, so the idea of going alone was more exciting than worrisome. Truth be told, the most stressful part of the whole deal for me was whether or not my hair looked good by the time I got to the branch, in case, you know. Not flattened by humidity or greasy if I'd slept in and missed my shower opportunity.

In reality, the daily grind of delivering papers was often mundane, and hauling a heavy wagon over curbs and up inclines physically demanding. And Tony was usually not at the branch. But each day was thrilling since he might be. And that was worth the walk and the extra grooming. On the days he was there I could relive every word he said on the way home, and on the days he wasn't, I could rehearse lines in my head in anticipation of the next time I did see him.

Despite the fact that most of the mental energy I spent on paper delivery revolved around Tony and my encounters with him, I did try to be a good paper girl. I did want my customers to be happy, mostly so they wouldn't call to complain or make me run another paper over after supper if I forgot one. I took care to place papers upright in the doors so they remained intact, to deliver them dry and wrinkle-free and to use the walkways. But while I did my deliveries, clattering along the walkways yelling out house numbers and offering encouragement to my helpers just like I'd seen Mark do, I was obliviously seated in my mental movie theatre, watching scenes that played and replayed, scenes of Tony cutting, Tony counting, Tony smiling, Tony wearing white T-shirts...

Mark continued to mentor me, and taught me about the proper tying down of plastic covering during rainstorms, because once a paper got wet, it was ruined. He also taught me about negotiating the pay for helpers and paying them more on Saturdays and Wednesdays when the papers were heavy with magazines and ads. Most kids were happy to work for a nickel and a partially squashed ice cream treat. Frannie Nickerson was willing to work for ice cream alone, but she could only remember one house at a time and nattered constantly. And I didn't want her coming to the branch with me. Younger kids didn't seem to notice my obvious infatuation and stalling when he was there. Frannie certainly would. In that department, she was quite astute, already wearing a B-cup bra, seemingly very aware of who was looking at who. And once she got an idea in her head, there was no stopping her mouth.

On Tuesday evenings, I shared the kitchen table with Mark, our stashes separated by the line that split to add the extra leaf, sorting, piling, counting and planning on ways to spend. When the profits were tallied, Mark put his into an empty Cheese Whiz jar. Mine went into a pink jewellery box handed down to me from Ruth, with a pop up twirling ballerina that played a tinkley minuet. I didn't particularly like ballerinas or the music and had no jewellery, but it came with a key and stored my treasures; postcards from our travels, some sea glass, a meagre collection of rabbits' feet, and my weekly profits.

Mom and Dad gave me "the talk" about opening a savings account, being a responsible consumer, planning ahead for college, and tithing (donating a percentage of my earnings to the church). I nodded and looked agreeable while thinking "it's a long time until college." Fortunately, Mom and Dad were busy with community involvements and didn't keep tabs on our savings accounts. As long as we put money into the collection plate at church and made some regular deposits at the bank, they didn't meddle.

I did try to save and tithe and be a responsible consumer, but things were different now. I entered stores differently, not like a poor sad waif, but as a person with options. I could choose a record album or a T- shirt, or a sweater, or new socks or my own brand of shampoo. My siblings and I were accustomed to walking or taking the bus uptown to shop with each other or friends, so Mom and Dad didn't always see what we bought. Our front door was right next to the stairs going up to our rooms, so getting things into the house wasn't too difficult, except in the summer when it was so hot we couldn't justify carrying jackets.

Mark and I had a quiet agreement. "Just don't tell them about your tips," he whispered. "When you get a tip, put it into your pocket. Then no one knows."

"Brilliant," I said.

"But don't do it with all of them, or they'll get suspicious. Do about half, maybe a bit more. In two or three weeks, you should have enough for a record album," he said.

"Is it deceitful?" I asked.

"Tips are tips," he said. "We're the ones going out every day, rain or snow. No one should tell us what to do with our tips."

One momentous day when I was in grade seven, Marcel got his mechanic's license. The exhilaration factor associated with picking up papers went way up. I only needed to be cautious about being at the branch when Mark was there. Generally, I timed it so I could arrive at the branch just as he was leaving. I used the extra moments at home to check my hair and apply a trace of eyeliner, mindful to smudge it off before I got home for supper.

By then, I was a seasoned newspaper girl. My knees still felt loose every time Tony smiled at me, but I managed to speak in full sentences, look him in the eye, and even make him laugh sometimes. I knew there was about as much hope he'd become interested in a slightly chubby eleven-year-old girl as there was of gold nuggets dropping from the sky. But somehow, that didn't matter. He was obviously flattered by my unwavering admiration. The only other delivery girl was quiet, with coarse red hair, a deep widow's peak and pop bottle glasses. She and her brother collected their papers and left in mouse-like fashion, so as far as female competition for his attention went, there was little if any.

Each moment I spent at the branch was dream-like and vitally alive at the same time. I felt as though I was floating, as though the air was full of honey and I was breathing it in. Every gesture, every word that came out of his mouth was magical for me, charged with energy, something to treasure. He asked questions, like. "How many do you want today?" and I'd say, "How many did I get yesterday?" and he would consult his clipboard, then say a number and then I'd say, "How many can I have?" Bliss.

Often, he'd pretend to lose track when counting my papers and have to start over again. Sometimes, he jumped over the table to help me load up my hideous wagon, upon which he was kind enough not to remark. I let other kids go ahead of me in line, pretending to be polite. Of course, organizing my wagon needed all kinds of time, time to shift and tuck, fiddle and cover with garbage bags if a cloud might be present in the sky.

I never told anyone about him. Not one soul. I couldn't cope with the idea of having my sisters torment me endlessly. And I couldn't have the girls at school talking behind my back. I knew it was absolutely impossible that he would ever become my boyfriend. For one thing, it was unthinkable that I would even mention the idea of having a boyfriend at home: Mom and Dad wouldn't hear of it. I might as well have said, "I'm going to school naked tomorrow." And he could have had his pick of absolutely anyone. And even if I had been stunningly beautiful with the world's best personality, I was far too young for him.

The flirting thing was just that. We moved to another part of the city before I was old enough to date. But for two and a half years, picking up newspapers was an event for me, like the World Series was to Dad. I knew in my heart that I wasn't going to win the big prize, yet I wasn't deterred from playing the game, cheering myself along inside my head, appreciating the opportunity to learn the art of maintaining my composure in the presence of extraordinary male beauty.

THE DONNY OSMOND FAN CLUB

Now that I had a steady income, I finally had money to join the *Donny Osmond Fan Club*. For a two dollar membership fee, I was promised an autographed eight by ten glossy photo and a letter from Donny.

Our family had been watching *The Andy Williams Show* for a while. Ironically, it was Mom who started the weekly ritual, being a fan of Andy's big toothy smile and his crooning rendition of *Moon River*. It immediately became my favourite show, but not because of *Moon River*. It was the weekly appearance of the Osmond Brothers, singing and dancing in a five brother, shiny-fringed-suit line-up who got my attention. Ecstatic they had Mom's endorsement, I drooled subtly and kept most of my comments to myself, knowing the repercussions of excessive gushing. I never left the living room during the show, taking care not to drink much at supper so I wouldn't have to use the bathroom, for fear of missing one second of seeing the Osmond Brothers. Donny was my star of the lot, even though he didn't stand out as absolutely the best looking, because they all kind of looked the same. He was smaller, "pint-sized", Mom said, and a bit older than me – just right to be my future husband. Mom didn't mind that I had a crush on Donny since she had crushes on Jimmy Stewart and Dick Van Dyke. But she would have freaked if she had known about my magazine collection.

I'd been secretly reading about Donny's favourite healthy snacks and about how he spent his Sunday afternoons. Along with all the other Hollywood teen idols, Donny apparently loved the idea of spending his free time walking in the woods with a special, intelligent girl with a sense of humour, claiming to be not the least bit concerned about her appearance – a "natural" girl who just wanted to be herself. I took the magazines to school, huddling with the girls on the playground while we debated and voted on whether Donny Osmond, Bobby Sherman or Mark Lester was the cutest.

I was probably a magazine addict because I knew exactly which day they arrived at the corner store. The clerks saw me coming, too. They knew they had to get out the *X-Acto* knife immediately and cut the freshly delivered bundle; otherwise I'd squat down right there, trying to read the front cover, blocking the aisle, oblivious to the needs of others who might want to get around me. I needed my fix. I needed to know everything.

And I wanted to be just like Marcia Brady. She had green eyes and blond hair and long legs. And even though I had none of those qualities, I thought that if I read enough about her, they might miraculously transfer to me, then the kids at school would think I was beautiful and my siblings would admire me and ask my advice, and we'd have a housekeeper.

I also needed to belong to Donny's fan club. I don't really know why, but I did. One magazine promised that Donny liked to personally answer special letters, especially from members of his fan club. I decided to join the fan club and at the same time, write one of those special letters. My letter told him how much I liked his singing and dancing, and that my favourite song was *Yo-Yo*. I asked him what movies he liked and what his favourite meal was. I told him how much it would mean to me to have a letter to hang on my wall. I did not, however, tell him that if he sent me a letter I would have to hide it under my mattress. I felt confident he would write me back. I filled out the form and placed it inside the envelope with a two dollar bill and the letter. Then I dropped the envelope into the mailbox.

Seconds after I released the envelope, alarm bells sounded inside my head. "MOM!" I screamed to myself. "What will Mom do when she discovers the eight by ten envelope delivered to our address??" In spite of all the time I'd spent planning to join the fan club, this thought had not occurred to me. Suddenly, I pictured Mom examining the package, marching toward me and demanding, "You sent how much money to this fan club, for this????" then, compelled to look for explanations, discover my magazine stash...and "oh my, oh my," and a tirade about being led from the narrow path of righteousness onto the broad highway to Hollywood glitter and ungodliness.

I felt sick.

I took some consolation from knowing there was a bit of safe time, one week for sure, two weeks perhaps, while they processed the order. But thoughts and questions began to torment me: How bad was it joining a fan club? How bad was reading those magazines? What was the degree of this particular sin? All around me people were doing things they shouldn't. I knew Ruth and the twins read magazines where they went babysitting, though they didn't buy them. Rita stole cigarettes from her mom's purse to smoke with Sophie. Liz kissed Joe Arcangelo and had a hickey under her turtleneck. Beverley's aunt had a baby and wasn't married. A whole bunch of people around here drank and smoked and swore.

After a week, I began to really worry. Not about going to hell when I died, because I knew my sin wasn't that bad. I didn't fear the wrath of God so much as the wrath of Mom.

I already knew Mom's lecture about corporate giants taking advantage, using magazines and television for brainwashing the public to follow fashion fads and buy stuff they don't need, about using resources from underprivileged countries where people worked for practically nothing and reaped no benefits for their efforts. I imagined myself questioning her about what this had to do with buying magazines and imagined her saying these television stars were getting richer, and as the rich got richer, the poor got poorer and it always came back to the big business, multinational corporate bureaucratic industrial giants, exploitation and squashing the poor. I had heard these words so many times and though I didn't really know what all of them meant, I had a pretty good idea. I knew it would all end in massive feelings of guilt.

And worse, Mom would make me stop buying magazines and that would be worse than horrible.

I began to pray again in earnest...that the photo would arrive on a morning when Mom was at sewing class or Bible Study, or out welfare cheque shopping with the ladies group. A morning when Mom was too busy to look closely at the mail, though how she might miss a large envelope with *Do Not Bend* printed across the front was beyond me. Or that it would arrive on a day that she was late coming home to meet us for lunch, so I might get there first. Or that she would scoop the pile and throw it into the basket on top of the piano to peruse later when she "put her feet up".

I began to dread coming home for lunch as much as I'd once dreaded going to school. I was losing sleep again and seeking comfort in ice cream. I was pretty sure Donny wouldn't be thrilled about maintaining correspondence with a chubby girl, once he asked me to send a picture his way, but I couldn't help it.

After two and a half weeks, I cracked. I couldn't take the pressure of worrying alone. I told my sisters I would receive a large envelope and I needed them to help by hiding it when it arrived. I told them about the letter and the two dollars.

That was a mistake.

"Do you really think Donny is going to write you a letter?" asked Sarah, like she was speaking to an imbecile.

"It says he answers a lot of his fan mail personally," I said. "It says he loves to keep in touch with his fans."

"Who says?" asked Ruth.

"It says in the magazine."

"Donny's not going to write you a letter," Trudy said flatly.

"And Donny Osmond wouldn't take the time to sign all those pictures, either," Ruth said. "He just signs one and they photocopy it for all the silly little girls in North America who send in two dollars."

I was shocked at the idea that they would copy Donny's signature, and equally offended by the implication that all his fans were silly little girls. I wanted to yell at them, tell them they were so wrong. I would receive a picture signed by Donny. And maybe I would be one of the lucky fans to receive a real letter. Instead, I begged them not to tell. They smiled at me in a way that suggested they knew I was at their mercy and loved it.

Mealtime became painful. "Got any good mail lately?" Trudy would ask in my direction, or, "Heard from Donny lately?" making my face burn as I choked down mashed potatoes. But as much as they tormented me, they also proved to have hearts. When Dad said, "Donny who?" Ruth jumped in and started talking about how she was being considered to be a contestant on *High Q*, our local television station's game show for smart high school students.

After almost four weeks of nerve-racking walks home, I opened the door to see the envelope among the mail, kicked to the side in the front entrance. "Thank you Lord," I sighed, "for hearing my desperate prayers."

I could hear Mom fiddling with the electric can opener.

"Hi Mom," I said, grabbing the envelope and sliding it inside my jacket.

"How was school?"

"I'll be right down," I called, as I ran up the stairs. "I've got to use the bathroom."

I locked the bathroom door and pulled out the envelope. My hands were shaking as I tore at the corner, careful not to rip the photo, careful to preserve the *Donny Osmond Fan Club* seal. My heart was pounding when I finally felt the smooth surface of the photo. With reverence, I pulled it out, knowing this was something special, the moment I had been waiting for. The photo was a black-and-white pose of Donny from the waist up, leaning on one elbow, semi-reclined in a white shirt, partly unbuttoned, and a sash belt. On the bottom right hand corner was the signature, "With love, Donny". I touched the autograph, sighed, and flushed the toilet.

It wasn't until after I finished my paper route and dinner that I got a really good look at the letter and the photo. The letter was addressed, "Dear Fan". It was typed and did not answer any of the questions I asked in my letter. I wondered if it was even from Donny, though his name was signed at the bottom. The letter said thanks for joining and a bunch of stuff that wasn't very interesting. It looked fake, and copied.

The photo was okay. I loved the eyes and hair, but the teeth were pretty big. I decided Donny was cuter when he was on television, singing and dancing with his brothers. The autograph looked like a copy, too, but I decided not to care and taped it to the bottom of the top bunk so I could stare at it for a few days, even though I wasted two dollars and spent almost a month being a nervous wreck.

DANCING

Mennonites should not dance. Whether it is written or simply understood, in those days I wasn't clear, since any discussion of dancing was discouraged. The founding father, Menno Simons, apparently required additional commandments: Number 11, "Thou shall not go to war." Number 12, "Thou shall not play cards." Number 13, "Thou shall not dance." And there were others.

My parent's theology fully embraced commandment 11, the war one. Number 12, they completely ignored because they loved games, and their thinking on number 13, hovered in a grey area. There seemed to be a continuum of responses from them on the rare occasion when the issue of dancing surfaced in our household. Somewhere along that continuum was a cut off point, a place to slam the door and say, "No more. We have gone too far." I just wasn't exactly sure where the line was drawn.

To my parents, some forms of dance were not only acceptable, but revered. One of them was the waltz, where dignified, full-skirted women and tuxedoed men swirled to the music of Johann Strauss. Square dancing also fell within the realm of the respectable— wholesome country folk dressed in plaid shirts and ruffled skirts, enthusiastic hand-clapping and foot-stomping around well-lit, hay-strewn barns, body contact limited to "grab your partner by the hand… now swing around and do-si-do," allowing little time to kiss or squeeze.

Dancing within epic musical productions like *Oklahoma* and *The Music Man* was not only accepted, but applauded. Mom loved it, though she never actually said, "I love the dancing in musicals". But we could tell. Her face glowed when Marian, "Madame Librarian", danced over tables in the River City Library. Her eyes beamed when Dick Van Dyke danced on London rooftops with the chimney sweeps while Mary Poppins floated above. The munchkins were "adorable," dancing joyfully along the Yellow Brick Road. Oklahomans on wind-swept plains, Fred and Ginger among the Christmas lights, nothing wrong with that. Mom even liked the Osmond Brothers, I think because they were brothers with enthusiastic smiles and matching outfits.

Mom even laughed with delight during *L'il Abner* while a stage full of young hillbilly women shook their half-dressed booties, flaunting cleavage to peppy fiddle music. She watched ballet misty-eyed, the male dancers' genitalia shockingly big and bulgy in their skin-tight leotards. But when Elvis Presley appeared on *The Ed Sullivan Show* in a white tasselled suit, gyrating his hips and singing rock-and-roll, Mom was out of her chair like a shot to change the channel, blocking the screen while she did so, then delivering a speech on decency and basic human morality.

There were advantages to living across the street from the Welcome Inn. While Mom and Dad spent many evenings and weekend afternoons there, we were now able to watch "racy" TV programs like *The Monkees, American Bandstand* and *Laugh In*, or listen to records or rock music on the radio without the sound carrying down through the floors. Around the time we expected our parents to come home, a lookout was stationed in an upstairs window. When the warning was sounded, a mad scramble followed to change the TV channel or hide records or change the radio dial to CBC.

Our first rock-and-roll album was *Bob Dylan's Greatest Hits*. Ruth found it scratched and missing the record jacket, lying in the middle of James Street. She snuck it into the house under her coat. "Hey Mister Tambourine Man" got stuck and repeated, I'm not sleepy and there ain't... I'm not sleepy and there ain't... but the other songs played well enough, despite scratches. We kept it hidden among Dad's extensive record collection. Being a great fan of the great classical composers, male choirs and gospel singers like George Beverly Shea, Dad had purchased a fairly decent cabinet stereo, with a record player and lift up lid.

In our parents' absence, with the curtains closed, we practiced the dance steps we saw on TV. We started with simple foot movements; step sideways with right foot, bring left foot to join right, step sideways with left, bring right foot to join, and repeat. Once we had the rhythm, arm movements were added; pump right arm up, then down, pump left arm up, then down and repeat. Ruth taught us the twist. She said to pretend we were holding the end of a towel in each hand and dry our behinds in time with the rhythm. Trudy and Sarah showed us the Bunny Hop, which we'd do in a tight circle. *American Bandstand* gave us more moves, like *The Pony*. The moves on *Soul Train*, we found, were more advanced, maybe too much for our repressed souls to emulate. Often someone sat in the vinyl lemon-lime-plaid recliner to provide commentary and constructive criticism.

Not all the songs on our Bob Dylan record were ideal dance numbers, and the radio didn't always play what we wanted so we began to smuggle records into the house.

The difficulty lay in getting them in undetected. It isn't easy to hide an album under clothing. Like, yes that blouse looks lovely, but it seems to be somewhat flat and square. Colder months were slightly easier with the aid of jackets, and newspapers provided a cover, since we always had extras. I kept the old cart parked on our backyard patio, never for a moment worried about it being stolen. Who would want it? Besides, it'd be fairly easy to track down. So, a record could be hidden in the cart under plastic and old papers overnight if necessary.

Keeping the albums hidden was also a challenge. Our collective blood pressure rose when Dad wanted to listen to Beethoven and started sifting through the stack. One of us would jump up to assist, saying, "What'll it be, Dad? I'll get it on for you". That became more difficult as the number of albums increased, and hiding records in our bedrooms was risky due to Mom's spontaneous episodes of, "I am sick of the state of your rooms", in which case, she'd be down on her hands and knees hauling out clutter from under our beds. Nor were our closets safe, subject to unpredictable overhauls where all un-hung items were heaped onto our bedroom floors to be sorted and put away properly. The basement was an option with assorted storage boxes and suitcases, but proved to be too much trouble when you had to factor in running up and down the stairs.

There came a time when we had too many records to keep hidden. And we all wanted to join *The Columbia Record Club*, where you get four records free if you agree to get the brochures each month. We decided it was time to break Mom and Dad in and introduce some modern music into the home. Our debut album was Simon and Garfunkel's,

Sounds of Silence. The plan was to let it play. If they asked, or mentioned that something new was playing, we were to call it "folk music", which it was. They didn't notice, or if they did, they didn't mention it.

So we played some Joni Mitchell and Gordon Lightfoot, even though they weren't the greatest for dancing. Ruth said it was good transitional music. After that, we introduced Crosby, Stills, Nash and Young and Neil Diamond. We kept the volume low and at the same time, grabbed brooms, dust clothes, and Lemon Pledge and did housework, so it would appear the music was actually good for us. Whenever one of our records was playing we remained calm and relaxed, making sure not to bicker or call each other names, to demonstrate the positive effects of modern music.

This all happened gradually. There were times we knew to take a record off before it was over, or skip certain songs. We knew when either Mom or Dad might have no tolerance, in which case, we stuck to television. And many albums were never played while they were home, like The Rolling Stones. That would be disastrous. Even Credence Clearwater Revival and *K-Tel's 20 Explosive Hits* were pushing it. We had to make sure not to bring out more than one new record a month, and equally important, to share ownership amongst ourselves to avoid the "wasting money on nonsense" lecture.

We began to give each other records at Christmas, so in a way, they slipped into the house through loopholes. Mom and Dad couldn't really get down on us for buying gifts at Christmas. And receiving albums openly was such a treat that, our spirits so buoyant, we joyfully peeled potatoes, cut up onions for stuffing and washed greasy pots. I was so happy to receive *The Partridge Family Album* one Christmas morning that I volunteered to shovel the sidewalk.

The dancing continued behind closed doors. But after all that secrecy, the times in our house were a' changin' enough that I would soon be allowed to go to my first dance. And confidently too, since having done so much practicing, I wasn't a bad dancer. At that time, I knew that dancing was still taboo in most Mennonite circles because it threatened the ideals of modesty and piety, so I considered myself fortunate.

I laughed, but with some reservation, when I heard a joke many years later. Because it's probably true:

"Why don't Mennonites have sex standing up?"

"Because it might lead to dancing."

SHALL WE MOVE?

One day, near the end of grade seven, I was home alone when Dad arrived with a newspaper tucked under his arm. He had circled an ad and said he needed to make a phone call. While he dialled the number I went upstairs to read *Tiger Beat*.

When he hung up the phone, he yelled up the stairs, "Want to go look at a house?"

"Where's the house?" I yelled back.

"Up by St. Joseph's Hospital," he answered. Ooh, I thought, a way nicer part of town.

"Sure," I said.

"Why are we looking at a house?" I asked as Dad started the car.

"Mom and I've been thinking," he said. I looked at him for more information.

"A Group Home," he said.

"A group home?" I asked.

"Foster children," he said. "They call it a group home if you take in more than four at once."

"Like living with us?" I asked.

"Exactly."

Dad pulled up to a stately but run-down brick house with a prominent veranda. It was at least as tall as the Welcome Inn with large bay windows on the first and second floors. "Wow, it's big!" I said.

"Seven bedrooms," Dad said.

Inside, was a long hallway with stairs running up on one side with a banister that looked as though it came right out of Scarlet O'Hara's house, curved and ornate. I explored while Dad tapped along the walls, jumped up and down in the corners, turned on every tap, flushed all four toilets and stuck his head under all the sinks. I was reminded of our first Welcome Inn tour, looking at the same high ceilings, wood trim and mouldings, knowing that if Mom was along she would be beside herself over the stained glass windows in the entrance and the floors throughout, exclaiming over the endless "possibilities".

I smiled, even though I was alone, when I reached the third floor; much bigger than the Welcome Inn's, divided into two rooms with an alcove in the front, and a bathroom with a skylight. I imagined my sisters and me being delegated to this floor and explored the closets, two of which were large enough to walk around in. Since I knew the twins would be interested, I went out the door in the back room onto the fire escape to view the rooflines and potential areas for sun-tanning.

That summer we took our annual camping holiday, this one to the eastern states, which included tours of Gettysburg and the Mayflower. We tried to gain entrance into the compound at Hyannis Port, but the guard on duty didn't believe Dad's story that we had been invited to lunch with the Kennedy's. When we got home, we spent many of the remaining days of summer holidays painting, scraping floors and mouldings, hauling garbage and hanging wallpaper, because Mom and Dad had received another "calling".

By the time school started in September, we were living in our new seven bedroom house. We were all enrolled in our new neighbourhood schools; me at the Junior High, Tina at the elementary school and the older four at the High School.

By the end of November, we had six new family members, each taking residence in three of the bedrooms on the second floor, joining the line-up for showers, sitting with us at meals and vying for seats in front of the television. Until then, I thought deciding on a television show among six siblings was a challenge. Add six more and choosing a TV show could turn into a wrestling match. Which is one of the reasons Dad bought boxing gloves that first Christmas for two of the 'foster brothers', so they could "settle their differences" in the basement. The opening of that gift had me raising my eyebrows on Christmas morning. But then again, I had two weeks earlier, been allowed to go to my first dance — which I had enjoyed immensely. Maybe because I was a 'new girl' at school, I had been asked to dance to more than half the songs. Even to several "slow" numbers, my hands looped over my partner's shoulders, my cheek occasionally brushing against his. Yes, the times they were a' changin'. But some things remained constant. With Mom and Dad it was their willingness to follow God's callings. And where God led them, we followed along.

After the mortgage papers were signed, and Dad had made the announcement at dinner that we would be opening a 'Group Home', I tried again to imagine what God's voice sounded like. I had closed my eyes and listened. But the only words I heard inside my head were, "Here we go again"...